P.
Vera D. Lewis

HOUGHTON MIFFLIN

WORLD REGIONAL STUDIES

Unless we know about the traditions and ways of life of people in other nations, we cannot develop an adequate understanding of the
present-day world. The goal of the World Regional Studies series is
to provide a well-rounded picture of human experience in these six
areas of the world:

The Middle East
Africa
China
India
Japan
Russia

Using history as the organizing principle, the books in this series incorporate concepts and skills from the social sciences and from the
humanities. Political and economic systems, geography, social organization and human values, the fine arts, and religion are all discussed in depth.

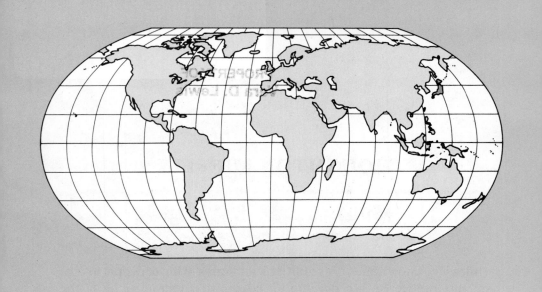

WORLD REGIONAL STUDIES

Japan

Third Edition

Michael Kublin
Hyman Kublin

HOUGHTON MIFFLIN COMPANY / **Boston**

Atlanta / Dallas / Geneva, Illinois / Palo Alto / Princeton / Toronto

Michael Kublin

Dr. Kublin received his Ph.D in History from New York University. He also has an MBA from Pace University. He is currently Assistant Professor of International Business at the University of New Haven and taught history previously at Kingsborough Community College in Brooklyn, New York. Dr. Kublin is also general editor for the Houghton Mifflin World Regional Studies series.

Hyman Kublin

A specialist in the history of East Asia, Dr. Kublin received his Ph.D from Harvard University. Formerly Professor of History at Brooklyn College of the City University of New York, Dr. Kublin also taught at the University of Hawaii and Waseda University in Japan. He wrote many articles on Japan and China for scholarly and educational publications and several other titles in the Houghton Mifflin World Regional Studies Series.

Howard R. Anderson

Dr. Anderson, consulting editor, taught social studies in Michigan, Iowa, and New York. He also taught at the University of Iowa and at Cornell University, and served as President of the National Council for the Social Studies.

Special thanks to Allison Lipski and Christine Walnycky, reference librarians at the University of New Haven Library, who were extremely helpful; and to Janet Blaustein Kublin, who did extensive research and editing. For valuable advice and assistance, the authors and publisher are indebted to Caryn White, Outreach Director, Council on East Asian Studies, Yale University, New Haven, Connecticut.

Cover photo: Golden Pavilion in Kyoto

The chapter opener art on the first page of every chapter was adpated from a design on a kimono worn by popular Japanese writer and artist Santo Kyoden in a portrait of him, circa 1790.

Printed in the U.S.A.

ISBN: 0–395–47079–X

ABCDEFGHIJ-M-9876543210/89

CONTENTS

MAPS

CHARTS, GRAPHS, AND TABLES

PHOTO ESSAYS

INTRODUCTION

A thoroughgoing revolution has long been under way in Japan. From both the short-range and the long-range points of view, the Japanese way of life has undergone a steady change. Little evidence has surfaced to indicate that the pace of change in Japan will slacken during the foreseeable future. Japan is now a major economic superpower. Its emergence as an economic powerhouse ranks among the most important worldwide developments of the second half of the twentieth century. Many people are saying that just as the twentieth century was an era of American greatness, so the twenty-first century will belong to Japan.

A Latecomer to the Modern Age

Until a century ago, the Japanese were among the least known of the peoples of Asia. They lived in self-imposed seclusion and refused to engage in diplomatic relations with other nations. They had to be coaxed, even intimidated into joining the community of nations. But once they entered into that community, they responded to the new challenges they encountered with enthusiasm and determination and still managed to hold on to their cherished traditions and heritage.

In earlier centuries, the Japanese had periodically "borrowed" institutions, ideas, and techniques that were more culturally advanced than their own. From the late 1800's to the present, the Japanese have continued their knack for selective cultural borrowing. Adopting what they needed as their own, they patiently put together the structure of a modern state and society. Within 50 years after they had opened their doors to the world, the Japanese had attained a place among the foremost nations of the world participating as a great power at the peace conference ending World War I.

The Quest for Empire

After World War I Japan tied its economic success to the quest for empire, seeking to control the sources of the raw materials that its burgeoning industries needed. Military leaders took control of Japan's government, committing aggressions against their neighbors in East Asia in the 1930's and thereafter. The outcome of Japan's military aggressions was a tragic war against the Allied nations that left Japan's islands in ruins. Moreover, Japan lost its far-flung overseas empire, welded together during the previous 75 years.

Postwar Achievements

Rarely in all of Japan's history had the future seemed so bleak as in August 1945 when Hirohito, as the emperor of Japan, announced his decision to surrender to the Allied nations. With the country's leaders in disgrace, the economy at a standstill, and the morale of the people at a low ebb, the Japanese were further humiliated by the presence of the Army of Occupation. But Japan's speedy recovery from the ashes of war, including the atomic destruction of Hiroshima and Nagasaki, was almost without parallel in world history. Prodded by their conquerors, the Japanese undertook to revamp their way of life. In place of militarism, imperialism, and authoritarianism, the people substituted the ideals of democracy, peace, and the welfare of the people as national goals. By 1952 the Army of Occupation was gone. Within a decade, the old order and the debris of war had been swept away.

An Industrial Giant

One of the most notable features of Japan's postwar resurgence has been its economic growth. Japan enjoys the greatest favorable balance of trade of any nation in the world today. It ranks first in many areas of industrial production. Its investments span the globe. Its people, too, have benefited with a rising standard of living and a growing affluence. Along with economic prosperity, however, have come a host of new challenges.

While industrialization and urbanization have created many benefits, they also have contributed to such problems as environmental pollution, overcrowding, traffic congestion, and disruption of traditional values and home life. Although Japan's annual per capita gross national product is close to $20,000, surpassing that of the United States, prices in Japan are skyrocketing. The Japanese must pay more than three times what Americans do for food and twice as much for other products. Rice, a staple of the Japanese diet, costs ten times more in Japan than it does in other parts of the world. Property in Japan is about four times more expensive than in the United States and an entire generation of young people are finding it impossible to buy homes.

Seemingly content to play a secondary role in international affairs, Japan has begun to increase its foreign aid to newly industrialized countries and those still struggling to industrialize.

When Emperor Hirohito died, dignitaries from all around the world attended his funeral. The attendance by so many world leaders symbolized not only Japan's growth into an economic colossus, but also the respect and admiration people the world over have for this island nation and its people.

Political Developments in the Late 1980's

During the summer and fall of 1988, scandal rocked the parliamentary government of Prime Minister Takeshita Noburu. The scandal involved the private sale of stock to various politicians and business executives before the stock was sold to the public. Those who purchased the stock before the public offering made considerable profits once they resold the stock after it became available to the public. Aides to former Prime Minister Nakasone and members of Prime Minister Takeshita's cabinet were among those implicated in the stock scandal.

Takeshita attempted to quell the growing public outrage in December 1988 when he replaced 15 members of his 21–member cabinet. This cabinet shuffle backfired, however, and Takeshita resigned in April 1989, taking full responsibility for the stock scandal.

Takehsita's successor, former Foreign Minister Uno Sousuke, resigned after only two months in office when revelations about his involvement in an affair with a geisha led to his party's stunning defeat at the polls. Both Takeshita and Uno were members of the Liberal Democratic Party, which had dominated the government for 34 years. In mid-summer of 1989, the voters showed their displeasure with the party by electing only 36 Liberal Democrats to the upper house of the Diet. With 126 seats available, the Socialist Party took 46 seats, giving Japan's opposition parties control of one of the houses of the Diet for the first time. By the fall of 1989, the Liberal Democrats remained in control of the lower house and had named a new prime minister, Kaifu Toshiki. Kaifu's goal to bring the Liberal Democratic Party back to its dominant position is a challenging one indeed.

1

Japan and Its Peoples

In terms of Asian settlement, Japan was a frontier region for many centuries. Civilization spread from the great river valleys of Asia into other fertile plains long before it reached Japan. Peoples of Asia began migrating to Japan in significant numbers only a little more than 2,000 years ago. By that time India and China had been civilized for many hundreds of years. A major reason for Japan's lack of contact with other parts of the world was the many miles of ocean separating the islands from the Asian mainland.

The physical makeup of Japan had a great influence on the people who eventually settled there. The absence of rich farm-lands and a lack of natural resources made the islanders rely on their own ingenuity. They developed a sense of practicality that enabled them to make the most of their opportunities. Their separation from the Asian mainland also had its effects. The Japanese acquired a fierce pride in the "Japanese way." With their sense of practicality, the Japanese were often inclined to borrow freely from any culture that offered them something they did not have. Their relative isolation from the mainland enabled them to adopt what they wanted and adapt it at their own pace.

Over the centuries, Japan has changed rapidly and intense-ly. Today it is the most westernized and economically advanced nation in Asia. Despite its small size, Japan has become an economic giant, rivaling countries much larger in size.

1. The Physical Geography of Japan

The Japanese **archipelago** is part of the easternmost area of Asia. The archipelago's location in relation to the vast Asian landmass is similar to that of the British Isles, the island frontier of Western Europe. Until a little more than a century ago, Japan's inhabitants and their way of life were mostly unknown to such close Asian neighbors as the Koreans and the Chinese, as well as to Westerners. Accordingly, Japan's cultural isolation as well as its history have been strongly influenced by the country's geographical location.

A Nation of Islands

The Japanese archipelago consists of about 3,400 islands. Scattered over a vast expanse of ocean, the islands skirt the coast of northeast Asia. While the islands include more territory than Korea, Japan's closest neighbor, the archipelago is less than one-twenty-fifth the size of China. Japan is larger than Great Britain or Italy but smaller than France or Spain. The island chain is shaped like a crescent curving from the north to the west, with the outermost tips of the island chain separated by almost 1,400 miles. This is about the distance between North America's Great Lakes and the Gulf of Mexico.

Most of the islands in the Japanese archipelago are little more than barren and uninhabited rocks scarcely protruding above the sea. There are just four main islands. Stretching from north to west, they are Hokkaido (hah-KYD-oh), Honshu (HAHN-shoo), Kyushu (kee-OO-shoo), and Shikoku (shih-KOH-koo). Hokkaido, the northernmost and the second largest island, has an inhospitable terrain and a rather severe winter climate, factors that have discouraged heavy settlement. Much of Hokkaido is still covered with forests.

Located immediately south of Hokkaido is the main island of Honshu. Having more than 60 percent of the land area of the archipelago, Honshu is home to the great majority of the people. Farther west is the small island of Kyushu, second in importance only to Honshu. The tiny island of Shikoku, slightly larger than the state of Hawaii, completes the foursome of important islands. It lies northeast of Kyushu and just south of Honshu.

Other Island Groups

The Japanese archipelago forms a hub from which several other islands and island chains radiate. Lying off the coast of eastern

Siberia in the northwest is the large island of Sakhalin (SAHK-uh-leen). Stretching away to the northeast is a long chain of bleak and rocky islands known as the Kuriles (KOO-uhr-eelz). This name, of Russian origin, means "The Smokies," and refers to the heavy fog banks that often blanket the islands. To the southwest is another extensive island chain, the Ryukyus (ree-YOOK-yooz), which are also called the Nansei Shoto. At the southern point of this chain is Okinawa, the main island of the Ryukyus. Okinawa was occupied by the United States as a military base after World War II. The island of Taiwan, now the home of the Nationalist Republic of China, lies just southwest of the Ryukyus.

For several centuries the various island groups stretching away from Japan were the targets of Japanese expansion. Japan did not have the natural resources of its own to be a major world power, but Japanese government leaders ultimately refused to accept anything less. During the half century ending with World War II, the Japanese attempted to conquer nearby and then distant territories. In 1942, when the Japanese Empire was at its height, Japan controlled a land area of 3,250,000 square miles, an area somewhat larger than the continental United States. Most of this territory, including all holdings on the Asian mainland, were lost in 1945. In the early 1950's the United States, which had occupied the Ryukyus since 1945, arranged to return the northern islands of the chain to the Japanese government. In 1968, the United States government returned Iwo Jima and other islands in the Bonin Islands group. In 1972, it returned Okinawa.

A Land of Hills and Mountains

In most pictures or paintings of Japanese landscapes, hills and mountains immediately catch the eye. In Japanese poetry, mountain peaks and passes are conspicuous among the similes and metaphors commonly used. For example, in the following lines from *The Manyoshu; the Nippon Gakujutsu Shinkokai Translation of One Thousand Poems,* an aristocrat of ancient Japan mourns the death of his wife:

> In the autumn mountains
> The yellow leaves are so thick.
> Alas, how shall I seek my love
> Who has wandered away?—
> I know not the mountain track.

JAPAN: AN ISLAND NATION

CHINA
MANCHURIA

Vladivostok

NORTH KOREA

KOREA
BAY

★ Pyongyang

38°

SEA OF
JAPAN

YELLOW
SEA

★ Seoul

SOUTH KOREA

34°

126°

STRAIT

KOREA

Fukui

Kitakyushu
Shimonoseki
Hiroshima
Kobe Kyoto
Sasebo Fukuoka
INLAND SEA
Osaka
Nagasaki
Matsuyama
Takamatsu
Nara
Oita
Kochi
Tokushima
Kumamoto
KYUSHU
SHIKOKU

EAST CHINA
SEA

Kagoshima
Miyazaki

30°

130°

Ryukyu Islands

134°

4

USSR

SAKHALIN
(USSR)

138°

46°

N
W · E
S

SEA OF
OKHOTSK

Asahikawa

Ishikari R.

HOKKAIDO

Sapporo

Kurile Is.

Nemuro

Muroran

Hakodate

42°

Aomori

PACIFIC
OCEAN

Akita

Kitakami R.

Sendai

Niigata

38°

Shinano R.

HONSHU

anazawa

Japanese Alps

Kiso R.

KANTO PLAIN

Mito

joya

Tengu R.

Mt. Fuji

Tokyo

Shizuoka

Kamakura

Chiba

Kawasaki

Yokohama

SE
INES

142°

38°

0   100
Approx. scale of miles

KEY
Megalopolis/metropolitan area
▲ Mountain peak

Area: 145,800 square miles

Population: 123 million (1989 estimate). Japan has a population density of 844 people per square mile.

Cities Over One Million in Population (1986 estimate): Tokyo (8.4), Yokohama (3.0), Osaka (2.6), Nagoya (2.1), Kyoto (1.5), Sapporo (1.5), Kobe (1.4), Fukuoka (1.2), Kawasaki (1.1), Kitakyushu (1.1)

Capital: Tokyo

Government: Constitutional Monarchy. The emperor is Akihito. The Japanese Parliament is called the Diet. Executive power is vested in the prime minister and cabinet.

Political Parties: The majority party is the Liberal Democratic Party. Minority parties include the Socialist Party, the Clean Government Party, the Communist Party, and the Democrat Socialist Party.

Currency: the Yen. The value of the yen against the United States dollar fluctuates on the world money market. On January 5, 1989, the number of yen equal to one United States dollar was 125.80.

Estimated 1986 Per capita income (in United States dollars): $21,820

Estimated 1986 Gross National Product (in United States dollars): $2,664 billion

Labor Force: In agriculture it is 8 percent; in industry it is 33 percent; in trade and services it is 51%.

Chief Industries: shipbuilding, motor vehicles, electronics, precision instruments, steel, textiles, chemicals, aircraft, ceramics, rolling stock (locomotives and coaches), fisheries

Literacy Rate: 99 percent

Major Religions: Shintoism, Buddhism

The Japanese islands are actually the crests of mountains jutting out of the sea from the ocean floor. The summit of famed Mt. Fuji, the highest in the islands, soars almost 12,500 feet into the sky. But most mountains in the islands are less than half as high. Japan's rugged appearance stems from the immense number of its mountains rather than their height above sea level. The distance from coast to coast is less than 200 miles everywhere in the archipelago, but the terrain of every island is broken by mountain peaks and chains of stubby hills.

Scarcity of Habitable Land

The search for habitable and tillable land has for centuries taxed the energies and ingenuity of the Japanese people. They have settled wherever they have found plains and plateaus. On level land are located most of the country's thousands of towns and villages as well as the great cities—Tokyo, Osaka, Nagoya, and Yokohama. The plains were also the first extensive areas to be converted into farming land. In recent decades, as urban centers have steadily expanded, cities have encroached on the farm-land. Rarely are cities separated from the surrounding country-side by suburbs, as is true in the United States. Tillable land is so scarce that planted fields extend to the very boundaries of some cities. For example, Tokyo and Yokohama have become so large that their suburbs actually adjoin one another in a giant **megalopolis** with as many as 26 million people.

The Japanese have proved themselves adept at transforming undesirable sites into prosperous farms and towns. In coastal areas the Japanese have reclaimed much land from the sea. In mountainous regions the hills have been terraced to provide more land for growing crops. There is much unoccupied land in Japan, but most of it is totally unsuitable for habitation. Only in Hokkaido are there still large tracts of tillable land yet to be developed.

Reliance on Rice

Rice has long been the core of Japanese agriculture. In their ancient myths the Japanese referred to their country as "Land of the Ten Thousand Ears of Rice." For longer than they them-selves can remember their staple crop has been rice. In some respects Japan is ideal for growth of this grain. The country has a warm climate for many months of the year plus ample rainfall. Both of these are necessary in rice production. But because rice is raised on irrigated **paddies,** level tracts of land are required. Unfortunately, only about 1 percent of the land area of Japan with a suitable climate for rice is also level.

With good farmland in limited supply, the Japanese rice paddy is quite unique in many respects. Seldom do farmers have more than a few acres of land. Numerous farms in Japan con-sist of several tiny plots that are often widely scattered. The Japanese farmers give their rice fields loving care. Each plot is abundantly fertilized. Only the best grades of rice are planted, and no grass or weeds are allowed to strangle the plants. Be-cause of the care the Japanese give their rice fields, the per-acre yield of rice in Japan is the highest in the world.

Not all land in Japan is devoted to rice. Barley, millet, soy beans, and a great variety of vegetables are raised. Land that is not suitable for rice, such as slopes and hills, is terraced and planted in tea, fruit trees, or mulberry trees. In recent decades

LAND USE. The scarcity of good farmland in Japan has forced the Japanese to make use of what they have. Mountainsides terraced for rice paddies and contoured plots are shown in the photographs at right and above. In some areas land has been reclaimed from the sea (below). What is Japan's average population density?

grazing and dairying have become important on the island of Hokkaido. But despite a diversity of crops, rice fields still account for more than half the land farmed in Japan.

Natural Forces in Japan

Like other island groups off the eastern coast of Asia, Japan is studded with volcanoes. Most of them are extinct or inactive, but occasionally an eruption takes place in an active volcano. Fortunately, none of the active volcanoes are near heavily settled areas. Earthquakes, however, frequently affect settled areas. About 1,500 shocks and tremors are recorded each year. The vast majority of the tremors are so slight that they are not even felt by the people. Periodically, though, Japan experiences a major earthquake. While the quakes may do little structural damage to homes and office buildings, they often set off fires that destroy life and property. Volcanoes that erupt on the sea floor and earthquakes that strike the sea floor, even thousands of miles away, sometimes form a **tsunami** (soo-NAHM-ee), a great sea wave that sweeps across the Pacific Ocean and causes tremendous damage when it hits coastal areas of Japan. A tsunami may also be responsible for much loss of human life.

Japan is also in the path of severe wind and rainstorms called typhoons, which are similar to hurricanes in the United States. These typhoons form over ocean waters, and sometimes take a path that sweeps over the archipelago's eastern coast. They destroy buildings and crops, disrupt communications and transportation, and start floods and landslides, sometimes with the loss of life.

The Japanese dread the forces of nature that again and again vent their fury upon the islands. But they have learned to live with their sometimes inhospitable environment. Whenever the Japanese suffer a disaster, they quickly set about repairing damages. In a very short time, they have returned to their normal routines of life.

Rivers and the Sea

Hundreds of streams race from the highlands of the interior to the sea. Japan's rivers are short and swift. The longest, the Shinano, is only 229 miles in length. Because most of them are navigable for only a few miles, these streams have little importance for transportation. Indeed, more often than not, they have been barriers to travel and trade. Because there were few bridges until modern times, crossing a stream was a nuisance and at times dangerous. But throughout the history of the land,

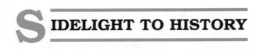

Earthquakes and Building Heights

For centuries, ever mindful of the dangers of earthquakes, people in Japan rarely erected buildings higher than one or two stories. Even the grand mansions and palaces of court nobles and feudal lords followed this pattern. If a building with only one or two stories collapsed from a severe earthquake, people had a better chance of escaping without harm than from a skyscraper. The cities of Japan thus grew outward rather than upward and covered immense spaces as a result.

But in 1923 this pattern began to change. That year saw the opening of the Imperial Hotel in Tokyo. Designed by the American architect, Frank Lloyd Wright, the new hotel was designed to withstand severe earthquake damage. When the Great Tokyo Earthquake struck in September of that year, the hotel was scarcely damaged. Wright's building demonstrated that earthquake-proof skyscrapers could be built and this led to the building of more skyscrapers and a change in the skyline of Tokyo and other major Japanese cities. Until the late 1950's, however, the highest buildings in Japan still rose no more than ten stories above the ground.

In 1958, the Japanese broke through the "height barrier" when they completed the 1,093-foot Tokyo Tower, used as an observation platform for tourists and for television transmission. In subsequent years, the Japanese have built far taller buildings using a new technique of flexibility called *jukozo* developed by a Japanese architect. The area around Tokyo's Shinjuku train station boasts numerous high-rise hotels, stores, and office buildings. Included in this high-rise area are the 47-story Keio Plaza Hotel, the 52-story Sumitomo Building, and the 55-story Mitsui office building. Another fast-growing commercial center in Tokyo, Ikebukuro, is home to the 60-story Sunshine Building, completed in 1980. With almost all outward-growing space in Japan's crowded cities filled, Japan continues to grow upward. Now Japanese builders must be mindful of the city's sunshine right, or *nisshoken*, a law that requires builders to compensate nearby residents who live in the shadows of Tokyo's growing number of tall buildings.

the countless rivers have provided water for irrigating rice in the paddies. In the twentieth century Japan's many rivers have become a valuable economic asset for still another reason. By harnessing their power, the country has acquired another urgently needed source of electricity for homes and industry.

As an island nation, Japan has always relied heavily upon the sea. Its long coasts are broken by numberless bays and coves. The larger harbors, such as those at Tokyo–Yokohama and Nagoya, have become major centers of commerce. The smaller ones serve the needs of the hundreds of fishing villages that dot the shores of the islands. Japan's "main street" is its huge Inland Sea, a body of water that separates three of the main islands of Japan. (See map on pages 4–5.) Along the sheltered banks of the Inland Sea are located hundreds of small fishing villages as well as some of Japan's leading industrial areas. The importance of the Inland Sea for commerce scarcely can be measured. In addition to being the main avenue for trade within Japan, the Inland Sea serves as a hub for foreign commerce. So many foreign ships pass through Japan's waters that the ports of Kobe and Osaka rank among the world's leading seaports.

The sea also serves the transportation needs of Japan. Outside the great metropolitan areas, Japan suffers from a scarcity of first-class highways and roads. In the past century an excellent system of railways, largely confined to the coastal regions, has been constructed. In the post-World War II period, Japan developed an excellent system of foreign and domestic airways. However, the Japanese continue to depend heavily upon ships for transportation, both among the islands themselves and between the islands and foreign countries.

Japan as an Island Nation

Like Britain, Japan found that the seas between itself and the rest of the world were an effective barrier. Japan was able to absorb much of its culture from the nearby countries of Korea and China without falling under the control of those states. In the 1600's Japan decided to limit severely its contact with the rest of the world. Except for a few carefully watched Dutch and Chinese traders, it successfully kept out all foreigners for more than two centuries. For most of Japan's history no would-be conqueror was able to overcome the water barrier and seize Japan. It was not until 1945, when Japan was defeated in World War II, that foreign troops occupied Japanese soil. Today modern forms of transportation link Japan with the rest of the world, and the sea remains vital to Japan for commerce, industry, fishing, and transportation.

Check Your Understanding

1. What are the four main islands of the Japanese archipelago?
2. **a.** In what way is Japan similar to the other large islands and island chains that are nearby? **b.** What part have these island chains played in Japan's history?
3. How have Japan's landforms influenced agriculture and its patterns of settlement?
4. How have natural disasters influenced Japan?
5. Why are rivers and seas of major importance to Japan?
6. **Thinking Critically:** What role did the sea serve for Japan before the nineteenth century? What role does the sea serve for Japan today?

2. Cultural Characteristics of Japan

In terms of the long span of world history, the Japanese are a young people. The civilizations of Egypt, Persia (present-day Iran), India, and China were many centuries old before a unified Japanese **culture** began to take shape. The history of the island country unfolded during the same time period as that of Western Europe. Just as Greece and Rome helped foster the growth of Western European culture, China influenced the **institutions** and people of Japan. Physically, and in many ways culturally, the Japanese resemble the Chinese. Other peoples, especially the Koreans, have left lasting marks on Japan, but none to the extent the Chinese have.

Physical Characteristics

About 350 years ago a Jesuit missionary living in Japan wrote a description of the Japanese people. Part of his account reads:

> The Japanese are white, although not excessively pale as the northern nations but just moderately so. They have goodly, somewhat round features, and as regards facial appearance they look like the genuine Chinese of the interior

[of the Chinese Empire], not like those of Canton [on the southeast coast]; they also resemble the Koreans on account of their hair, dark eyes, and small noses. Thus they greatly wonder at big and long noses, thick beards and red or fair hair [so common among Westerners], and consider all these things as so many defects. And so it comes about that they do not think very highly of beards, and if a man has a thick one he pulls it out . . . . [Michael Cooper, ed., *They Came to Japan: an Anthology of European Reports of Japan, 1543–1640.*]

The Japanese, Koreans, and Chinese share certain physical characteristics. Short in stature, they have straight black hair and dark, almond-shaped eyes. Their skin color ranges from fair, to yellowish, to brown. The Japanese strongly resemble the northern Chinese. But, as the above description states, the Japanese also tend to resemble the Koreans. This is understandable, because Korea is the mainland nation closest to Japan. Over the centuries many Koreans have settled in the islands.

Many Japanese also exhibit physical characteristics of other peoples in East Asia. In the northwest, the island of Sakhalin was a convenient stepping stone from mainland Asia to Japan. Many people crossed it and entered the island country. As a result, some Japanese resemble the people found in what is today the eastern area of the Soviet Union. Migrants from Southeast Asia also may have reached the archipelago by traveling northward along the island chains. It is possible, therefore, that the Japanese have absorbed physical characteristics from that region also.

The Ainu

One set of people in Japan cannot conveniently be placed in any **ethnic group.** They are the Ainu, a rapidly disappearing people who live on the island of Hokkaido. In physical appearance the Ainu are short and heavily built and have ruddy complexions. Unlike typical Japanese, Ainu men have much body hair. They are easily recognized by their long, thick beards and flowing mustaches.

At one time the Ainu were scattered throughout much of the Japanese archipelago. They were some of the earliest inhabitants of the islands. About 5,000 years ago they were drawn into a long fight for their lives and lands. Newer arrivals from the Asian mainland, ancestors of the modern Japanese, began to war with the Ainu, gradually forcing them northward. About 400 or 500

THE PEOPLE OF JAPAN. The bearded man at the right is an Ainu. Despite recent modernization, the Japanese still reflect traditions of the past. The farm couple above bow in respect to their employer, while the women below are not at all self-conscious shopping in their traditional kimonos.

years ago the Ainu withdrew to Hokkaido. There the last descendants of this people live today. Their distinctive characteristics, however, are rapidly being lost as they are absorbed into the Japanese community.

The Unity of Language

In ancient times many dialects were spoken in the Japanese islands, but these have largely disappeared during the past 1,000 years. Cultural and political unity has been fostered because the same language prevails everywhere in the country. Unlike China, the Soviet Union, or India, Japan has not been troubled by problems of language disunity.

The origins of the Japanese language have not yet been determined. Although its structure seems to relate it to such languages as Mongol and Turkic, some aspects of its vocabulary indicate a connection with languages spoken in Polynesia. The only Asian languages clearly related to Japanese are Okinawan and, to some extent, Korean. At any rate, Japanese is completely different in its structure and grammar from Chinese. When, as we shall see later, the Japanese adopted the Chinese system of writing, this difference created problems that still exist.

Japanese is not difficult to speak and pronounce. The native words, those not borrowed from other languages, are mainly polysyllabic, that is, composed of more than one syllable. Each syllable, moreover, is made up either of a single vowel or a consonant followed by a vowel. The following chart illustrates the composition of some typical Japanese words. The *n* that appears after a vowel should be sounded as a separate syllable.

Japanese	Syllable Make-up	Meaning
yama	ya ma	mountain
kimono	ki mo no	clothing
kamikaze	ka mi ka ze	"Wind of the Gods"
samurai	sa mu ra i	knight or warrior
sake	sa ke	rice-wine
banzai	ba n za i	Long live! Hurray! (literally "10,000 years")

Ordinarily, no syllable in a Japanese word is accented. For this reason the language has a very monotonous sound to people unfamiliar with Japanese.

Written Japanese

The strong Chinese influence on Japan is reflected in the Japanese system of writing. For centuries the Japanese practiced an **oral tradition** because they had no way of writing down their language. They memorized events and traditions and passed them on to the next generation by word of mouth. After a time, through their contacts with China, they discovered the advantages of writing and began to borrow the Chinese system. In this system each character stands for an idea or object, rather than for a sound, as in the Roman alphabet. This means that in order to be able to read and write, a student must memorize literally hundreds of different characters. At the same time, one such character could be read and understood by both Chinese and Japanese readers, even though neither could speak the other's language.

But many Japanese did learn to speak Chinese, and many Chinese words were adopted and became part of the Japanese language. As a result, the borrowed characters have at least two pronunciations, one Chinese and one Japanese. Usually, but not always, the meaning is the same with either pronunciation. For example, "Japan" is written 日本 in Chinese characters. The Chinese pronunciation for the word is "JIH-PEN," but the two characters are pronounced "NI-HON" or Nippon by the Japanese. In both the Chinese and the Japanese systems 日 means "sun," while 本 is the character for "root or origin." Literally, the two characters together mean "where the sun has its origin" or "Land of the Rising Sun."

Certain difficulties soon became apparent when the Japanese tried to use this Chinese system to write their own language. The characters had developed to fit the requirements of a language very different in its structure from Japanese, and could not always fill the needs of the new language. For example, Japanese, unlike Chinese, makes great use of post-positions. These are words that follow another word to indicate such things as ownership of an object, or the function of a word within the sentence. For instance, "wa" following a word indicates that the word is the subject of the sentence. Thus "watakushi wa Americajin desu" means "I am an American." "Kara" resembles the English word *from*, thus "kyo kara" means "after today" or "from today." Written Chinese did not have such signs and made no provisions for them. To solve problems such as this, the Japanese developed not one, but two writing systems of their own. Called **kana**, they were the creations of Buddhist monks of the ninth century. Both were **syllabaries,** alphabets

16

composed of symbols that represented the various syllables of Japanese words. Because most Japanese words are composed of several syllables, kana is well suited for writing Japanese.

The two Japanese syllabaries are known as *hiragana* and *katakana*. Hiragana is used in much the same way that we use cursive handwriting (script), while katakana resembles our Roman or block printing. In each system of kana there are 48 symbols, which are really abbreviations of Chinese characters. The appearance and method of spelling in kana may be noted by the following examples:

English spelling	Hiragana	Katakana
hi ra ga na	ひらがな	ヒラガナ
ka ta ka na	かたかな	カタカナ
Ya ma to	やまと	ヤマト
He i a n	へいあん	ヘイアン

Although the kana are far simpler than the Chinese characters and in some ways better suited to expressing Japanese in writing, they have never supplanted the Chinese characters. Instead, the Japanese use both characters and kana in the same sentence. The character is used for the noun or verb, for instance, and the kana is used for the post-position or other grammatical indication. If writers do not know the Chinese character for a word, they spell it out in the simpler kana. Thus for "of the mountain" writers may write either やまの or 山の.

The Japanese also use the Roman alphabet for certain limited purposes. Along the railways for instance, the names of stations are often shown on billboards in three systems of writing—Chinese, kana, and Roman letters. Because many Japanese read at least some English, such signs are not confusing to them.

Check Your Understanding

1. Where is China's influence on Japan most clearly seen?
2. Explain the differences between the Japanese and the Ainu.
3. Why did the Japanese develop a strong oral tradition?
4. **Thinking Critically:** What role has cultural adaptation played in the development of a unified Japanese language?

3. Shinto and Buddhism

Early in Japanese history, the people of the archipelago held religious beliefs about nature and its mysteries that were similar to the beliefs of other early peoples in northeast Asia. This nature worship of the early Japanese had no name until Buddhism reached Japan. There was little need for a name because nature worship had no founder, no ministers, no shrines, no formal creed, and no competition.

The term *Shinto*, literally "way of the kami," or forces of nature, was adopted to differentiate the native religion from Buddhism, the religion that was brought into the archipelago by Buddhist monks from India. Eventually Buddhism gained millions of followers in Japan. Today Shinto and Buddhism are the two faiths that hold the loyalty of most of the Japanese people.

Shinto—the Worship of Nature

For as far back as people can remember, Japanese people have practiced Shinto, a religion that is based upon the mysteries of nature. The Japanese adherence to Shinto is hardly surprising considering the various physical forces that are often at work on the islands. The howling typhoons, the treacherous tsunami, the erupting volcanoes, and the frequent earthquakes are the unseen forces of nature that rule the lives of the Japanese. Seeking a way to exercise some control over these destructive natural forces without understanding why they occurred, the Japanese practiced Shinto.

The Japanese call these unseen forces of nature **kami**. The light of the sun, the roar of thunder, the flash of lightning are all attributed to various kami. So too are all aspects of nature that arouse fear, awe, admiration, and love. Things that reflect unexplainable forces are all held in reverence. Virtually nothing in nature is separate from kami.

Originally a Shinto believer worshiped kami only in nature. Today in Japan, the kami are worshiped in shrines, an outgrowth of the influence of Buddhism. The shrines are often simple buildings surrounded by groves of trees. Before approaching a shrine, worshipers purify themselves by washing their hands and rinsing their mouths. Then, without ceremony, they offer food or other gifts to the kami of the shrine. A short prayer is then said. The following prayer is one recited in shrines at planting time:

If you receive in your hearts tranquilly and peacefully
   The noble offerings thus presented
      As offerings of ease,
      As offerings of abundance,
And if you spare all the products harvested by the
   common people of the kingdom
      From bad winds and rough waters
      And prosper them and bring them to fruition—
Then the first fruits, raising high the soaring necks
   Of the countless wine vessels, filled to the brim,
      Will be set up, in both liquor and stalks,
      Eight hundred ears [of rice], a thousand ears,
And will be presented in the autumn festival.

[Donald L. Philippi. *Norito: a New Translation of the Ancient Japanese Ritual Prayers.*]

The prayer urges the kami to withhold bad weather so that the new crop can grow. The worshipers then promise the kami a generous offering of first fruits in the fall if the crop is spared. But nowhere in this prayer, or in any Japanese prayer, is fear of the kami expressed.

Official sponsorship of Shinto was an important aspect of the Meiji Restoration of 1868. (See page 121.) In what came to be known as State Shinto, the Meiji government installed a system of national shrines and an office of Shinto worship and required Shinto to be taught in schools. The union of church and state took on an increasingly nationalistic flavor and became an integral part of the mobilization effort before and during World War II.

Buddhism in Japan

Buddhism, which was founded in India some 2,500 years ago, entered Japan in the sixth century A.D. (See page 51.) Today it has almost as many followers in Japan as Shinto. Actually, many Japanese are followers of both religions. Neither Shinto nor Buddhism is so rigid in its requirements that a person must adopt its ideas and practices to the exclusion of everything else. Many Japanese Buddhists also make offerings at Shinto shrines.

Buddhism did not become a major faith in Japan until about a thousand years after it developed in India. Japanese peasants did not begin to accept Buddhism until much later. For several centuries the new religion was the faith of the upper classes, people who appreciated the colorful Buddhist ceremonies and the stirring works of Buddhist artists. Rulers and nobles erected

JAPANESE SHRINES.   Many Japanese are followers of both Shinto and Buddhism. A pilgrimage to the Imperial Shrines at Ise (above) might also take the believer to the Buddhist temple called the Byodoin (below), located in the town of Uji.

Buddhist temples and monasteries and commissioned artists and sculptors to symbolize Buddhist beliefs. Much of Japan's architecture, art, and sculpture still shows strong Buddhist influence.

The common people did not at first accept Buddhism because it conflicted with their traditions. Valuing family life and children, peasants could not approve of a religion that prohibited the marriage of priests. Moreover, Buddhism was perhaps too moody and pessimistic for most Japanese. Changes in the spirit and practice of this imported religion had to be made before it could gain large numbers of converts. Such modifications came in the 1100's and 1200's, when religious leaders founded new Buddhist sects, better suited to the Japanese personality. The changes embodied in the sects, which are treated in Chapter 3, helped Buddhism to sweep through the country. Ever since that time, Buddhism has enjoyed an important place in Japanese life.

Other Faiths in Japan

Although almost all Japanese are either Buddhists or Shintoists, most have also been influenced by other beliefs. Confucianism, the elaborate moral and philosophical code of China, has had a considerable impact upon Japanese thought and behavior. Ranking behind Shinto and Buddhism in Japan is Christianity. After Christianity was brought to the islands by missionaries in the 1500's, it grew slowly for about a hundred years. But from 1637 to 1873, Christianity was banned in Japan. Trying to wipe it out completely, the Japanese government had thousands of Christians killed. Since the ban was lifted, however, Christianity in Japan has shown a somewhat steady growth, especially in the years since World War II. Today some 1.7 million Japanese are Christians.

Check Your Understanding

1. What is the relationship between kami and Shinto?
2. Why were most Japanese not attracted to Buddhism when it was first introduced?
3. **Thinking Critically:** How did the introduction of Buddhism into Japan influence Shinto?

CHAPTER REVIEW

■ **Chapter Summary**

Section 1. Life in the Japanese archipelago has been a challenge for its inhabitants. A mountainous terrain, little tillable land, and inadequate natural resources have encouraged the island people to become industrious, resourceful, and fiercely proud of their homeland. The sea has served them well as a source of food, as a highway for travel and commerce, and as a barrier against invasion. It also has facilitated cultural borrowing from China and Korea.

Section 2. Although spoken Japanese is unrelated to other Asian tongues, the writing system shows strong Chinese influence. Lacking a writing system, the Japanese adopted that of their neighbors. The problems involved in taking a system of writing developed for the Chinese and adapting it to fit another language led the Japanese to develop their own systems of writing. These kana, as they are called, may replace the Chinese characters but ordinarily are used in conjunction with them.

Section 3. The Japanese have two main faiths. The native Shinto is founded on nature worship. Aspects of nature that arouse fear, awe, admiration, or love are worshiped as kami. Prayers are said and offerings are made in order to reap benefits. Buddhism came to Japan from the mainland in the sixth century A.D. At first the common people showed no interest in the gloomy outlook and teachings of Buddhism, which were in direct conflict with the happier outlook of the Japanese. But in time new Buddhist sects, better suited to the Japanese personality, arose. Today Buddhism ranks with the native Shinto as one of the two major religions of Japan. Other religions, including Christianity, have entered Japanese life but none have achieved the widespread acceptance given to Buddhism and Shinto.

■ **Vocabulary Review**

Define: archipelago, megalopolis, paddy, tsunami, culture, institution, ethnic group, oral tradition, kana, syllabaries, kami

Places to Locate

Locate: Hokkaido, Honshu, Kyushu, Shikoku, Kurile Islands, Ryukyus Islands, Sakhalin, Mr. Fuji, Inland Sea, Tokyo

People to Know

Identify: Ainu

Thinking Critically

1. Why did Japan remain a frontier region for many centuries?
2. Why is Japan called a "Nation of Islands"?
3. How did Japan's island location affect its relations with other nations?
4. Why is reverence for nature an important characteristic of the Japanese people?
5. Why do ancient Japanese myths refer to the country as the "Land of the Ten Thousand Ears of Rice"?
6. How have natural forces helped shape the physical environment of Japan?

Extending and Applying Your Knowledge

1. Use encyclopedias and the *Readers' Guide to Periodical Literature* to research tsunami. Find out how many have struck Japan in recent history and where and how destructive they were. Make a diagram to show how a tsunami is created and gathers force. Use this information for a bulletin board display.
2. Write to the Japanese consulate or JAL airlines or find pictures of Japanese skyscrapers in magazines for a bulletin board display.

2
Formation of an Island Monarchy

For many centuries the inhabitants of Japan lived much like the prehistoric peoples of western and central Europe. Organized as small tribes, the Japanese lived on an archipelago off the Asian mainland. They lived along the islands' coasts and in interior valleys. The early Japanese had no system of writing and used no metals. Not until the early centuries A.D. did the Japanese come in contact with the advanced cultures on the Asian mainland and begin to adapt these cultures to their own distinctive ways of life.

From the fifth century A.D. onward, various facets of Chinese civilization met an ever-increasing acceptance among the upper classes in Japan. In the 600's, leaders in Yamato, a state in central Honshu, organized Japan's first central government with an **emperor** at its head. They stepped up the introduction of Chinese ways into Japan through a series of reforms that made revolutionary changes in Japan. Although the Yamato government claimed authority throughout the archipelago, it lacked the military strength and economic resources to command widespread obedience. Because it needed the backing of important court families to maintain control of Japan, the imperial government allowed itself to be used by these families. But outside the court in the outlying provinces, powerful warrior families were quietly amassing power of their own. Their power finally emerged in 1156. For many centuries thereafter, imperial rule, though continuing to exist in name, became a powerless shadow of its former self.

1. The History of Early Japan

Japan's islands have been inhabited for thousands of years, but little is known about life in the archipelago during prehistoric times. Before World War II, very little archaeological research was conducted in Japan. Since then archaeologists have uncovered many sites. The information thus far assembled, however, has been fragmentary and incomplete. Knowledge of prehistoric Japan is based upon these remains, together with information gathered from Korean and Chinese accounts. It is highly doubtful that the story of early Japan will ever be fully known.

The Jomon Culture

Most of the early Japanese probably came from northeast Asia. Even in ancient times, it was not difficult to make the crossing from the mainland of Asia to Japan. The earliest people of Japan seem to have entered the archipelago mainly by way of Sakhalin and Korea. The island of Sakhalin provided a stepping stone for migration from the north. (See page 3.) Moreover, the western island of Kyushu is separated from the Korean Peninsula by less than 100 miles of sea. Available evidence also indicates that southeast Asian migrants reached the archipelago by traveling northward along the islands south of Japan. These ancestors of the Japanese ultimately developed Middle–Stone–Age cultures. (See page 27.) These ancestors maintained themselves by hunt-

TIMETABLE

Development of the Japanese State

8000–300 B.C.	Jomon Culture
300 B.C.–A.D. 300	Yayoi Culture
300–700	Tomb Culture
593–622	Reign of Shotoku
646	Reform Edict
645–710	Taika period
710–784	Nara period
720	*Nihongi* completed
794–857	Early Heian period
857–1160	Late Heian (Fujiwara) period
1156	End of the Fujiwara period

EARLY CULTURES. This Jomon "cat lady" to the right is representative of the Stone Age culture supplanted by the Yayoi Bronze Age. It is typified by the bronze mirror above.

ing and fishing. Their tools were made of polished stone, and their homes, like those of many people on the Asian mainland, were pits that were dug in the earth and then roofed over. These prehistoric inhabitants produced beautiful pottery, the surfaces of which were decorated with rope-like designs. Archaeologists call their way of life the Jomon Culture and estimate its date as about 8000–300 B.C.

The Yayoi and Tomb Cultures

About the third or second century B.C., new waves of immigrants began to enter the islands from the Korean Peninsula. Their ways of living were more advanced than those of the people already living in the archipelago. The newcomers introduced agriculture, and especially the cultivation of rice, into Japan. They also brought metalworking in bronze, probably having learned this skill from the Chinese. But the Japanese Bronze Age was of short duration. The final immigrations brought iron workers into the islands. Over the course of several centuries these newer settlers helped change the existing cultures. The new way of life, which lasted approximately 600 years, is called the Yayoi Culture.

The Tomb Culture, the most advanced of prehistoric Japan, developed from the Yayoi Culture. The name *Tomb Culture* is given to this way of life because much of the information about it comes from burial mounds. These huge earth-mounds may still be seen today in scattered locations around the Inland Sea and even as far westward as northern Kyushu. Square, round, or keyhole shaped, the mounds are located on the tops of hills

S IDELIGHT TO HISTORY

The Ages of Prehistory

The period of time before people kept written records is called prehistory. For the world as a whole, the period of prehistory varies, depending on the people and the region of the world being studied. For some people, prehistory has never ended because in remote regions of the world today people exist who have never developed a system of writing or learned to work with metals. The period of prehistory is usually called the Stone Age, which is generally divided into three subperiods—the Old Stone Age, the Middle Stone Age, and the New Stone Age.

People living in the Old Stone Age, or Paleolithic period, obtained their food by hunting and gathering and lived in naturally formed shelters such as caves. They used stone tools, sometimes chipping them to form sharp edges. On the walls of their shelters, they sometimes painted or drew scenes that showed how they lived. Such cave drawings have been found in France and Spain.

The Middle Stone Age, also called the Mesolithic period, was usually a transition period that led to the New Stone Age or Neolithic period. During the Middle Stone Age, in Europe, changes took place that led to the development of new tools such as the ax and the bow and arrow. Fishing became important as people settled along river banks and seashores. While this period in Europe ended about 8000 B.C., in Japan people were still living in the Mesolithic period about 300 B.C.

In the New Stone Age, people changed from food gatherers to food producers by learning to grow their own food and to domesticate animals. They settled in permanent villages. They then developed even more advanced tools, began to specialize in different occupations, and learned how to barter, or trade, with one another.

Eventually people learned metalworking, ushering in the Age of Metals. First they learned how to work with copper, then with bronze—a mixture of copper and tin. Finally they learned how to work with iron, an even harder and more useful metal. In Europe the New Stone Age had ended and the Age of Metals had begun by 3000 B.C. In Japan the Age of Metals began about A.D. 200.

and in the center of large plains. Archaeologists believe they are the tombs of local chieftains who lived from the third to the seventh centuries A.D. The largest of these artificial mounds is 120 feet high and 1,500 feet long. Such immensity hints at the great power once wielded by the chieftains buried within them. Rulers would need effective control over thousands of people to build mounds that size.

Many kinds of artifacts, including iron weapons and tools, have been found in the burial crypts of Japan's ancient mound builders. These artifacts make it clear that many technological advances had taken place in Japan since the days of the earlier prehistoric cultures. These improvements in weapons and tools were the work of later immigrants rather than that of people long resident on the islands.

Clay figurines, or **haniwa,** are among the most interesting artifacts found in the mound burial crypts. According to Japanese legend, the servants of a dead ruler were sacrificed at their master's funeral so they might serve him in the next world. An early emperor, it is said, rebelled against this practice and ordered that it be stopped. The haniwa were placed in the tombs as symbolic servants for the ruler in the next life. The haniwa also represented animals, houses, boats, and other objects the ruler might use in the next life. The haniwa tell much about the life and culture of the times. The types of clothing, weapons, and armor engraved on the figurines are further proof that these ancestors of the Japanese borrowed much from Korea and other parts of mainland Asia. The haniwa are disarmingly simple in design and exhibit a liveliness captured only in the best art and sculpture. Many critics rate the haniwa as the finest artistic creations of ancient Japan.

Chinese Accounts About Japanese Life

During the time of the Tomb Culture, references to Japan began to appear in the Chinese histories of the day. The Chinese regarded the early Japanese as barbarians, or uncultured people. *Wa,* the name the Chinese gave Japan in this period, means, in effect, "dwarf." Written references are brief. The following account appears in the history of a Chinese dynasty that ruled from A.D. 220 to 265.

> The land of Wa [Japan] is warm and mild. In winter as in summer the people live on raw vegetables and go about barefooted. . . . They smear their bodies with pink and scarlet, just as the Chinese use powder. They serve food

TOMB CULTURE. The life and culture of the Tomb Age are recorded in the clay figurines (haniwa) of the period. This alert warrior and his steed reveal the importance of the mounted knight in Tomb Age society, and give details of arms and dress.

on bamboo and wooden trays, helping themselves with their fingers. When a person dies, they prepare a single coffin, without an inner one. They cover the graves with earth to make a mound. When death occurs, mourning is observed for more than ten days, during which period they do not eat meat. The head mourners wail and lament, while friends sing, dance, and drink liquor. When the funeral is over, all members of the family go into the water to cleanse themselves in a bath of purification. . . .

In their meetings and in their deportment, there is no distinction between father and son or between men and women. They are fond of liquor. In their worship, men of importance simply clap their hands instead of kneeling or bowing. The people live long, some to one hundred and others to eighty or ninety years. Ordinarily, men of importance have four or five wives; the lesser ones two or three. Women are not loose in morals or jealous. In case of violation of law, the light offender loses his wife and children by confiscation; as for the grave offender, the members of his household and also his kinsmen are exterminated.

[Ryusaku Tsunoda, William T. de Bary, and Donald Keene, *Sources of Japanese Tradition.*]

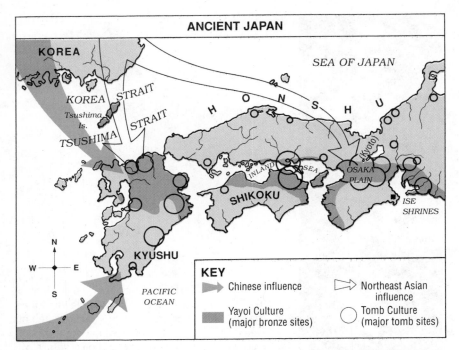

ANCIENT JAPAN

KEY

Chinese influence

Northeast Asian influence

Yayoi Culture (major bronze sites)

Tomb Culture (major tomb sites)

MOVEMENT: THE SPREAD OF CULTURES. The spread of the Yayoi and Tomb cultures in Japan brought such advances as agriculture and bronze-working to the islands. These advances probably reached Kyushu first, via Korea or the Ryukyus, and moved northward until they reached the Osaka Plain. The rich soil of the plain soon made it the new center of wealth and power.

Chinese accounts also provide insight into the political structure of early Japan. Evidently there was little political unity among the Japanese. In the year A.D. 57, according to a Chinese record, Japan consisted of more than 100 scattered tribal communities. The various chieftains fought one another for territory. By 220 the number of communities had been reduced to about 40, as the larger states overpowered their weaker neighbors. During the next 200 years, a region in west central Honshu, called Yamato (yah-MAH-toh), began to emerge as the most powerful state in Japan. The historian of the Chinese dynasty that ruled from 420 to 479 relates that the Chinese emperor recognized the Yamato ruler as king of the Wa. Still, even at this late date, the basic social unit of Yamato society was the **uji.**

Korean and Chinese Influences

Most of early Japan's contacts with Chinese civilization came through Korea. Korean monarchies had adopted various Chinese customs while Japan was still a prehistoric land. Since Korean monarchs often asked Japanese rulers for help in time of war, many Japanese visitors to the Korean Peninsula observed first-hand the borrowed Chinese customs. Eventually, Japanese chieftains invaded the Korean Peninsula, and by the mid–400's, the Japanese occupied considerable Korean territory. The Japanese subsequently lost these lands. But the Japanese developed a liking for the modified Chinese culture they found during their stay in Korea.

Yamato, the most important Japanese state, took the lead in introducing Chinese culture. Envoys from the Yamato court visited the court of the Chinese emperor, returning with glowing reports of the cultural advances found there. Moreover, scholars, craftsworkers, artists, and Buddhist monks came from China and Korea to Japan. Influential nobles at the Yamato court recognized that these people possessed a richer cultural background than their own.

Chinese civilization was especially respected by Prince Shotoku, **regent** of Yamato from 593 to 622. Although legends have colored his accomplishments, Prince Shotoku was a remarkable person. He had a deep appreciation for Chinese history, philosophy, religion, and art. Shotoku deliberately set out to build a Japanese state based on the Chinese model. He sent missions to China to study landholding and tax systems, law codes, and governmental and military organization. He also approved the spread of Buddhism, a religion that some decades earlier had

Prince Shotoku, the regent of Yamato from 593 to 622, is credited with speeding up acceptance of Chinese culture in Japan. This portrait of the Prince and two of his sons shows them dressed in the style of the Chinese court.

Buddhism's Introduction into Japan

Twenty-five centuries ago a young Indian nobleman named Gautama left his comfortable palace to seek the meaning of life. Six years of self-sacrifice and solitude brought him no closer to the answer. Then, as Gautama sat under a tree in deep meditation, he received a revelation that the "Eightfold Path of Right Living" was the only way to find peace.

Gautama suddenly saw that a life of suffering and impermanence was caused by selfish desires, and that only the destruction of these desires could bring peace. With this revelation Gautama became the Buddha, or Enlightened One, and he set out to convince others to follow the Eightfold Path. Although Buddha's teachings spread slowly during his lifetime, after his death they reached many parts of Asia. Over the course of a few centuries, the words of Gautama were transformed into the teachings of Buddhism, the leading religion of the East.

According to tradition, Buddhism reached Japan in A.D. 552. In that year a Korean monarch is said to have turned to the Japanese for military help against Korea's enemies. To gain favor, the monarch sent the Japanese some gifts: a bronze Buddha, Buddhist scriptures, and an explanation of the faith. Actually, however, Buddhism had entered Japan several decades earlier, but had met with little success.

The Japanese responded in different ways to the new faith. Many feared Buddhism as a threat to the Japanese way of life. Others in Japan saw Buddhism as an opportunity to learn more about the cultural advances on the Asian mainland. Curiosity about the new faith won out, and Buddhist temples and monasteries began to appear in Japan. The Buddhist monasteries became seats of Chinese learning, and a whole new world of art, literature, and language was opened to the Japanese. Today the Japanese belong to many Buddhist sects. (See pages 65–69.) The most popular is Nichiren. Other important sects are Zen, Jodo (Pure Land), True Pure Land, and Shingon.

entered Japan via Korea. By the end of his reign more than 800 monks were promoting Buddhism among the upper classes.

Shotoku's program of cultural borrowing was not approved by everyone. Some powerful families at the court opposed the introduction of foreign ways. Having inherited various privileges in the government and in society, these families felt threatened by political and social changes. They liked to look upon themselves as the guardians of Japan's long-standing **traditions.** After Shotoku died, these opponents of reform took over the reins of government. For more than 20 years little was done to promote Chinese culture in Japan. Those Japanese who admired Chinese civilization had no alternative but to wait for a better opportunity to put Shotoku's ideas into practice.

Check Your Understanding

1. **a.** Who developed the Jomon Culture? **b.** Describe it.
2. How did the Yayoi Culture differ from the Jomon Culture?
3. What have archaeologists learned about early Japan from the Tomb Culture?
4. What insights do Chinese accounts of prehistoric Japan provide about the people and the political life?
5. How did early Japan make contact with Chinese civilization?
6. *Thinking Critically:* How did the emergence of Yamato as the most powerful state in early Japan speed up acceptance of Chinese culture in the archipelago? How was this acceptance brought about?

2. Japan Under the Taika Program

In 645 several leading nobles, enthusiasts of Chinese culture, joined forces to seize power in Yamato. After establishing an emperor of their choice, they began an unusually ambitious series of political, social, and economic changes. Known in Japanese history as the Taika (TY-kah), or Great Reforms, program, the changes were carried forward for more than a century. Although many of the reforms were never completed and others were abandoned as unworkable, the spirit and flavor of the reforms had a lasting effect on Japanese life.

Setting Up the Program

The reformers moved fast to set up their program. The leaders who aspired to control the Yamato state gave their potential challengers little opportunity for a countermove. First, the leaders ruthlessly killed or imprisoned those who favored the deposed regime. Then they called a meeting of the leaders of the great uji, or clans, that controlled most of the land. At this gathering the reformers outlined the changes they had in mind and gained support for the program. At this meeting they also proclaimed the Yamato ruler the emperor of all Japan.

In 646, acting in the name of the emperor, the reform leaders issued the famous Reform Edict. This edict consisted of four main points. It established Yamato as the seat of imperial rule. It abolished private ownership of land, making all territory the property of the imperial government. The Edict also announced that all cultivated lands in Japan were to be retained by the peasants who worked them. Finally, the Edict abolished the old methods of taxation and established a completely new system. Clearly, the reformers, through the Taika program, sought to revolutionize Japanese life.

A New System of Government

The Taika reformers established a new system of government. The main branch of the large imperial family was to form the **dynasty**, but members of all branches were given grand titles. So, too, were high-ranking nobles of other important uji in and around Yamato. Both the system of rank and the titles were borrowed from the Chinese court. Most offices carried more honor than power, but the officeholders enjoyed favor with the emperor—a consideration that became increasingly important as time passed. The emperor ruled supreme only in theory. In practice, the nobles representing the great clans around Yamato had considerable influence over his decisions.

The central government tried gradually to extend its authority into the outlying areas. Under the provisions of the reform program all regions that formerly were independent states became **provinces** in the Japanese Empire. When possible, the imperial regime appointed its own trusted officials as governors of provinces. However, if resistance seemed likely, the emperor gave the traditional ruler a new title (usually vice-governor), making him an imperial officer. In such cases the emperor continued to appoint a governor from the ranks of the court nobility. However, many governors never bothered to perform their duties, preferring a life of ease made possible by income from

This graceful Buddha of Mercy from the Horyuji Temple, carved in the early 600's, is an example of the artistic and cultural wealth that surrounded the new city of Nara from the start.

their offices. Such offices became hereditary, and were passed on from father to son for generations.

Official Histories

The Taika reformers introduced another practice borrowed from the Chinese court. Scholars were assigned the task of writing an official history. Since none existed for early Japan, the court historians patiently collected, organized, and recorded many ancient myths, legends, and documents. The result was the *Kojiki*, or *Record of Ancient Matters*, a rather fanciful account largely of the Yamato people and their rulers since the beginning of the universe. This work was completed in 712. Further literary polishing and corrections transformed the *Kojiki* into the *Nihongi*, or *Chronicles of Japan*, a project finished in 720. In these histories, heroes and others who made outstanding contributions were given the status of supernatural beings. Their ancestry was traced to powerful kami, the forces behind nature. (See page 18.)

The preparation of the official history was an important part of the Taika program. As part of their effort to add increased legitimacy to Yamato rulers, the writers elevated the emperor to a position of divinity and unquestioned supremacy. According to the *Nihongi*, the rulers of Yamato were descended from a kami of the sun, a female named Amaterasu, meaning "Heavenly Shining One." Her parents, also kami, had created the islands of Japan, and Amaterasu had bestowed them upon her descendants for all time. The grandson of Amaterasu left heaven to establish a monarchy in the islands. Since the emperor was of divine origin, no ordinary mortal dared challenge him. And since the imperial family had received the islands as a gift from the gods, imperial ownership of all land could not be questioned. In time the divine origin of the imperial family was accepted throughout Japan.

Building an Imperial Capital

The architects of the new Japanese state decided that their ruler must have a permanent residence in keeping with his exalted position. At the time Japan had no cities and only a few towns, and no state in Japan had a permanent capital. Instead the seat of government was the current ruler's estate. When a ruler died, the place of residence of the succeeding ruler became the new capital.

After a few years, the reformers began building Nara, a city patterned after Chang'an, the capital of the Chinese Empire. But Nara, the capital of Japan from 710 to 784, was built on a much smaller scale because Japan lacked the wealth to duplicate China's magnificent capital. During this period, Buddhist monks became influential at court. Partly to escape Buddhist domination, the emperor in 784 moved his court from Nara to a temporary capital in a nearby town.

Soon after this move, the construction of a new capital city called Heian (HAY-AHN) began on a site about 30 miles from Nara. Like Nara, Heian was planned to be a miniature version of the Chinese capital. But unlike Nara, Heian was to be built on a larger scale. First occupied in 794, Heian later came to be called Kyoto, which means "the capital." Kyoto became a great cultural center and served as the capital of Japan until 1868. In that year the seat of government was moved to Tokyo, Japan's present capital.

Imperial Needs and Demands

To meet its many needs, the imperial government imposed taxes on produce, demanded a labor tax, and required military service from its subjects. The produce tax called for a share of the crops from each tract of land. The labor tax required peasants to work on the building of Nara and other government projects.

Yamato—Its Legendary Beginnings

The myths of the *Nihongi* are of interest to the archaeologists who wish to trace the affairs of early Japan. These legends reflect the struggles of the Yamato people to establish their claim to the throne of all Japan. Yamato was not without rivals, and the story of its triumph may be gleaned from the myths surrounding the foundation of the imperial dynasty, "unbroken from ages eternal."

A central story of the *Nihongi* deals with the conflict between the sun goddess, Amaterasu, the patron, or ancestress, of the Yamato clan, and her younger brother Susa-no-o, the storm god. Susa-no-o, violent and impious, offended Amaterasu so greatly that she shut herself away in a cave, leaving the world in darkness and cold. Though the other deities cleverly lured her forth again, Susa-no-o was banished to earth. He settled in the region of Izumo, on the west coast of Honshu.

Here Susa-no-o seems to have reformed, for he and his descendants are said to have brought the knowledge of law and of medicine to the people of Izumo. They built boats, and traded with Korea. Indeed, so well did they rule that many Koreans were led to emigrate to Japan. But the people of Izumo were unable to control all the evil elements in the Japanese Islands. Finally Amaterasu decided to send her own grandson to found an imperial line that would rule Japan forever. Susa-no-o and his sons willingly yielded their positions to the imperial grandson, and received in reward the Great Shrine of Izumo as their home.

This story about the real rivalry that existed between Ameratsu and Susa-no-o evidently represents a rivalry between Yamato and another strong clan located in Izumo. The people of Izumo seem to have had close ties with Korea and to have served as transmitters of new skills and knowledge from the mainland to the rest of Japan. Yamato finally won the contest for supremacy from his rival by a narrow margin, which suggests a reason why the Great Shrine of Izumo is among the most revered in all Japan. Only the Grand Imperial Shrine of the sun goddess at Ise has surpassed it in popularity.

To maintain its authority and defend its frontiers, the state had need for many citizen-soldiers. Moreover, many emperors sought to push the Ainu out of the northern territories in order to resettle Japanese in this area. (See page 13.) To achieve their military goals, the government had to depend almost completely upon **conscription**, which placed a heavy burden on the peasants. Peasants drafted during the growing season were in danger of losing their entire rice crop. Not only did the conscripts have to provide their own food, their own tools, and their own weapons, but they also had to provide and feed the horses that were needed by the government. So burdensome was military service to the peasants that many of them fled from their lands rather than serve in the army.

By the late 700's, it was clear even to the emperor that conscription was not the answer to Japan's military needs. Instead of conscripting citizens, the emperor appointed a commander to recruit soldiers in the eastern provinces. Soldiers from this area already had won a reputation for bravery in campaigns in Korea and against the Ainu. The commander was given the high-sounding title of "Barbarian–Quelling Generalissimo" for the duration of a campaign. For short, the commander was simply referred to as **shogun**, or general. Holders of the title, who had to be related to the imperial family, exercised the military authority of the emperor. But once a campaign ended, the title of shogun was restored to the emperor. Despite this limitation, the title of shogun became one of the most sought after in the realm.

Failure of Some Reforms

Even during the Taika period (645–710), it became obvious that much of the reform program was unsuitable for Japan. Having great admiration for Chinese civilization, the reformers tried to reproduce it as a whole rather than adopt only those laws and those procedures that were actually appropriate for Japan. As a result, the reformers were not always successful in achieving their goals.

A case in point were the land laws. Following the pattern that had been established by the Tang rulers of China, the reformers declared that all of the land in Japan was part of the imperial domain. Moreover, the land was assigned to the peasants who worked it. But in implementing imperial land laws, the reformers had to contend with the uji. The uji had controlled most of Japan's land and people for centuries and resented the loss of their lands and their power. To gain the support of the uji, the Taika reformers appointed the leaders of the chief clans as governors or vice-governors of the lands they formerly ruled. The clan leaders collected taxes from the peasants, sent the revenues to the imperial court, and then received them back in the form of salaries and gifts. In actuality, little had really changed.

Taken as a whole, the land reform laws were not a complete success. Some land was redistributed among the peasants, but in most cases the government simply confirmed the right of landowners and peasants to use the land as they had before the Reform Edict was passed. Little cultivated land was actually added to the imperial estates, except in the frontier areas, because the government was not strong enough to wrest it from the traditional owners. Quite a bit of marginal land was reclaimed for rice and other crops. But most of this work was done by private developers, and the reclaimed land became, in effect, private property. Finally, the government reduced its own revenue from land by granting immunity from taxation to a number of imperial officers, nobles, and Buddhist temples. By the beginning of the Nara period (710–784), the inadequacies of the land reform laws were apparent. Japan was plagued with problems of landholding until after World War II, when the American Occupation pushed through an effective land reform law. (See page 185.)

Lasting Influences of Reform

Because many proposals were never carried out, and others involved little more than calling old things by new names, the hard core of traditional Japanese culture remained unbroken. Despite these shortcomings, the Taika reform program produced revolutionary changes in Japan. It firmly established the primacy of the ruling house of Yamato, and upper-class Japanese culture came to reflect that of China.

At the beginning of the early Heian period (794–857), most of the laws embodied in the Taika program were still on the books, although many of them were being ignored in practice. Further changes were likely to be produced as the central government was being forced to surrender its authority to the Fujiwara clan. In addition, in the outlying provinces, several of the uji had developed into powerful warrior clans. How this warrior class supplanted the imperial rulers will be told in later sections of this chapter.

Check Your Understanding

1. What were the four main points of the Taika Reform Edict?
2. How did the Taika program reform the government of Japan?
3. How did the reform program promote the traditions and legends of Japan?
4. What steps did the imperial government take to meet: **a.** its revenue needs? **b.** its military needs?
5. Why were the land reform laws only partially successful?
6. *Thinking Critically:* How significant was the building of a permanent capital in achieving the political successes of the reform program?

3. The Era of Fujiwara Domination

From the mid–800's to the mid–1100's the Fujiwara family so dominated the imperial government that it gave its name to the period. This Fujiwara clan was established by Kamatari, one of the leaders in the "palace revolt" of 645. (See page 33.) Throughout the period of reform (645–710), the Nara period (710–784), and the early Heian period (794–857), the Fujiwara steadily gained influence. Consequently the eventual Fujiwara takeover was no surprise. The Fujiwara period, also called the late Heian period (857–1160), lasted until warrior families from the outlying provinces took over the imperial court.

The Fujiwara

The 200 years following the Reform Edict were marked by fierce competition among the various court families for imperial favor. The prize was worth seeking, for imperial favor carried with it broad powers. One of the court families, the Fujiwara, regularly succeeded in outsmarting its rivals. A favorite maneuver was to marry into the imperial line. Fujiwara leaders were able to marry their daughters to young emperors and to claimants to the throne. For most of the Nara and early Heian periods the fathers-in-law to the emperor were Fujiwara. Usually, the father-in-law was also the emperor's closest adviser. As a result of such close influence, by 850 the Fujiwara were able to fill all important offices of state with their relatives.

40

Despite their overwhelming power, the Fujiwara never attempted to overturn the imperial dynasty. Indeed, the right of the imperial line to reign has never really been challenged, even in modern times. The emperors of Japan were to be stripped of their authority for centuries on end, but never were there rivals who sought to oust the imperial family from the throne. The Japanese rightly claim that theirs is the world's oldest ruling dynasty. Evidence of the unique position of the imperial line is that it has only one family or dynastic name. Every other person of importance in Japan has two names—the family name, which comes first, and the given name.

Draining Imperial Resources

In 858 a descendant of Kamatari placed his nine-year-old grandson on the throne and had himself named as regent. For centuries thereafter, whenever an emperor abdicated or died, the new ruler often was a minor. It became customary for the grandfather, always a Fujiwara, to gain appointment as regent. At times the Fujiwara boldly forced the emperor to step down from his throne, thus making way for a child-emperor who would be less likely to make trouble.

Once the Fujiwara made the emperors into **puppet rulers,** they and other court families proceeded to plunder many of the imperial estates and to take over the government's sources of revenue. These court families also secured special imperial charters that granted them the right to own estates and to be free from the payment of taxes. By such moves, a large part of the imperial domain came under the control or ownership of the Fujiwara and other influential clans. All these moves violated the intent of the Taika program. Thus both the emperor's power and his source of wealth were steadily drained away.

The Growth of the Aristocracy

Away from Heian, in the areas that formerly had been independent states, descendants of the original uji still held considerable influence. They scorned the frivolous life in the capital and held the "dandies" at the imperial court in contempt. Proud of their traditions and customs, the descendants of the uji gloried in their rough and simple ways of living as warriors who fought one another, the imperial forces, and the Ainu. Their most highly esteemed virtues were valor and strength in the face of battle, and skill in the use of arms. The most admired men were the **samurai,** the elite of the cavalry, who strove to possess these virtues. (See page 44.)

The vast and often widely scattered estates of the Kyoto families required efficient management if they were to produce income for their owners. Often this task fell to junior members of a court family, men whose chances for advancement in the capital were slim. Many such men, including descendants of the imperial family, acquired lands of their own and settled permanently in the provinces. These junior members frequently married into or allied themselves with members of the provincial warrior families. Thus there developed a new **aristocracy**, prestigious because of its ties with the imperial court but with its base of power in the countryside. The most powerful of these provincial families were the Taira and the Minamoto, both of whom were founded by descendants of the imperial family itself.

The Beginnings of a Feudal System

As the court nobility and the warrior families enlarged their landholdings at the expense of the imperial government, the power structure in the provinces began to change. The control of the central government was weakened, and violence and disorder increased. Owners of small farms in rural districts, long accustomed to taking up arms in defense of their homes, could no longer cope with the situation. They saw little advantage in paying taxes to a government that no longer could protect them. The large and often tax-exempt estates held by powerful nobles and warrior chiefs provided the answer to their problem. Farmers could commend their land to the holder of such an estate. **Commendation** meant that the farmers gave up claim to their lands to nobles, who then made these lands part of their estates. The peasants continued to work their lands as before, paying a small fee for this right. In return the farmers gained wealthy and powerful protectors, while the nobles and warrior chiefs gained additional income and control over more land and people. Everyone profited except the imperial government.

As imperial government control continued to weaken, the strength of the provincial military class grew. Using the farmers under their protection, the local aristocracy and the stewards of Kyoto-owned estates created and maintained private armies. They used these armies to defend their lands from the increasing disorders in the provinces and often to extend their holdings. Many aristocrats and stewards became skillful military commanders. Certain families gained power in large areas, forcing lesser nobles to ally themselves with one another. By the end of the ninth century, the beginnings of a system similar in many ways to European **feudalism** was well established in the provinces. Farmers paid in military service and rice for the protection of a warrior chieftain, who in turn might owe loyalty and service as a **vassal** to a more powerful lord.

Decline of Fujiwara Domination

A Japanese proverb says: "Even monkeys fall from trees." While the warrior families were gaining control in the provinces, the Fujiwara were gradually losing control over the imperial government. In 1027, all but two of the 24 highest offices in the government were filled by Fujiwara. By the early 1100's, fully half of the offices were occupied by members of the provincial Minamoto family.

The reversal in the fortunes of the Fujiwara had several causes. One was a new imperial practice that evolved during the mid–1100's. Frustrated by the ceremonial functions that prevented them from ruling effectively, emperors began to abdicate at the height of their reigns and retire to monasteries. Then a retired emperor, having appointed a successor, would continue to rule as a **cloistered emperor,** making all important decisions. The successor became known as the **titular emperor** and performed all ceremonial obligations. The Fujiwara continued to hold the highest titles at the Heian court because the elaborate system of titles, ranks, and privileges had been built around the titular emperor. The cloistered emperor, who was the real ruler, was now free to choose his advisers without regard for rank or family. Some appointees were Fujiwara or members of other court families. But many were Taira or Minamoto. Actually Taira, Minamoto, and Fujiwara were all represented in both the titular and cloistered groups. Rivalry still prevailed within the clans and among the clans. Usually the Taira predominated in the group around one emperor, while the Minamoto predominated in the group around the other.

The rise of the Taira and Minamoto was especially damaging to the Fujiwara cause. These families controlled much land and wealth, as well as many warriors. As their holdings began to exceed those of the Fujiwara, the emperors, both titular and cloistered, increasingly turned to the Taira and Minamoto families for help and advice. Indeed, the Fujiwara family itself developed strong ties with the Minamoto. Although most of the Taira and Minamoto remained in the provinces, building up their strength and influence, some came to Heian where they gained appointments to key posts in the two imperial governments. Every time a Taira or Minamoto was appointed to office, the position of the Fujiwara was weakened a little more.

The Samurai

The samurai was the hereditary warrior class of feudal Japan. The word *samurai* comes from the Japanese verb *samurau,* which means "to serve." At first the imperial guard were the only warriors referred to as samurai. But as feudalism developed, the shogun rose to power, and warrior chieftains commanded other warriors. The term *samurai* then came to include the entire warrior class— samurai warriors, warrior chieftains, and the shogun.

As feudalism developed and flourished in Japan through three military shogunates, the samurai class dominated Japanese society. Members of the imperial court and the shogunate were all samurai or members of samurai families. Military life revolved around Bushido (boo-SHEE-doh), the samurai code of behavior. Bushido stressed unwavering loyalty to one's lord, the highest degree of courage on the battlefield, exceptional self-control, indifference to pain and worldly wealth, and above all, honor. To preserve personal honor or that of their lord or to atone for a wrong, a samurai committed seppuku (seh-POO-koo), a ceremonial suicide performed with one of the two swords worn by all samurai.

The samurai treated their swords, which they wore crossed at the left hip, with great reverence. To the samurai, the sword was far more than a weapon. It was the symbol of their rank and their honor. It was also a great work of art. Swordsmiths forged and tempered the steel of each sword's blade and balanced it for use in battle. They also adorned the hilt and the blade of each sword with rich fittings of gold and silver and ornamental lacquerwork. Samurai swords were handed down from father to son. Today in Japan, samurai swords are considered national treasures and may not be taken from the country.

As feudalism was replaced with more modern social structures, the samurai lost their positions as warriors. Some accepted positions as officials of the government. Others became interested in scholarship or turned to business. Today many of the leaders of Japan's most productive businesses are descendants of samurai.

The Supremacy of Warrior Rule

In 1156 the court nobles committed a blunder that changed the course of Japanese history. When the emperor died, the two imperial **factions** disagreed on a successor. Unable to settle the issue, the faction in which the Minamoto dominated turned to a Minamoto chieftain. The other faction asked for help from a Taira chieftain. After a brief but hard-fought struggle in the streets of the capital, the Taira were victorious. A few years later, the Taira leaders put down an attempted **coup** by the Minamoto. This second victory assured the Taira-led group of control over imperial affairs.

The Taira victories paved the way for the supremacy of warriors in Japanese government. Although Taira warriors did not remain in control for long, Japan was ruled for more than 700 years by military families. Already supreme in the provinces, these "knights on horseback" could not be ousted from power once they reduced the imperial government's power and made it subject to their bidding. It is true that the emperor continued to command considerable prestige despite the exalted position of the warriors. Furthermore, Fujiwara nobles, and, to a lesser degree, other nobles, continued to hold high offices in government. But all in all, the Taira takeover marked the eclipse of the Japanese emperors and the noble families at court. From 1156 to 1868 it was provincial lords, not Heian aristocrats, that governed Japan.

The unsuccessful coup of the Minamoto clan began in 1159 with the violent abduction of the cloistered emperor. This episode, pictured below, truly symbolized the overthrow of the civil authority by the warrior class. What was the role of the cloistered emperor?

Check Your Understanding

1. **a.** How did the Fujiwara gain and maintain their positions of power and influence? **b.** How did they lose them?
2. What led to the development of a warrior aristocracy and the beginnings of a feudal system?
3. *Thinking Critically:* Cite evidence from the section to prove or refute this statement: *The emperor and the imperial court's rivalries led to the rise of warrior rule.*

4. The World of the Heian Court

The world of the Heian court has had few, if any, counterparts in history. Its chief goal was living well. Rituals, ceremonies, conversation, singing, and the recitation of poetry occupied the days and evenings of the princes, nobles, imperial officers, and ladies-in-waiting. Far removed from such realities as warfare and poverty, these aristocrats led a unique life and provided a fascinating page in the history of Japan.

Cultural Borrowing from China

For several centuries the aristocrats at the Heian court steeped themselves in the arts and literature of China. Familiarity with Chinese culture was deemed the indispensable mark of good taste and manners. Courtiers and ladies-in-waiting vied with one another to exhibit the newest fashions and interests of China. In matters of architecture, interior decoration, and gardening, the tastes of the Heian aristocrats were delicate and refined. These princes, officers, courtiers, and ladies-in-waiting were alert to every detail of their costumes and hairstyles. Beautiful flowers and trees were greatly admired, and moon-watching was a popular diversion. Excited by the universe about them, the aristocrats never tired of expressing their enjoyment of nature in poem and song. In time, the Heian court became a remark-able center of cultural sophistication, even though the rest of Japan followed a simple, rural life-style. The Japanese process of cultural borrowing has been summed up in the phrase *adopt, adapt, adept.* The ability of the Japanese people to be open-minded to foreign ways has often served them well.

Writing and Poetry

Heian's favorite means of cultural expression was the written word. The mark of the well-bred aristocrat at the Heian court was the ability to record stirring ideas and sentiments in Chinese and Japanese. During Heian times, gentlemen writers snubbed the kana systems, scorning them as unfit for the expression of noble thoughts. Much Japanese literature during the Heian period and for centuries thereafter was written in Chinese and was the work of men. Like Chinese scholars, they spent long hours perfecting their **calligraphy.** Even today expert use of the brush is admired in Japan.

The composition and recitation of poetry was a favorite form of recreation among Heian aristocrats. Poems—whether original or memorized—were at the heart of every message exchanged between lovers. Much formal poetry was written in Chinese. Many poems of the Heian period, as well as later periods, were written in kana. For centuries kana systems were used by aristocratic women, who were not expected to know elegant Chinese. (See pages 15–17.) These women were supposed to use their time mastering arts and skills that were deemed appropriate to their sex. Modern critics have focused much of their attention on the poetry written in kana since it is representative of an enduring Japanese literary form. Because of this, many of the best-remembered poets of the Heian period are women.

Works familiar to every Heian aristocrat were collected in anthologies. The most famous collection was the *Manyoshu*, or *Collection of Ten Thousand Leaves.* Completed about the year 760, the anthology contains more than 4,000 poems and songs dating from ancient times to the eighth century. The theme of frustrated love, so typical of many Japanese poems, appears in the following selections:

> I will think of you, love
> On evenings when the gray mist
> Rises above the rushes,
> And chill sounds the voice
> Of the wild ducks crying.
>
> That you like me not
> It may well be—
> Yet will you not come
> Even to see the orange tree
> Abloom in the courtyard?

[Donald Keene, comp. and ed., *Anthology of Japanese Literature.*]

Although the ability to write a distinguished hand is no longer as all-important in present-day Japan as it was to the Heian courtier, good calligraphy is still admired. Here a Japanese student is learning the art of calligraphy.

Poetry written in Chinese followed the standard Chinese forms. Japanese verse, however, was composed in traditional Japanese styles. The most popular of the Japanese forms was the **tanka,** or short poem. The tanka is made up of five lines. In each line the total number of syllables of all words must follow the fixed pattern of 5, 7, 5, 7, 7. Being limited to 31 syllables, the tanka usually contains about 10 words. Many of the surviving short poems of early Japan are tankas written in Japanese that lose their meter when translated into English.

Personal Diaries

Many women and men of the court kept accounts of their activities, impressions, fancies, and prejudices. Poems, especially tankas, also embellish the pages of these diaries. It is from these books that the clearest picture of Heian aristocracy emerges.

The Pillow Book of Sei Shonagon, the most famous of the court diaries, was written during the late 900's and early 1000's by Sei Shonagon, a lady-in-waiting to an empress. Sei Shonagon recorded more than 300 observations. Taken together, these observations recreate Heian court life. Included in her observations is this one about her arrival at court.

When I first entered her Majesty's service, I felt indescribably shy, and was indeed constantly on the verge of tears. When I came on duty the first evening, the empress was sitting with only a three-foot screen in front of her, and so nervous was I that when she passed me some picture or book to look at, I was hardly capable of putting out my hand to take it. While she was talking about what she wanted me to see—telling me what it was or who had made it—I was all the time wondering whether my hair was in order. For the lamp was not in the middle of the room, but on a stand immediately beside where we sat, and we were more exposed than we should have been even by daylight. It was all I could do to fix my attention on what I was looking at. Only part of her Majesty's hand showed, for the weather was very cold and she had muffled herself in her sleeves; but I could see that it was pink and lovely. I gazed and gazed. To an inexperienced homebred girl like me it was a wonderful surprise to discover that such people as this existed on earth at all. At dawn I hurried away, but the empress called after me, saying I seemed to be as frightened of the daylight as the ugly old God of Katsuragi (who is so unhappy about his appearance that he hides all day and only comes out at night).

I lay down again, purposely choosing an attitude in which she could not get a full view of me. The shutters had not yet been opened. But soon one of the ladies came along and the empress called out to her, "Please open those things!" She was beginning to do so, when the empress suddenly said, "Not now!" and, laughing, the lackey withdrew.

Her Majesty then engaged me in conversation for some time, and said at last: "Well, I expect you are wanting to be off. Go as soon as you like. And come back in good time tonight," she added. It was so late when I got back to my room that I found it all tidied and opened up for the day. The snow outside was lovely. Presently there came a message from the empress saying it was a good opportunity for me to wait upon her in the morning. "The snow-clouds make it so dark," she said, "that you will be almost invisible." I could not bring myself to go, and the message was repeated several times. At last the head-girl of our room said: "You mustn't shut yourself up here all the time. You ought to be thankful to get a chance like this. Her Majesty would not ask for you unless she really wanted you, and she will think it very bad manners if you do not go." So I hustled off, and arrived once more in the Imperial Presence, in a state of miserable embarrassment and confusion. [*The Pillow Book of Sei Shonagon*, translated by Arthur Waley.]

Japan's Greatest Novel

One of the classics of world literature is *Genji Monogatari*, or *The Tale of Genji*, written in the early 1000's of the Heian period by Lady Murasaki Shikibu. Lady Murasaki was a lady-in-waiting to an empress, one of two wives of the reigning emperor. Sei Shonagon, the author of *The Pillow Book*, was a lady-in-waiting to the other wife. Each wife occupied a separate palace and endeavored to surround herself with the most beautiful and talented ladies-in-waiting.

Through the adventures and romances of Prince Genji, Lady Murasaki's hero, the reader is taken on a guided tour of Heian at the peak of its glory and into the tiny world of elegance and beauty in which the Heian aristocrats lived. *The Tale of Genji* is the earliest and considered the greatest of Japan's novels. Often it is acclaimed as the world's first novel because it appeared more than 800 years before Henry Fielding's *Tom Jones*, the forerunner of the modern novel in the West.

A massive work, *The Tale of Genji* consists of six parts and has more than 1,000 pages in the English translation. Moreover, after killing off Genji at the age of 51, Lady Murasaki wrote a second series about the adventures of one of his sons that continued for another 3,000 pages. The fame of *The Tale of Genji* rests in its vivid descriptions of the people, the rituals and ceremonies, and the customs of Japan's aristocratic upper class. The novel has been read in whole or in part by generation after generation of Japanese and has done much to keep alive the memory of the almost make-believe life at the Heian court.

Since Heian times, the delicate elegance of the Heian lifestyle has been reflected in the traditional furnishings of a Japanese home. In the photo below rooms are separated by beautifully decorated screens.

Not all courtiers were interested in the fine points of Buddhist doctrine, but most found pleasure in the art that accompanied it. This painting, done in gold and silver ink on a deep purple background, illustrates a scroll of one of the Buddhist sutras (scriptures). Such ornate scrolls were given as gifts or used in important rituals.

The Influence of Buddhism on Court Life

The courtiers took up Buddhism with the same enthusiasm with which they had seized on anything Chinese. Some became scholars and authors of learned commentaries on Buddhist texts. But most aristocrats were more attracted to the elaborate and colorful rituals of the temples than to the new beliefs expressed in Buddhism, finding the voice and manner of the preacher of greater interest than his words. Nevertheless, the Buddhist philosophy greatly affected the outlook of the Heian court. Very early in Heian times, the Buddhist prohibition against the taking of life led to banishment as a substitution for the death penalty. It also led to a decline in other cruel punishments.

In some Buddhist temples and monasteries, priests and monks spent their days in meditation and the study of Buddhist texts. But these places were few. Most others, such as the powerful monastery on Mount Hiei just outside Kyoto, had more interest in the pursuit of wealth and power than in doctrine. These institutions became military camps. From them armies of monks and provincial **mercenaries** attacked rival establishments or forced the unarmed court into helpless obedience to their demands for lands and privileges. These monasteries wielded great political power and provided one of the very few ways by which an able man of the lower classes might rise to influence and wealth. However, the monasteries had little interest in gaining converts to their faith. As a result, the bulk of the rural and provincial population had little contact with Buddhism until almost the end of the Heian period.

Check Your Understanding

1. Why did Heian aristocrats steep themselves in the arts and literature of China?
2. Why have modern critics focused much of their attention on the poetry written in kana?
3. Why is *The Pillow Book of Sei Shonagon* important?
4. On what does the fame of *The Tale of Genji* rest?
5. **Thinking Critically:** Why did Buddhism in Heian times only influence the aristocratic upper class?

CHAPTER REVIEW

■ Chapter Summary

Section 1. The Japanese archipelago was settled mainly by immigrants from the mainland of northeast Asia, who came to the islands over a period of many thousands of years. Archaeological artifacts and other unearthed evidence of the Jomon, Yayoi, and Tomb cultures, as well as myths and legends of Japan and accounts of Japanese life found in China, lead to the conclusion that the political and social organization of early Japan remained quite simple until about 1,500 years ago. In time small monarchies developed in various parts of the islands. Some of these monarchies had contacts with the nearby states of China and Korea. Especially influential in introducing Chinese civilization into the Japanese archipelago was the state of Yamato.

Section 2. The foundations of Yamato were laid in the seventh century A.D. through the institution of a series of reforms called the Taika Program. This program took its inspiration from the Tang Empire of China. The program's reforms placed the Yamato rulers at the helm of a centralized government and brought lasting changes to many aspects of Japanese life. It established the claim of the Yamato rulers to the throne of Japan. It produced official histories, one effect of which was to elevate the emperor to the status of a divine being. The Yamato government also established Japan's first permanent capital and made the military commander, or shogun, an important part of Japan's political life.

Section 3. From the mid–800's to the mid–1100's, the Fujiwara family dominated the imperial court. In effect the emperors became puppet rulers, and an imperial aristocracy arose around court life. Maneuverings for power by families in the outlying provinces who shunned court life led to the beginnings of a feudal system that was similar in some ways to European feudalism. The competition produced by the Taira and Minamoto families eventually brought to an end the domination of the Fujiwara family in Japan. In the 1100's rural warriors seized control of the government. These samurai chieftains swept the imperial regime to one side. Their coming to power marked the beginning of a new era in Japanese history.

Section 4. Japanese cultural borrowing from China came into full bloom at the imperial capital of Heian, later called Kyoto. Court aristocrats created a cult of beauty and fashion that demonstrated their good taste as well as their amazing skill in adapting Chinese models to Japanese needs. During the height of Heian's glory many forms of literary expression were produced. Foremost among them is *The Tale of Genji*, which is considered the world's first novel. Buddhism, imported from China, also took firm hold at the Heian court, but left untouched the bulk of Japan's population at this time.

■ **Vocabulary Review**

Define: emperor, haniwa, uji, regent, tradition, dynasty, province, conscription, shogun, puppet ruler, samurai, aristocracy, commendation, feudalism, vassal, cloistered emperor, titular emperor, faction, coup, calligraphy, tanka, mercenary

■ **Places to Locate**

Locate: Sea of Japan, Korea, Izumo, Nara, Heian (Kyoto)

■ **People to Know**

Identify: Shotoku, Buddha, Amaterasu, Fujiwara, Taira, Minamoto, Sei Shonagon, Lady Murasaki Shikibu

■ Thinking Critically

1. How did the development of agriculture change early Japan?
2. Rank in order of importance the successes of the Taika Program. Then explain the reasons for your ranking.
3. Why do you think that the right of the imperial family to reign has never been challenged in Japanese history, even during the era of Fujiwara domination?
4. Explain what is meant about Japan's cultural borrowing in the phrase *adopt, adapt, adept.* How is this phrase indicative of Heian poetry?

■ Extending and Applying Your Knowledge

1. Use the *Readers' Guide to Periodical Literature* to research articles on archaeology in Japan. Prepare an oral report based on the information you find. Make diagrams of the sites and drawings of some of the more important finds.
2. The text says that the early beginnings of Japan may never be completely known. Research archaeology in Japan and write a one-page explanation of why this is true.
3. Using art books from the library, prepare an oral report on the art of the Heian period.

3

The Beginnings of Warrior Rule

The rise of warrior families to supplant the Fujiwara, Taira, and Minamoto domination marked a significant change in Japanese life. The blows delivered by the warrior families to imperial officialdom were decisive. After the warrior families achieved political and social leadership, they retained their dominant position for 700 years. But dominance did not mean unity. Operating within the social and economic system known as feudalism, the warrior families spent the first 400 years scrambling for control of land and peasants. Eventually power became concentrated in a few warrior families. Even the mightiest of these families, however, found it difficult to keep rivals, and even their allies, in line. Not until the 1500's, when Japan was unified by the campaigns of three great generals, was the archipelago to enjoy a measure of peace and order.

The dominance of the warrior families in Japan had a lasting effect on Japanese life and culture. The sword-carrying samurai became the elite of society, with special rank and privileges. Simultaneously, the position of the emperor and the imperial nobility underwent a steady decline. With the islands torn by constant warfare, the Japanese turned increasingly to the spiritual solace of Buddhism. From these times on, Buddhism won a firm hold on warriors and peasants alike.

Much of Japan's traditional culture may be traced to the turbulent centuries of the country's early feudal age. Even though warrior rule had its disadvantages, it resulted in many social and economic advances.

1. Japan's New Direction Under Feudalism

Ruthless ambition and greed led to the downfall of the Taira soon after their momentous victories. When Yoritomo, the eldest surviving son of the defeated Minamoto leader, rose in revolt, he had support from the many warriors who resented the arrogance of the Taira family. Victorious in his turn, Yoritomo seized the reins of government. Following the establishment of his capital at Kamakura, he obtained the title of shogun from the emperor and founded a military dynasty, the first of three that were to rule in Japan over the next seven centuries. With Yoritomo showing the way, Japanese feudalism began to evolve into a highly effective system. Certain offices and practices that he developed survived long after his own dynastic line had disappeared.

Revolt Against the Taira

Taira rule was short-lived despite the ruthlessness of its chief, who ordered the vanquished Minamoto to be hunted down and slain. The Taira chief, however, made the mistake of sparing several sons of the Minamoto leader, two of whom were sent to the provinces and kept under guard. The eldest boy, Yoritomo, 13 years old at the time, was first held in Kyoto. There he first became aware of a growing resentment among the warrior families over the ruthless ambitions and strong-arm methods of the Taira.

As Yoritomo grew older, he began to forge an **alliance** among the enemies of the Taira. When he finally took action in 1180,

Under Minamoto Yoritomo, the government of Japan took on the form that it was to retain for 700 years. Obtaining the title of shogun for himself and his descendants, he founded the first of the three military dynasties that overshadowed the imperial government until the mid–1800's.

Feudal Japan

1180–85	Taira–Minamoto wars
1185–1333	Kamakura Bakufu
1274, 1281	Mongol invasions
1338–1573	Ashikaga Bakufu
1543	Arrival of Portuguese
1549	Arrival of Francis Xavier and Christianity
1467–1568	Warring States Period
1567–1600	Period of unification

the entire country became engulfed in war. For five years the Minamoto and their allies fought the Taira on land and sea. When the struggle came to a close in 1185, Yoritomo was the victor. These wars have ever since grasped the imagination of the Japanese people, giving rise to legends of chivalry and daring that have been retold repeatedly in literature, on the stage, and in movies.

A Dual System of Government

The little seaside town of Kamakura, near present-day Tokyo, had once been headquarters for a branch of the Minamoto family. When victory over the Taira came, Yoritomo decided to keep his government headquarters at Kamakura rather than move it to Kyoto. Yoritomo felt that the Taira warriors had been softened by life in Kyoto and divided by its intrigues, and he did not want the same fate to overtake his own warriors. More important, Kamakura was located in the eastern provinces, which were the traditional domain of both Yoritomo and the allies of the Minamoto. In addition, it was from the eastern provinces that Yoritomo had recruited his most trusted soldiers. In an age when treachery was common, this loyalty could prove to be a decisive advantage.

The military government founded at Kamakura by Yoritomo was called the **Bakufu.** The Kamakura Bakufu was the real government of Japan from 1185 until 1333. The imperial government at Kyoto remained, however, and the emperor was kept in place, as were the imperial courtiers. The office of emperor was firmly entrenched in Japanese tradition. Yoritomo knew he would only hurt his cause by destroying it. With the imperial offices under his firm control, Yoritomo saw no need to eliminate them. Instead he shrewdly used the emperor and the other imperial offices to gain legitimacy for his authority.

Yoritomo saw to it that one of his own Fujiwara allies was placed at the head of the imperial government. This man, acting as regent for the child emperor, granted Yoritomo the title of shogun. Imperial princes who had held the title before had held it only for brief periods. (See page 38.) Yoritomo, however, received it for life. He was also granted the right to pass it on to his descendants.

A Significant Move

Giving Yoritomo the title of shogun with hereditary rights turned out to be one of the most significant moves in Japanese history. As shogun, Yoritomo and his successors possessed legal authority over all of the military houses and all of the samurai in Japan. For the emperor, however, the action proved to be disastrous because the regent had deprived the emperor of the right to select the future shoguns. In effect, the emperor and his successors had lost all chance of regaining their former power and prestige.

Yoritomo's dual system of military and imperial government endured with occasional lapses well into the 1800's. Yoritomo established the ascendancy of the military government by amply rewarding those in his service. Vassals were allowed to retain lands acquired by force. Faithful generals were granted special tax rights in land confiscated from the Taira. Chosen associates were also made stewards and constables in the provinces. The stewards managed estates for Yoritomo, and the constables were military governors. Both positions were offices of great prestige and power.

Yoritomo was so generous with his close followers and supporters that even those men who could never hope to become **go-kenin** were able to become wealthy. On the other hand, while the imperial aristocrats retained their privileges, titles, and incomes, they had almost no influence outside the capital city. Yoritomo had permanently reduced the importance of the emperor's court.

FEUDAL WAYS. Japanese feudalism was similar in many ways to the European feudal system (see chart on facing page). Many of the differences can be attributed to differences in the locations of Japan and France. Japan was isolated by ocean, whereas France was surrounded by other nations.

FEUDALISM—A COMPARISON

JAPAN	FRANCE
Background	
History of tribal loyalties	History of tribal loyalties
Decline of Heian power through internal warfare	Decline of Roman power through warfare and invasion
Development of Feudalism	
Enlistment of professional warriors as samurai; swearing of allegiance by vassals in return for protection	Enlistment of professional warriors as knights; swearing of allegiance by vassals in return for protection
Development of hierarchy of lord-vassal relationships	Development of hierarchy of lord-vassal relationships
Appointment of Yoritomo as shogun, most powerful position in Japan; change of emperor into mere figurehead	Coronation of Charlemagne as first king; creation of the Holy Roman Empire, a new state
Control of land ownership by the shogunate	Control of land ownership by the monarchy
Little outside pressure	Constantly changing boundaries through conflicts
Feudal Code	
Loyalty to feudal lord	Loyalty to feudal lord
Bravery on the battlefield	Bravery on the battlefield
Little religious influence	Influenced by Christianity
High regard for past culture	Little regard for past culture
Disintegration of Feudalism	
Continuous warfare during period of weak Ashikaga Shogunate and strong lords	Period of competition between weak kings and strong lords
Sudden resurgence and centralization of shogunate power by Tokugawa	Centralization of power by Capetian monarchs
Limits placed on daimyo power	Transfer of loyalty to monarchs through checks on vassals
Creation by Tokugawa of unified state using centralized feudalism	Replacement of feudal loyalties with national loyalties
Rise of towns; growth of independent craftsworkers, guilds, merchants, and money economy	Rise of towns; growth of independent craftsworkers, guilds, merchants, and money economy
Intermediate period of strongly centralized isolated feudalism; return to emperor's rule and modernization	Development of absolute monarchy

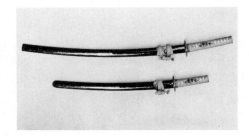

SAMURAI. The arms and armor of a Japanese samurai were elaborate and colorful. His armor, made of strips of steel laced with brightly colored cords, gave excellent protection while allowing freedom of movement. Why were a samurai's swords so important?

A New Feudalism

Even before obtaining the title of shogun, Yoritomo was becoming the founder of a new Japanese feudalism. The early feudal structure fell apart because the Taira–Minamoto struggles loosened the blood ties among individual military houses. (See page 42.) During and after the Taira–Minamoto wars, samurai from many different backgrounds and from all parts of Japan became allied with one side or the other. Yoritomo himself made vassals of many warrior chiefs who were not of the Minamoto family. Eventually every major military house, including remnants of the Taira, came under Yoritomo's influence at Kamakura. At the same time that Yoritomo forged new alliances, he refined the feudal codes so that every vassal would know his place in the emerging military society.

The feudal society that eventually took shape was based on Minamoto house laws. The Kamakura Bakufu tightly controlled the feudal aristocracy. At the top were the go-kenin, retainers who were bound to the Minamoto house by blood ties or by ties of loyalty and service so strong that they were almost the equal of blood ties. From this group Yoritomo drew the staff of his government bureaus. It was from this group, too, that Yoritomo filled important openings in the provinces. Many of the vassals applied for admission to the ranks of go-kenin, but few were accepted.

Second in honor to the go-kenin were the samurai, another rank that was not easily attained. Only the shogun, or later, a representative of the shogun, could elevate a warrior to the rank of samurai. Below the samurai were several ranks of foot soldiers and armed retainers. These men were farmers or ex-farmers and were not a part of the nobility.

A stern code of ethics held the feudal society together. The feudal code made loyalty and obedience the highest virtues. A samurai was expected to sacrifice his life, his possessions, and even his family for his lord without question or hope of reward. Foot soldiers and retainers were bound by the same requirements as the samurai. So stern were the demands that treachery against a master was never permitted, even from the vassal of an enemy. Yoritomo was known to execute enemy warriors who approached him for reward after having slain their leaders. In later years, treachery became common, but never during the reign of Yoritomo.

Government from Behind the Screen

During and shortly after the struggles that gave birth to the Bakufu, most leaders of the Minamoto house had been slain. Yoritomo contributed to this situation himself by following the Japanese custom of having his own brothers killed so they would not be able to conspire against him. When Yoritomo died in 1199, few members of the direct Minamoto line were still living. Twenty years later in 1219 the last Minamoto shogun died without having produced an heir. But the Hojo family, from whom Yoritomo had chosen a wife, stepped in to take control of the Bakufu.

The Hojo family never sought the title of shogun. They preferred to act through puppet rulers, appointing loyal members of the Fujiwara family or imperial princes as shoguns. An extraordinary situation thus resulted in a custom that has been called "government from behind the screen." The custom of ruling through puppets persisted in Japan for many centuries. Although strong and forceful men sometimes occupied the office of shogun, it was frequently difficult to pinpoint the actual center of authority. As it has been observed:

The inability of the Kamakura Bakufu to reward samurai like the one above for their services during the Mongol invasions exposed and increased its weakness. Discontented vassals later overthrew the impoverished regime.

> During the rest of the Kamakura period, the Kyoto hierarchy consisted of an emperor, who had lost his power to a regent, who in turn had lost control of the court to a retired (cloistered) emperor, while the real power had been handed over to a shogun, who now had been supplanted by his Hojo regent. [Edwin O. Reischauer and John K. Fairbanks, *East Asia, the Great Tradition*]

Mongol Invasion Attempts

While Yoritomo was seizing power in Japan, the Mongols under Genghis Khan (JENG-ghis KHAHN) were creating a vast Asian empire. During the time of the Hojo Regency, the Mongol realm stretched from the Pacific Ocean to eastern Europe. The Japanese archipelago, India, and Southeast Asia were the only lands not overrun by the Mongol armies. During the late 1200's Kublai (KOO-bly) Khan, a descendant of Genghis Khan, demanded that the Japanese also recognize the Mongol overlordship. When they refused, Kublai Khan decided to force the Japanese to submit.

Kublai dispatched a fleet of ships to Japan in 1274 and again in 1281. Although the elite Mongol cavalry units that landed in Japan were the best in the world, the hardy Japanese warriors were able to hold their own. But victory for the Mongols seemed certain. The crucial difference for the Japanese was the weather. The first invasion failed when a severe storm threat-

Brothers in Conflict

Yoritomo and Yoshitsune (YAHSH-ihts-OO-nee) started out as brothers allied in the fight against the Taira. But they ended as brothers in conflict. After the leaders of the Minamoto family were killed by the Taira, the infant Yoshitsune was hidden away in a monastery. When he was older, he sought haven with a branch of the Fujiwara family. Later, wishing to avenge the death of his father, Yoshitsune joined his older brother, who at that time was preparing to challenge Taira power.

Yoshitsune displayed unusual military skill, and Yoritomo made him his personal aide and gave him important military commands that led to brilliant victories and fame throughout the country. But the cloistered emperor, hoping to create a feud between the two brothers and thus advance his own fortunes, singled out Yoshitsune for honors and congratulated him on his victories while ignoring Yoritomo. As a result, Yoritomo began to suspect Yoshitsune of conspiring against him.

Yoshitsune denied all the accusations against him and proclaimed complete loyalty to Yoritomo. At the same time, however, Yoshitsune demanded that Yoritomo praise him for his military feats. Yoritomo finally decided that his brother was a "traitor" who should be killed. The first attempt failed. Yoritomo then planned a new campaign against his brother. This time Yoshitsune was hunted down and, rather than face surrender, Yoshitsune took his own life.

The conflict between the two brothers has fascinated Japanese writers for over 700 years. Was Yoshitsune actually disloyal to his brother? Or was he merely guilty of excessive pride? Did Yoritomo follow his political instincts and do what he had to do to preserve his power for the glory of Japan? Or was he heartless and cruel in putting aside brotherly love for political power? In trying to answer these and other questions, Japanese writers have turned out a massive array of literature. While the questions probably will never be answered, Yoshitsune and Yoritomo both are honored by the Japanese people as two of their country's most famous heroes.

ened to wreck the Mongol fleet and forced the Mongols to leave before they were victorious.

The second fleet of ships carried an invading force of 150,000 Mongols. As the fleet approached Japan, typhoons unleashed their destructive winds, scattering and sinking many of the Mongol ships. The Japanese were so convinced that the typhoons had been sent by benevolent kami that they named the storms **kamikaze,** or "winds of the kami." The defeat of the Mongols gave rise to a belief that was cherished by the Japanese people for centuries thereafter that Japan was under divine protection, and they boasted that their islands could not be conquered.

This belief later played an important role in World War II. Toward the end of that war, when the Japanese were fighting desperately to defeat the Allies, they formed special squadrons of pilots who volunteered to fly explosive-laden planes into American warships. The pilots who flew these suicide missions were called kamikaze after the winds that had saved Japan from invasion almost 700 years before. So strong was this belief in divine protection that the Allied occupation of the country at the end of World War II came as a deep shock to the Japanese people.

Check Your Understanding

1. **a.** What effect did Yoritomo's victory over the Taira have on Japan's warrior class? **b.** What place did the emperor have in Yoritomo's plans?
2. **a.** What changes took place in the feudal system of Japan as a result of the Taira–Minamoto struggles? **b.** What further changes were made by Yoritomo?
3. Explain how the Hojo family came to be in control of the Bakufu.
4. **a.** How did the Hojo change the way Japan was governed? **b.** What was this change in governing called?
5. What lasting effect did the Mongol invasion have on Japan?
6. **Thinking Critically:** What are the similarities and differences between feudalism in Japan and feudalism in France?

2. Buddhism's Inroads During and After Kamakura Times

By the time the Kamakura Bakufu was founded, Buddhism in Japan was already six centuries old. But Buddhism had established itself as a faith of the upper classes. In this role, however, its influence on court life, thought, and policy had been significant. (See pages 51–52.) Buddhism's teachings were much too complicated and pessimistic to attract the great mass of Japan's people. Some basic changes in Buddhism were necessary before Buddhism could win over and become a major religion of Japan.

Buddhism's Broader Appeal

Modifications to Buddhism began to appear as early as the tenth century. By the twelfth and thirteenth centuries enough changes had been made to enable Buddhism to sink deep roots among the Japanese. The basic change was the emergence of Buddhist sects whose teachings and practices were easy to understand and accept. Of great importance was the tendency of the new sects to conform to traditional Japanese ways of life. For example, in the old Buddhist sects priests were not allowed to marry. Strongly attached as the Japanese were to family life, they took a rather dim view of this precondition for entering the ranks of the clergy. The new sects had no such restriction. Furthermore, the new sects built temples in small communities, whereas the older sects had thrived in or near the Nara and Kyoto capitals. People were more inclined to follow a religion that allowed them to take part in temple ceremonies and that allowed priests to participate actively in community affairs.

Toward the end of the Heian era, these new sects began to reach the countryside. Some Buddhist monks saw the need for a religion people could understand. They began to preach their doctrines throughout the provinces. Knowing that the villagers had neither the time nor the inclination to engage in long periods of study or to perform good works, these wandering preachers stressed only one fact. This was that believers need only demonstrate that they had faith in the saving grace of Buddha. By the end of the Kamakura period dozens of sects, each emphasizing simple faith in Buddha, had taken their place in the religious life of Japan.

The Pure–Land Sects

The most important of the new sects were those belonging to the Pure–Land school of Buddhism, which was popularized in

Japan through the efforts of the monk Eshin (942–1017). The Pure–Land school of Buddhism emphasized salvation through the grace of a Buddha known as Amida. Amida was believed to reign over the "True" or "Pure" land, that part of heaven known to the faithful as the "Western Paradise." Like other forms of Buddhism, the Pure–Land school had broken into a number of sects. However, all Pure–Land sects agreed on the basic method of gaining entry to the happy afterlife. This was by invoking the name of Amida, using such formulas as "Namu Amida Butsu," or Hail the Amida Buddha!

Making few demands on its followers, the Pure–Land sects, or Jodo, soon became the most popular of all the Buddhist sects in Japan. At first the new Buddhism, like the old, attracted mainly the courtiers at the capital. Lady Murasaki, the author of *The Tale of Genji,* was an early convert to Pure–Land Buddhism. But thanks to the efforts of Honen the Saint (1133–1212), a wandering evangelist, Jodo later swept the countryside as well.

Shinran (1173–1262), originally one of Honen's followers, made the new Buddhism even more attractive to the common people. Seeing no purpose in the required, endless repetitions of the Amida formula, Shinran taught that to call out "Namu Amida Butsu" once was sufficient for anyone who had true faith in the Buddha's mercy. The simplicity of this method of salvation understandably had wide appeal. Shinran's True Pure–Land sect, or Jodo Shinshu, gained a multitude of followers. During the centuries since Kamakura times, Jodo Shinshu has remained, together with its parent sect, one of the major forms of Buddhism in Japan.

Nichiren Buddhism

In sharp contrast to the mild, tolerant Jodo and Jodo Shinshu was the Hokke, or Lotus Flower, sect, founded by the firebrand Nichiren (1222–1282). A zealous and militant agitator, Nichiren proclaimed his beliefs wherever he could find an audience. He was notable among the Buddhist preachers for his intolerance. Any woes that befell Japan he attributed to the "false teachings" of the other Buddhist sects. Without hesitation, he denounced their advocates as thieves, rascals, and traitors, creating an uproar in Japan that no other religious leader either before or since has equaled.

In general, Nichiren followed traditional Buddhist teachings. The one exception was his insistence that the only source of salvation was the Sutra, or scripture, of the Lotus of the Wonderful Law. Japanese Buddhism was broadly tolerant of many points of view. But not even the most conservative Buddhist theologian of other Japanese sects accepted this interpretation. Nichiren used certain prophecies in the Lotus to prove that the world was headed for ruin, that it could be saved only by Buddhism—his brand of Buddhism—and that he himself was the reincarnation of the Buddha who was to bring about this salvation. Moreover, he warned that Japan would be severely punished, most likely by invasion from the Asian mainland, if it did not heed his message. When the Mongols descended upon the archipelago not long afterward, his prediction seemed to have been borne out.

Aside from his religious contributions, Nichiren is often given credit for planting the seeds of **nationalism** in Japan. By insisting that settlement of the impending world peril lay in the hands of the Japanese, he showed a patriotic fervor that had not been present previously in Japan. This nationalistic quality spread and continued to arouse nationalist feelings in many Japanese in the following centuries, so much so that the Nichiren sect has endured as one of the country's major Buddhist sects. After World War II many of Nichiren Buddhism's teachings were adopted by the new sect of Soka Gakkai, or Value Creating Society, which swept through Japan like a whirlwind. (See page 203.)

Zen During Kamakura Times

One of the many Buddhist sects that won adherents during the Kamakura period, Zen differed sharply from all other forms of Buddhism. The followers of Zen sought self-understanding called **satori.** They held that such traditional religious practices as prayers and rituals were a waste of time. They called analysis, logic, and reason barriers to understanding and said they must be discarded. According to Zen Buddhism, satori comes to the fortunate few through intuition, often in a sudden flash of insight. The principal ritual of Zen is meditation. To develop the proper frame of mind, one reflects upon a koan, or Zen riddle, such as "What is the sound of one hand clapping?" When the disciple of Zen Buddhism senses that analysis and deduction are futile in discovering an answer, for there is no answer, some progress toward achieving satori has been made.

The practice of Zen became especially popular among the samurai. For one thing, the practice of Zen required great self-discipline, a much-admired trait among the warriors. Also, practicing the ritual of meditation helped the samurai keep

ZEN ARTS. Zen has had a wide influence on Japanese culture. All of the arts illustrated here have been shaped in some way by Zen. The tea ceremony (above) is restrained and disciplined. Its object is to create a sense of tranquillity by concentrating upon the formal yet simple movements of the ceremony. Ink painting (right) and Nō drama (below), like Zen, make use of suggestion and restraint, and leave much of the interpretation to the observer.

themselves in a proper state of mind. Despite their rise in social rank and economic power during Kamakura times, the samurai often experienced feelings of insecurity. Their view of life was summed up in a Japanese saying that compared the samurai to the cherry blossom, a flower that died as quickly as it blossomed. The saying was "Among flowers the cherry blossom; among men the warrior." Acutely aware that death on the battlefield was their likely fate, the samurai found comfort in the peace that came with the practice of Zen.

Zen did not reach its full flowering until after the Kamakura age. Over the centuries Zen's natural wonder and simplicity has appealed strongly to artists and poets, as well as to athletes and warriors.

Check Your Understanding

1. What changes were made in Buddhism to give it more appeal to Japan's common people?
2. How did the Pure–Land sect of Buddhism differ from the True Pure–Land sect?
3. How did Nichiren view all other Buddhist sects?
4. *Thinking Critically:* What is the relationship between satori and the Zen Buddhist's rejection of analysis, logic, and reason? How did Zen Buddhism help samurai who were attracted to it?

3. The Ashikaga Age

After almost 150 years of rule, the Kamakura Shogunate was overthrown by a coalition of its greatest vassals and an ambitious member of the imperial house. An attempt to restore the imperial government to its former glory failed when the head of the Ashikaga family, a leader of the revolt, seized power for himself. The shogunate that he founded, however, was never able to control the unruly warrior lords. Although characterized by cultural and economic advances, the Ashikaga period was marked by almost unbroken war.

The End of the Kamakura Bakufu

The Bakufu established by Yoritomo never recovered from the Mongol invasions. The task of beating back Kublai Khan's invaders had drained the Bakufu's treasury. An equally disastrous effect was the Bakufu's loss of support among the warlords. Many of the warrior chiefs had gone to great expense to perform military service for the Hojo Regency, some sacrificing nearly everything they owned. These warrior chiefs became bitterly disappointed when they did not receive the customary land grants for their help. They lost confidence in the central government when the warriors saw Buddhist monasteries receive rich rewards for prayers offered during the invasions, while they themselves were given nothing. Finally after the last Mongol invasion in 1281, all Hojo regents were hopelessly incompetent and totally unfit for their tasks. Japan was at a point in its history when it was ready for a change of government.

In the early 1300's the alert and able emperor named Go–Daigo made moves to restore the political fortunes of his family. Soon after ascending the throne, Emperor Go–Daigo began plotting against the Kamakura Bakufu. In 1331 government leaders learned of the conspiracy and exiled Go–Daigo from the imperial capital, but a number of dissatisfied warrior chiefs came to his support.

Throughout the islands, loyalist troops began attacking Bakufu forces and winning victories. Finally Ashikaga Takauji, a leading Bakufu general, turned against the Kamakura shogun and cast his lot with Emperor Go–Daigo. This defection proved to be the turning point in the struggle between the Kamakura Bakufu and its former vassals. Soon Emperor Go–Daigo was able to return in triumph to the capital. By the end of 1333 all resistance had been crushed, the Hojo family was powerless, Japan's first line of shoguns was at an end, and much of Kamakura was in ashes.

The Ashikaga Military Dynasty

"Never summon a tiger to chase out a dog." The wisdom of this Japanese proverb became evident soon after Go–Daigo returned to power. Takauji, the head of the Ashikaga family and Emperor Go–Daigo's chief supporter, had ambitions of his own. After a fierce struggle Takauji occupied the imperial capital, declared the throne vacant, and appointed a successor to the throne from a rival branch of the imperial line. The royal puppet then granted Takauji the title of shogun in 1338. This act marked the official beginning of the Ashikaga Shogunate, Japan's second military dynasty. The new shogun established his headquarters in Kyoto, thus completing the eclipse of Kamakura as a force in national affairs. The Ashikaga Bakufu remained the official government in Japan for more than two centuries (1338–1573).

The Rise of the Daimyo

Despite its exalted position, the Ashikaga Shogunate was not able to exert much political power. Its authority never reached beyond the Home Provinces, the small group of states clustered around Kyoto. Throughout most of Japan, power was centered in constables, distant cousins of the imperial family and court nobility, and local aristocracy. (See page 60.) The family ties and loyalties between capital and provinces, however, were wearing thin. Over a period of many decades these local lords had assumed or had been granted more and more authority over the lands and farmers in their provinces.

By Ashikaga times most of the local people, including warriors who formerly dealt directly with the central government, were subject to the power of provincial lords. The strongest lords, called **daimyo** (DY-mee-oh), meaning "great names," had bands of samurai at their command. Since the equipment of the mounted samurai was expensive and their "salaries" fairly large, most daimyo also recruited peasants for their armies. They furnished these peasants with light weapons and trained them to serve as foot soldiers. Even before Ashikaga times the size of private armies easily surpassed that of armies available to the Bakufu. Only by working in league with the great daimyo were the Hojo regents able to maintain their positions.

At the same time, many daimyo relied on their relationship with the central government to hold their stronger vassals in check. These vassals, in turn, helped to protect the daimyo from aggressive neighbors. After 1467, however, Bakufu authority collapsed and was unable to contain the aggressive impulses of local lords because of a dispute over succession. With the system of checks on local power in disarray, the result was a period of political disintegration. During this period, the daimyo used every opportunity to attack their neighbors and seize their land.

The Growth of Towns

Despite the constant threat of violence, the number of towns increased noticeably during the Ashikaga age. Perhaps violence was a stimulus, rather than a hindrance, to the growth of towns. To protect themselves against attacks, feudal lords turned their homes into fortified castles. Peasants and craftsworkers, seeking protection or the chance to earn a living by providing goods and services to the daimyo and their retainers, settled near the castles. Many cities developed from the clusters of people, homes, and businesses that formed castle towns. Tokyo, Nagoya, Osaka, Okayama, and Nagasaki—all were once **castle towns.**

Towns also arose around markets, at convenient stopping places along trade routes, and where natural harbors encouraged shipping. **Market towns** and castle towns grew steadily, largely because of changed economic conditions. During the Kamakura period, new methods of cultivation had begun to create agricultural surpluses. During the Ashikaga period, this trend accelerated. At the same time, coined money came into use, although it did not replace the **barter system**. Also, artisans became more and more skilled in all types of production. An important development stemming from this advance in skills was the rise of **guilds**, each of which monopolized a particular product or service. By the end of the Ashikaga age, Japan still was mainly a rural land, but its castle towns and market towns contributed a great deal to the economy.

Gains in Domestic and Foreign Trade

Trade flourished in the unsettled times of Ashikaga Japan. Local trade actually benefited from the warring of the daimyo, for the vast armies had to be fed, clothed, and equipped. Many merchants grew wealthy by supplying the needs of the armies and became a strong force in Japanese life. Foreign trade also grew rapidly. Large quantities of raw silk, porcelain, pottery, and copper coins were imported from the Middle Kingdom because the fondness of the upper classes for Chinese wares continued. In return, the Japanese exported swords, finished silk, lacquer-

ware, and other delicate manufactures. Most foreign trade was carried on by the Ashikaga Shogunate, since that was the only Japanese agency licensed by the Ming dynasty to trade in China. Occasionally, the Ashikaga granted the highly valued trading permits to favored Buddhist temples.

But some foreign goods arrived in Japan in the ships of pirates. When daimyo were in urgent need of funds or wanted precious foreign goods, they often sent their warriors to sea. These samurai pirates were feared in a wide region from Korea to as far south as the Malay Peninsula. When they were unable to seize rich booty at sea, the pirates stormed ashore to plunder cities and towns on the seacoasts of China and Korea. In reprisal, the Ming government broke off official relations with Japan. The Ashikaga Bakufu could not stop the pirates, however, and freebooting continued into the early 1600's.

Trade and Christianity

During the late Ashikaga period, the seafaring Portuguese built a **monopoly** over the all-water trading routes between West and East. In 1543, Portuguese sailors arrived in Japan some 40 years after Vasco da Gama had sailed the first Portuguese ship around Africa to Calicut, India. The Portuguese were delighted with the reception they received and soon began to return in large numbers. Some daimyo saw in the Portuguese trade the revenue they needed for financing wars. Also, they were eager

The interest of the Portuguese traders in the many customs of Japan was matched by the fascination of the Japanese with their foreign visitors. No detail of the first meeting between the two groups escaped the brush of the artist who painted this screen. The Japanese were especially curious about the new faith brought by the foreigners. Why do you think the long-robed Christian priests are so prominently displayed?

to obtain the deadly firearms of the Portuguese. The Japanese were familiar with gunpowder, but they had never seen a weapon quite like the harquebus, an early type of musket that the foreigners could fire with deadly effect. The Portuguese, therefore, were invited to settle in the ports of feudal lords.

Before long the Portuguese merchants were followed by Jesuit missionaries. Francis Xavier had already served in India, the island of Ceylon (now the nation of Sri Lanka), and Indonesia. Famous as the "Apostle of the Indies," he was anxious to convert the Japanese. In 1549 Xavier made his way to the archipelago. Although he did win converts, Xavier also experienced many disappointments. Having observed that the culture of aristocratic Japanese was strongly influenced by China, he decided to transfer his activities to the Middle Kingdom. Once the Chinese accepted Christianity, he believed, it would follow the course Buddhism had taken and spread to Japan. But Xavier failed to gain entry to China. He died near Macau in 1552 and was later buried in Goa, India.

Other Jesuits adopted Xavier's zeal for converting Japan. Some daimyo who were interested in promoting foreign trade permitted the Jesuits to teach in their domains, and some became Christians themselves. But it was in western Japan, especially among the common people, that Christianity made its greatest inroads. A few years after the Ashikaga Shogunate ended, a Jesuit official visited the archipelago. He reported that Japan had only about 20 priests but it contained some 150,000 Christians. By 1600 this number had risen to 300,000.

Upper–Class Culture

Japanese culture bloomed during the period of the Ashikaga Bakufu. As during the Nara and Heian periods, the upper classes looked to the Asian mainland for inspiration. New art forms were imported from China, although traditional Japanese arts continued to flourish. The art of ikebana or flower arrangement, brought from China, won countless devotees. Enthusiasts of bonsai cultivated the art and techniques of slowing the growth of trees. These miniature trees, exact in every detail, might be a hundred years old but no larger than a potted plant. The tea ceremony also took its place in Japanese culture during this era. As developed by the great tea masters of Japan, it was an art form and not a means of offering refreshment. Every detail of participation was governed by tradition, and the ceremony was both a spiritual experience and a mental exercise. All three of these arts are still practiced in Japan.

Other arts sank deep roots in Japan during the Ashikaga age. The Japanese drew upon old traditions of music and dance to create a new form of drama, the Nō play. Similar to ancient Greek tragedy, Nō makes use of simple stage settings, against which performers move in stylized, subtle patterns. Landscape painting, inspired by the masters of Song China, depicted the simple majesty of nature. The Ashikaga Japanese also excelled in architecture, scroll painting, and poetry.

The Close of the Ashikaga Age

In Japanese history the years 1467–1568 are known as the Warring States Period. Armies were constantly on the move during these years, the final century of the Ashikaga Shogunate. Feudal lords now commanded large armies of mounted samurai and foot soldiers, and their resources for waging war were far greater than those available to earlier military captains.

To the Japanese of the 1500's, it was difficult to see rhyme or reason in the brutal struggles of the daimyo. As the feudal system had developed, the authority and prestige of both the emperor and the shogun had waned. From about 1490 through the 1500's both were only figureheads, and revenues of the Imperial House and shogunate declined until some rulers were short of funds. If unity were to be restored, it had to come from a source other than the shogunate or the Imperial House.

This period was not without daimyo striving to unify the archipelago. Of course, they were prompted chiefly by private ambition, not by a patriotic spirit or a simple desire to restore peace and order. From this struggle for complete power there arose powerful figures who finally brought unity to Japan.

Check Your Understanding

1. Why did the Kamakura Bakufu lose the support of its warrior chiefs?
2. How did the Kamakura Shogunate come to an end?
3. Why was the Ashikaga Shogunate not able to exercise much power?
4. How was Christianity introduced into Japan?
5. **Thinking Critically:** Why do you think that the Ashikaga Shogunate was a time of great cultural and economic gains? How might the structure of feudalism have helped bring about these gains?

4. The 1500's: From Disorder to Political Unity

The century of the 1500's produced three of the most famous names in Japanese history—Nobunaga (no-bu-NAH-ga), Hideyoshi (HID-ee-YOH-shee), and Ieyasu (ee-eh-YAH-soo). Each successively dominated the political and military scene, and each had distinct talents. Each differed from the others in personality and character. Through their combined efforts, they turned Japan into a strong, unified state. Nobunaga was a bold, forthright warrior, inclined to be blunt and belligerent. Hideyoshi, an unrivaled military commander, was notorious for his cunning. Ieyasu, who boasted descent from the famous Tokugawa family, was a peerless politician and administrator. A popular Japanese tradition underscores the differences of the three men. Nobunaga, so the tale goes, said: "If the cuckoo doesn't sing, I'll kill it." Hideyoshi was wiser. "If the cuckoo doesn't sing," he stated, "I'll show it how." Ieyasu showed the greatest patience of all. "If the cuckoo doesn't sing," he declared, "I'll wait until it does." Fortunately for Japan, each man was dominant at a time when his particular quality of character was most needed.

Nobunaga's Drive for a United Japan

The first to rise to power was Nobunaga, a minor daimyo in Honshu. In 1560 Nobunaga won several quick victories over stronger opponents in local feudal wars. Gathering support through marriage alliances and promises of reward, he took over lands of warlords near the capital. The emperor asked his help to regain imperial lands taken by feudal lords. About the same time, the shogun was murdered. One of his brothers asked for Nobunaga's aid in gaining the shogunate. Nobunaga responded to both requests, thus gaining the backing of the two most respected offices in Japan. In late 1568 Nobunaga defeated the last warlords who stood in the way of his drive toward the capital. With the emperor's blessings, he entered Kyoto, designating the Ashikaga pretender as his choice for shogun, and began consolidating his position in nearby provinces. Eventually Nobunaga defeated most opposing warlords, bringing about 20 provinces under his control.

Unification Under Hideyoshi

Hideyoshi, Nobunaga's successor, of humble birth, became a foot soldier in his youth. Quickly demonstrating unusual ability, he rose rapidly in the military ranks. In time he became one of Nobunaga's most successful field commanders and military advisers. In 1582, Nobunaga was treacherously slain by one of his own generals. Hideyoshi then was appointed to the council of regents named to rule until Nobunaga's grandson and heir reached adulthood. Hideyoshi, however, soon decided to look after his own interests. Already the most powerful warlord in Japan, he pushed aside his former commander's heir and took charge of the drive for unification. Thereafter Hideyoshi and his samurai allies were invincible on the field of battle. Within a few years they had control over the entire archipelago. After several centuries of disorder and civil war, Japan was at last free from feudal turmoil.

Dreams of an Asian Empire

Having made himself lord over all that was worth ruling in Japan, Hideyoshi looked longingly toward the rest of Asia. He briefly considered invading Taiwan and the Philippines. But his chief ambition was to gain control over the huge Chinese Empire. To reach China, he landed his samurai armies in nearby Korea in 1592. Although the Japanese advanced rapidly northward in the Korean Peninsula, the invasion was a failure. One reason was that the Korean navy intercepted and sank the ships that were bringing supplies and reinforcements from Japan. Also, the Chinese came to the aid of the Koreans, who waged relentless guerrilla warfare against Hideyoshi's forces. The net result was a deadlock that finally led to an armistice. Four years later, Hideyoshi ordered the resumption of the war. Again the Japanese forces were stopped, and the tremendous cost in Japanese lives forced the generals to evacuate their troops.

The effects of these wars were felt in Korea for many years to come. Much of the land was in ruins, and a heritage of bitterness against Japan was created that lasted for generations of Koreans. Hoping to spare their country from further suffering at the hands of aggressive foreigners, the Korean government adopted a policy of national isolation. For more than 250 years, the "Hermit Kingdom, as Korea came to be called," refused to have anything to do with outsiders.

The End of the Ashikaga Shogunate

With men of the caliber of Nobunaga and Hideyoshi in the forefront of Japanese life, the shogun was a mere figurehead. The fifteenth and last Ashikaga shogun assumed office in 1568, shortly after gaining the support of Nobunaga. Soon, however, the new shogun began plotting against his former benefactor. His plan was to rally the enemies of Nobunaga around himself and restore the shogunate to its former glorious position. Nobunaga learned of the intrigue. In 1573 Nobunaga abolished the machinery and the office of the shogunate and deposed its treacherous head. No successor was appointed.

After his downfall in 1573 the ousted Ashikaga shogun, who kept his title without having any office or authority, went into exile. Until Nobunaga's death in 1582, he continued to plot against Nobunaga, who ignored the shogun's futile attempts to create alliances. The shogun died in 1597, the year Hideyoshi's second campaign in Korea opened, and with his death the line of Ashikaga shoguns came to an end.

Breaking Buddhism's Military Might

Ever since Heian times the monasteries of certain Buddhist sects had exercised great power. With vast landholdings and control over thousands of peasants, some monasteries were as powerful as any warlord in Japan. Moreover, with short notice the monasteries' leaders could raise huge armies. Not only did they have scores of soldiers constantly under arms, but they could muster hundreds of armed peasants simply by ringing a bell. The leaders of these monasteries never hesitated to use force to advance their own interests.

Both Nobunaga and Hideyoshi sought to break up the militaristic Buddhist institutions. Nobunaga burned to the ground the famous monastery on the slopes of Mount Hiei, killing every man, woman, and child under the monestary's protection. Nobunaga used the same methods against the Ikko sect, a later form of Shinran's True Pure-Land sect. Hideyoshi was more tolerant of Buddhist sects, possibly because Nobunaga had broken much of their power. On occasion, however, Hideyoshi had to use force to bring the Buddhist armies under subjection, and in doing so was no less ruthless than Nobunaga. By the time of Hideyoshi's death, the Buddhist threat had been crushed.

The Continuation of Castle–Building

The period of castle-building that began in Ashikaga times continued into the late sixteenth century. (See page 71.) The castles of fifteenth-century warlords were designed strictly for defense, but by Nobunaga's time many warlords were building mansions designed as much for show as for war. Nobunaga built two castles, one of which, the fortress at Azuchi, was the greatest of its day. Hideyoshi, however, surpassed all castle-builders. He had a passion for castles, building or rebuilding three of them into great architectural monuments.

Although built for the practical purpose of defense, many of Japan's medieval castles were also beautiful examples of Japanese architecture. Near Osaka stands the castle of Himeji, known as the "White Heron" because of its outstanding grace and elegance.

The greatest of Hideyoshi's castles was the one at Osaka. It is well described by a noted expert on Japanese architecture:

> Construction of the castle began in 1583, when 30,000 men were put to work on it day and night. The number of workers was later doubled, and the castle was completed in three years. Strategically, the site was well chosen. . . . The circumference of the castle area, which contained a central compound and its surrounding second and third compounds, was approximately eight miles. . . . The castle itself had no fewer than 48 large towers and 76 smaller ones. The chief of these, a structure of some eight stories, stood on a stone base 75 feet high and rose above this to a height of 102 feet. It was topped with a roof of gilded tiles and ornamented in characteristic style with a pair of gold dolphins. Cranes and tigers, respectively symbolizing long life and prowess, decorated the exterior walls of the top floor. [John B. Kirby, Jr., *From Castle to Teahouse; Japanese Architecture of the Momoyama Period*]

Osaka castle, a masterpiece of fortification, was strong enough to withstand the most determined assaults. In 1614 the castle defenders successfully resisted an attack by an army of

NATIONAL TREASURES.

Intensely interested in their history, the Japanese have preserved religious and other buildings from their past and have erected monuments to important recent events. Shimogamo Shrine (bottom) at Kyoto is an outstanding example of Shinto religious architecture. Phoenix Hall (below), part of a Buddhist temple called Byodoin, was built at Uji near Kyoto during the Fujiwara Period. Peace Memorial Park (left) in Hiroshima preserves an area that was severely damaged by an atomic bomb in 1945. Why do you think the Japanese people would choose to preserve a reminder of this catastrophe?

150,000 men. Taken through an act of treachery shortly thereafter, Osaka castle was largely destroyed. Rebuilt on several occasions, the fortress now occupies a hill overlooking the industrial center of Osaka.

The Death of Hideyoshi

Hideyoshi died in 1598, shortly after issuing the order for the evacuation of Korea. Since his son and heir was only five years old at the time, five of Hideyoshi's principal vassals were named to form a council of regency for the boy. Almost immediately a struggle for power began between Tokugawa Ieyasu, the greatest vassal, and the other four. Some daimyo supported Hideyoshi's son, but others backed Ieyasu. After two years of political and military maneuvering, the issue was decided on the field of battle. In the year 1600, one of the crucial battles in Japanese history was fought at Sekigahara, a town near Kyoto. When Ieyasu triumphed over his foes, the way was clear for the Tokugawa family to establish the third and last military dynasty in Japan. Ieyasu had proved that it was worthwhile to wait for the cuckoo to sing.

Check Your Understanding

1. Compare the qualities of leadership that Nobunaga, Hideyoshi, and Ieyasu had that enabled each of them to contribute to the reunification of Japan.
2. How did Hideyoshi rise to power?
3. **a.** What effects did Hideyoshi's dream of an Asian empire have on Japan? **b.** on Korea?
4. **a.** How were the Buddhists a threat to the power of Nobunaga and Hideyoshi? **b.** How did the two leaders handle this threat?
5. What was one of Hideyoshi's great passions?
6. Why did a political crisis erupt when Hideyoshi died?
7. **Thinking Critically:** Review the traditional Japanese story about the cuckoo and the three Japanese leaders who helped reunify Japan. What do you think the cuckoo in the tale represented? Explain your thinking.

CHAPTER REVIEW

Chapter Summary

Section 1. Minamoto Yoritomo consolidated the victory of the military class in Japan. After defeating the rival house of Taira, he established a military government at Kamakura that exercised authority over a large part of the archipelago. When Yoritomo obtained for himself the title of shogun and the privilege of transmitting it to his heirs, the emperors were deprived of all military authority. In effect they became helpless puppets. So effectively did Yoritomo establish feudal institutions that many of them persisted long after the Minamoto family died out. The Kamakura Bakufu, or Shogunate, was finally overthrown when discontent caused by a heavy drain on the country's resources followed the Mongol invasions, the last of which took place in 1281.

Section 2. The rising popularity of Buddhism, brought about by the founding of many new sects, helped create a change in the mood and the outlook of the Japanese people during Kamakura times. These sects greatly simplified Buddhism by placing emphasis on faith as the principal means of salvation. The most popular of the new Buddhist sects were the Jodo, or Pure–Land sects, which emphasized salvation through the grace of a Buddha called Amida, and the True or Pure–Land sect. Shinran made Jodo Shinshu attractive to common people by reducing the endless repetitions of "Hail the Amida Buddha!" to one. Nichiren's Buddhist sect followed the interpretation of the Lotus flower as the only source of salvation, but Nichiren is also credited with arousing Japanese nationalism. Some members of the upper classes, especially the samurai, were strongly attracted to Zen and its reliance on self-enlightenment through meditation and insight rather than through analysis, reason, and logic.

Section 3. After the downfall of the Kamakura Bakufu brought about by the Emperor Go–Daigo in 1333, the Ashikaga family founded Japan's second military dynasty in 1338. The dynasty lasted until it was replaced in 1573. During its regime, feudalism was steadily extended in Japan. But warfare was almost continuous because the Ashikaga Shogunate was unable to control the powerful daimyo who controlled the local provinces.

The economy and cultural life, however, continued to flourish and advance. Castle towns, such as Tokyo, Nagoya,

Osaka, and Yokohama, developed where the daimyo and their retainers built large castles. Market towns arose at harbors and other convenient stopping places. The economy advanced through the creation of surplus goods, the use of coins in trade, and the establishment of guilds to foster training in new skills. Foreign trade with China was carried on by the Bakufu and by pirate daimyo. It was through trade with the Portuguese that Christianity was introduced into Japan. By 1600 Japan had about 300,000 Christian converts, many in western Japan.

The Ashikaga period was a time of cultural blooming as new art forms arose, especially among the upper classes. Developed at this time were bonsai culture, the tea ceremony, Nō drama, and various forms of painting and poetry.

Section 4. The disorder of the Ashikaga age was followed by the efforts of Nobunaga, Hideyoshi, and Ieyasu to turn Japan into a strong, unified state. Nobunaga is remembered for his abolition of the Ashikaga Shogunate and the destruction of Buddhist military power. Hideyoshi began as Nobunaga's top military adviser. On Nobunaga's death he rose to power, but his efforts to conquer Korea brought discontent to Japan's people. But it was Ieyasu of the house of Tokugawa who was to reap the richest rewards when he founded the third and last military dynasty in Japan.

■ Vocabulary Review

Define: alliance, Bakufu, go-kenin, kamikaze, nationalism, satori, daimyo, castle town, market town, barter system, guild, monopoly,

■ Places to Locate

Locate: Kamakura, Kyoto, Korean Peninsula, Osaka, Nagoya, China

■ People to Know

Identify: Yoritomo, Yoshitsune, Genghis Khan, Kublai Khan, Eshin, Honen the Saint, Shinran, Nichiren, Go–Daigo, Ashikaga Takauji, Francis Xavier, Nobunaga, Hideyoshi, Ieyasu

■ Thinking Critically

1. Defend or refute the statement, *Yoritomo deserves the title of "architect of feudalism."*

2. Was it wise for the Hojo regents not to seek the title of shogun? Why or why not?

3. What contributed to the failure of Go–Daigo to restore the imperial throne to a position of power? Was it possible for him to do this given Japan's feudal society at the time? Why or why not?

4. Japan has had some great leaders in its history. What part has feudalism played, if any, in the rise of Japan's leaders during the period of the Kamakura and Ashikaga shogunates?

5. Why do you think great art forms and a high degree of culture flourished in Japan despite the feudal warfare of the times?

Extending and Applying Your Knowledge

1. For an oral report, research the art of bonsai, using encyclopedias and other reference books. If possible, bring a sample of bonsai to the class.

2. Investigate the procedures of the Japanese tea ceremony. For a presentation to the class, explain the obligations of the one preparing the tea as well as of those who are to participate in the ceremony. Be sure to indicate the symbolism behind each gesture.

4

Japan Under Centralized Feudalism

Japan under the Tokugawa Shogunate retained many of the common characteristics of feudalism, but it also developed unique feudal features. Although Japan was ruled by a hereditary class of warriors, the samurai rarely had occasion to use their weapons. In contrast to the strife that was characteristic of feudalism elsewhere, Japan enjoyed several centuries of unbroken domestic peace. Whereas other feudal systems were characterized by decentralized rule, Tokugawa feudalism was notable for its **centralized government.**

Tokugawa Japan was a country that voluntarily kept its distance from other lands and peoples. Its policy of national seclusion was introduced at the very time the Japanese were moving to extend their commercial and cultural relations with the states of East and Southeast Asia. By keeping its distance from the rest of the world, Japan undoubtedly reaped certain benefits. Yet Japan ultimately paid a price for a policy that restricted foreign trade and contact with other cultures.

Denied the stimulus of foreign trade, the Japanese enjoyed a boom in agriculture and domestic trade during the seventeenth century and for some years thereafter. The movement of people from all social and economic classes to the growing cities greatly increased the production and exchange of goods and led to the establishment of many new types of business enterprises. But the gradual breakdown of the older, self-sufficient local economies, together with economic growth, created many new problems. The failure to cope with them effectively contributed to the overthrow of the Tokugawa Bakufu.

1. The Emergence of Centralized Feudalism

Under feudalism, political power usually is divided among many lords, not concentrated in a central government. The feudalism of Tokugawa Japan did not follow that pattern. Ieyasu and his immediate successors had the power to shake up, even perhaps to destroy, Japan's feudal system, but they used their power instead to centralize authority in themselves. Clever organizers and political manipulators, they were able to impose numerous checks and balances on the daimyo and to restrict contacts with the outer world. The seclusion and centralized feudalism that they imposed on Japan lasted for more than 200 years.

The Tokugawa Shogunate

Triumphant in the battle of Sekigahara, a town near Kyoto, Tokugawa Ieyasu moved quickly to follow up his victory, obtaining the title of shogun in 1603. Thus began the Tokugawa Shogunate (1603–1868), Japan's third. Having engineered the end of Hideyoshi's budding dynasty, Ieyasu knew he had to ensure the continuation of his own line. In 1605 he resigned as shogun in favor of his son but retained control of the Bakufu until his death. In 1614–1615 Ieyasu destroyed the last supporters of Hideyoshi's son, in the process taking over his rival's stronghold

Tokugawa Ieyasu seized the title of shogun and founded the last and most successful of Japan's three military dynasties. How did he gain power?

Tokugawa Japan

1603–1868	Tokugawa Shogunate
1633–1639	Establishment of isolationist policy
1853	Arrival of Perry; end of isolation
1854	Treaty of Kanagawa
1868	Replacement of shogunate by loyalist coalition

at Osaka. The downfall of Hideyoshi's son ended all effective resistance to Tokugawa ascendancy.

Ieyasu knew that several former opponents still liked to think of themselves as equals of the Tokugawa. Wise in the ways of feudal Japan, he also recognized that even allies do not always remain loyal. One of the tasks facing the Tokugawa regime, therefore, was to establish a method of controlling the daimyo.

Ieyasu and his successors had to tread carefully as they sought to curb the military and economic power of the lords. But by building on reforms started by Hideyoshi, they gradually increased the power and prestige of the Tokugawa Bakufu. Step by step they tightened existing restrictions on the daimyo or imposed new ones. By 1650 the Tokugawa system of government was complete and the relationship between the central government, the shogun, and the daimyo was firmly established.

The Relocation of Potential Rivals

Ieyasu and later shoguns were remarkably successful in dealing with the daimyo. One of Ieyasu's early moves was to establish his own Bakufu in a small coastal village in the Kanto Plain called Edo, which today is the large metropolis of Tokyo. Edo had been Ieyasu's capital while he was still a vassal of Hideyoshi. After Edo became headquarters for the Bakufu, Ieyasu reshuffled the surrounding **fiefs** to dilute the strength of the great lords. The lands immediately surrounding Edo either became "houselands," acreage that provided taxes for the support of the Tokugawa interests, or were redistributed to minor vassals. Lords related to the Tokugawa, as well as some of the greater hereditary vassals, were relocated on fiefs at least a day's march from Edo. These estates served as a **buffer zone** against surprise attacks. The estates together with their military, adminis-

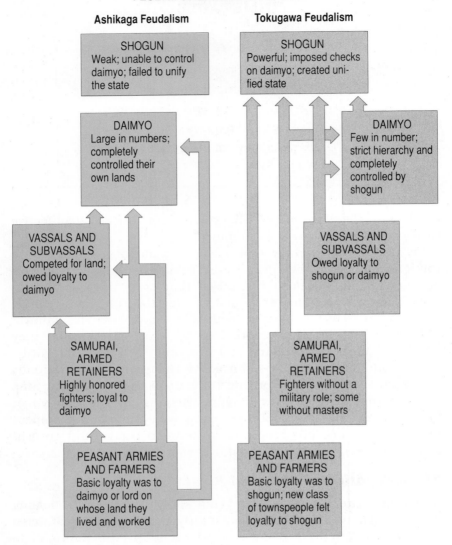

FEUDAL ORGANIZATION IN JAPAN

Ashikaga Feudalism

SHOGUN
Weak; unable to control daimyo; failed to unify the state

DAIMYO
Large in numbers; completely controlled their own lands

VASSALS AND SUBVASSALS
Competed for land; owed loyalty to daimyo

SAMURAI, ARMED RETAINERS
Highly honored fighters; loyal to daimyo

PEASANT ARMIES AND FARMERS
Basic loyalty was to daimyo or lord on whose land they lived and worked

Tokugawa Feudalism

SHOGUN
Powerful; imposed checks on daimyo; created unified state

DAIMYO
Few in number; strict hierarchy and completely controlled by shogun

VASSALS AND SUBVASSALS
Owed loyalty to shogun or daimyo

SAMURAI, ARMED RETAINERS
Fighters without a military role; some without masters

PEASANT ARMIES AND FARMERS
Basic loyalty was to shogun; new class of townspeople felt loyalty to shogun

CHANGES IN CONTROL. The structure of feudalism in Ashikaga and Tokugawa times is shown by the arrows, which indicate patterns of loyalty. In Ashikaga times loyalties were more divided than in Tokugawa times when almost all loyalties were tied directly to the shogun.

trative, and fiscal structures were referred to as **han.** Well outside the protective ring of fiefs were the estates of the **tozama.** Some of these tozama, or outside lords, had not acknowledged Ieyasu's supremacy until after the battle of Sekigahara. Others were deemed untrustworthy because their ties to the Tokugawa house were weak.

Townspeople kneel in respect as a daimyo and his followers enter Edo to take up the required annual residence. How did maintaining such a large following in Edo, while supporting a large household in the home province, lead to the impoverishment of the daimyo?

Controls on the Daimyo

The relocation of potential rivals was only one restraint imposed upon feudal lords by the early Tokugawa shoguns. By the mid–1600's a host of restrictions had been placed on the daimyo to discourage any thought of rebellion. A lord could not enter the fief of another lord without permission from the Bakufu. Nor could he repair his castle, take on additional vassals, or even arrange the marriage of a daughter without official approval.

But the most important method of control was the **sankin kotai.** Originally instituted by Hideyoshi to control his vassals, the sankin kotai was enlarged and strengthened by the Tokugawa. It required all daimyo to build a residence in Edo, to live there for a large part of every year, and to leave their wives and children in Edo at all times. In practice, the actual length and frequency of the required visits to Edo varied slightly with the status of the daimyo and the location of the fiefs. Sankin kotai helped to keep the daimyo out of political mischief. The daimyo realized that to plot against the shogun when away from Edo would endanger their families. The system also helped to drain away surplus funds that the daimyo otherwise might be tempted to use to finance a rebellion. The cost of the journey to and from Edo and the expense of living there was high, sometimes taking as much as 80 percent of a daimyo's annual income.

The shoguns had other methods of limiting the income of the daimyo. When the Tokugawa rulers learned that the daimyo were accumulating wealth, they would order the daimyo to make costly gifts or to improve roads and develop harbors. They also encouraged the daimyo to maintain luxurious households both in Edo and in their home provinces. Such tactics kept the daimyo poor and harmless.

Emperors Under the Tokugawa

Ieyasu and his successors respected the throne, if not the occupants. Following Hideyoshi's example, they granted new income to the court and treated the emperor with great honor. Shoguns married imperial princesses and asked advice of the emperor before naming their children. At the same time, however, they made sure that the court did not become a rallying point for discontented daimyo. The Bakufu maintained high officials in Kyoto to guard against conspiracies, and no daimyo was allowed an audience with the emperor without permission from the shogun. And during the entire Tokugawa period no emperor was allowed to leave the vicinity of Kyoto. So effectively was the imperial court sealed off that until the 1860's foreigners did not realize that Japan had an emperor.

Opposition to Christianity

By the time Ieyasu came to power, the days of Japanese Christianity were numbered. Fearful that Christianity would upset the existing social and political order, Hideyoshi had begun to harass foreign missionaries and Japanese converts. Ieyasu shared Hideyoshi's caution concerning Christianity. Like his predecessor, he issued anti-Christian edicts, but he did not enforce them until the last few years of his rule.

The darkest days for Christianity came after Ieyasu's death. His heirs were afraid that rebellious daimyo might conspire with Western traders and missionaries to secure firearms. They were also aware of European conquests in other parts of Asia. The shogunate, therefore, forbade missionaries to enter Japan on pain of death. Japanese converts were looked upon as possible allies of anti-Tokugawa daimyo or Western invaders and were ordered to renounce their faith. The converts who refused were

MOVEMENT: TOKUGAWA JAPAN. The distribution of fiefs under the early Tokugawa shoguns was carefully planned to strengthen the shogunate. Most of the best fields and almost all of the land around Edo were absorbed by the Tokugawa and their supporters. Tozama were isolated on the outer fringes.

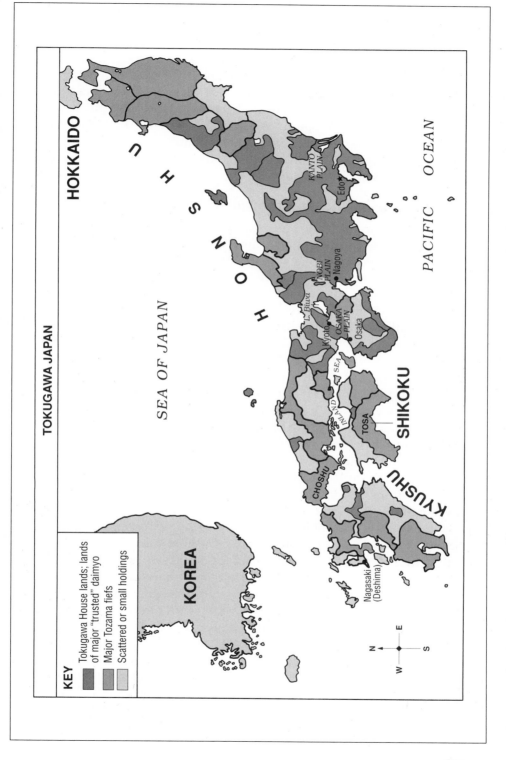

TOKUGAWA JAPAN

KEY
Tokugawa House lands; lands of major "trusted" daimyo
Major Tozama fiefs
Scattered or small holdings

KOREA

SEA OF JAPAN

HOKKAIDO

HONSHU

KANTO PLAIN
Edo★

Nagoya
NOBI PLAIN

L. Biwa
Kyoto
OSAKA PLAIN
Osaka

INLAND SEA

SHIKOKU

TOSA

CHOSHU

KYUSHU

Nagasaki (Deshima)

PACIFIC OCEAN

N
W — E
S

executed. By 1630 Christianity was all but wiped out in Japan, lingering mainly around Nagasaki.

The death blow to Christianity was delivered when a revolt broke out in late 1637 at Shimabara, a small peninsula near Nagasaki. The rebels were simple peasants aroused by oppressive treatment and heavy taxation. But many of them were also Christians, and soon the struggle became a battle for the survival of the Christian religion. When the forces of the shogunate prevailed, thousands of rebels and members of their families were slaughtered. The massacre destroyed the last significant pocket of Christianity in Japan.

Relations with the Outside World

Japan's decisions regarding relations with the outside world were closely tied to the shogunate's attitude toward Christianity. Ieyasu had favored foreign trade and his reluctance to enforce anti-Christian edicts stemmed from concern lest such actions should adversely affect that trade. The Portuguese particularly had brought both merchandise and the Christian religion to Japan. But in the early 1600's the Dutch and English, neither of whom had any interest in missionary activity, began trading with Japan. Realizing that his country now could accommodate Western traders without tolerating Christianity, Ieyasu had begun to suppress the foreign religion.

Ieyasu's successors not only clamped down on missionaries and Japanese Christians, they also attempted to tighten controls on foreign trade to minimize the possibility of a challenge to their rule from the outside world. In a series of **seclusion laws** between 1633 and 1639, the shogunate prohibited Japanese subjects from leaving the archipelago without seeking a valid license from the appropriate officials. Those who had already left Japan faced possible execution on their return to the archipelago. Fearful of the influence of Catholicism, the Tokugawa authorities expelled Spanish traders in 1624 and Portuguese traders in 1639. The English had already abandoned their trade with the Japanese because it was unprofitable for them. The Japanese continued to trade only with the Dutch, Chinese, Koreans, and Ryukyuans. Even this trade, however, was restricted. Dutch traders were confined to the island of Deshima in the harbor of Nagasaki. Merchants from China, who had actively traded with Japan for centuries, were also confined to this island. The Satsuma domain in southern Kyushu was given the exclusive right to trade with the Ryukyus, and trade with Korea remained in the hands of the shogun's special representatives.

For 200 years the Dutch and Chinese were the only major traders to enter Japan. In an attempt to regain trading privileges, the Portuguese sent a mission to Japan in 1640. All but 13 of the mission's 74 members were beheaded. The survivors were sent back to Macau (mah-KOW), the Portuguese trading base in China, to inform the other traders that the shogunate meant to enforce its laws. The Portuguese were warned, if "King Philip himself, or . . . [the] god of the Christians, or the great Buddha contravene this prohibition, they shall pay for it with their heads." Eventually, even the Dutch became irregular in their trading visits to Japan. Every year or so a Dutch ship arrived from Java. Before being unloaded, the foreign ship was carefully searched. The discovery of any objects by Japanese inspectors, which suggested that a Christian faith even existed aroused their suspicion. As soon as a cargo was unloaded at Deshima, the Dutch lost no time in preparing the ship for its return voyage. Because of diligence such as this and other ways of carefully observing the shogunate's policy, Japan's seclusion was as complete as the shoguns could make it.

Interest in Useful Knowledge

Once a year, the seclusion restrictions were lifted to enable the Dutch traders at Deshima to visit Edo and present gifts to the shogun. The imperial officials and the shogun took advantage of these visits to learn any European news the traders had picked up from Dutch ships. By the early 1700's the shogunate officials realized that strict seclusion laws kept out useful knowledge. A few samurai were encouraged to confer with the Dutch at Deshima. Having scholarly interests, these samurai were eager to learn about the world beyond their islands, and the bored traders were delighted to be their teachers. The first subject studied was the Dutch language. Next the samurai-scholars turned their attention to practical matters such as cartography, surveying, gunnery, military engineering, and various sciences. Western politics, government, and culture were largely ignored in these studies.

The writings of these students of Dutch learning were studied by daimyo and samurai interested in other than traditional Japanese military and scientific learning. Dutch was the only European language really studied in Japan during the long era of national seclusion. When the policy of seclusion was abandoned in the mid-nineteenth century, Dutch became, for a brief time, a principal means of communication between the Japanese and Westerners.

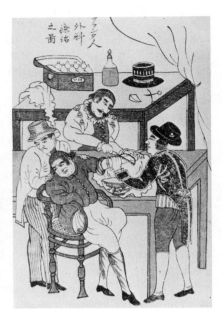

WESTERN INFLUENCE. Despite their seclusion, many Japanese showed interest in the West. A book on Dutch learning (right) was livened by a print showing a Western surgeon at work. The plate (left) is decorated with scenes about Dutch trading.

The Effects of Seclusion

The rigid controls exercised by the shogunate over Japan had both advantages and disadvantages for the Japanese. By keeping the Westerners at arm's length, the shoguns may have helped to spare the Japanese the intrigues and aggressions that marked Western colonial intrusions into the Americas, Africa, and Asia. On the other hand, because of their seclusion the Japanese were deprived of important means of enriching their culture and their economy. Seclusion also denied the Japanese opportunities to develop large-scale foreign trade. As it was, it was necessary for the people of Japan to fall back on themselves and rely on their own limited resources to enrich their way of life. Lack of contact with other lands and cultures at this time denied the Japanese much of the scientific and technological knowledge that was transforming ways of living in Western lands. Finally, the centuries of self-imposed seclusion doubtless contributed to the feelings of uneasiness that some Japanese still have when dealing with foreigners.

Check Your Understanding

1. What were the main tasks facing the Tokugawa Shogunate when it took control of Japan?
2. Why did Ieyasu reshuffle the fiefs surrounding Edo?
3. How did the sankin kotai help Ieyasu control the daimyo?
4. How were Tokugawa opposition to Christianity and the Tokugawa seclusion policy related?
5. In what ways did the Japanese obtain some useful knowledge about the outside world?
6. *Thinking Critically:* What effects did centralized feudalism and Japan's seclusion policy have on the Japanese people?

2. Class Divisions in Tokugawa Society

The main goal of Ieyasu and the advisers close to him was to ensure the continuation of the Tokugawa regime. Social mobility, the movement between classes, might disturb the established social order. Consequently steps were taken to make it difficult for people to move upward from one social class to another. The Tokugawa had good reasons to fear rapid social change and to keep people within the bounds of their own class. The Tokugawa knew all too well that an ambitious leader might mold undisciplined samurai or peasants into an effective army. As long as the ambitions of the people were restricted and limits placed on the number of arms-bearing men, the Tokugawa believed that they could maintain control.

The Tokugawa Social Structure

The Bakufu sought to regulate the activities of each class and to prevent movement from one class to another. Children were born into the class of their parents. Sons usually carried on the occupations of their fathers because class determined the work or service one performed. The rigid class lines were not imposed overnight. The laws freezing class lines were formulated over a period of many years and reflected conditions that had developed over a much longer period. Bushido, the code of the samurai, which developed in the mid–1600's, became the base of the Tokugawa social structure. (See page 44.) This code was strongly influenced by new interpretations of Confucian teaching that

95

emphasized the duty of everyone to respect and honor those above them in the social structure. (See page 97.) In Japan this obligation required the samurai to obey their overlords, the people to respect the samurai, and children to revere their fathers and elders. The Tokugawa Bakufu, dominated as it was by the samurai mentality, enacted laws designed to ensure the supremacy of men over women.

The Status of Women

In Tokugawa Japan the status of women declined from what it had been in earlier times, particularly before the Warring States period. Several reasons account for this decline. By its very nature, the military class admired the martial arts and martial ability. Thus anyone who did not practice the martial arts was considered in an inferior status. Besides the samurai mentality, two other important influences in Japanese life—Confucianism and Buddhism—also accorded women a subordinate status to men.

In general a woman's role was defined in terms of the "three obediences." The woman was to obey her father before marriage and her husband after marriage. If widowed, the woman was to obey her sons. A wife was expected to be frugal and industrious. She was also expected to be self-sacrificing, especially for her children. A man could be unfaithful to his wife, but a woman's behavior at all times had to be above suspicion.

Within the samurai family, women were subject to the absolute authority of the male head of the household. In the artisan and merchant classes, women led less restrictive lives, perhaps because women in these classes often worked alongside the male members of the family. Peasant families, however, tended to be influenced in their attitudes by the samurai class. Still in most peasant households, women were held in a relatively higher status than they were in samurai families.

The Peasant Class

Eight out of ten Japanese of the Tokugawa period were peasants—farmers working the fiefs of the daimyo. The peasants ranked below the warrior class on the social scale, but a vast gulf separated the two classes. Even samurai faced with poverty looked down on the peasants. All peasants were legally bound to the land, but some were wealthier than others. Those who were modestly wealthy were greatly respected by other peasants. Poorer peasants had barely enough rice left to feed their families after taking out the share owed to their lords. The poorest peas-

The Influence of Confucius

Confucius was born about 551 B.C. in North China. Confucius believed that people would behave properly in everyday life, if they knew how to live together in peace and harmony. To help people accomplish this, he determined the basic relationships of human life and defined the duties of the partners in each relationship. The five basic relationships were between parents and children, rulers and subjects, husbands and wives, older children and younger children, and members of the community with other members.

Confucius said that the most important of these basic relationships were the ones between parents and children and between rulers and subjects. Filial piety, the devotion and obedience of children to their parents, was the greatest and most basic of Confucian virtues. The state was a huge family. Rulers were like parents. Their subjects were their children. Subjects owed the same loyalty and obedience to their rulers as children did to their parents. But parents and rulers as superiors must use their authority with justice, love, and concern for the welfare of their inferiors. Superiors must set an example, for if the superiors were not virtuous, their inferiors could not be expected to behave properly.

Confucius believed that education was necessary to help people achieve virtue. Confucian educators emphasized proper behavior, believing that once taught to behave properly, people's outward actions would influence their inner attitudes. As a result, manners and ritual came to have great importance.

Confucius died in 479 B.C. His philosophy had enormous influence in China and throughout East Asia. His ideas first began to enter Japan in the fifth century A.D. In the twelfth century, a Chinese philosopher named Zhuxi (Chu Hsi) reformulated Confucianism to include Buddhism and Daoism. This reformulated Confucianism, which came to be called Neo-Confucianism, emphasized people's obligation to obey their ruler and to accept their social status. Neo-Confucianism fit in well with Tokugawa plans to freeze Japanese society in place. As a result, the Tokugawa welcomed its teachings as philosophical support for their policies.

ants owed the lords their entire harvest of rice and then had to subsist on barley and potatoes.

Most peasants made their own tools and household goods because they rarely had enough money to purchase such goods from others. The Tokugawa government, which kept a close watch on the peasants, directed them to live frugally. They also directed them to spend their free time in silkmaking and other useful pursuits, to dress in cheap clothing, and to care for their rice fields with the utmost dedication.

The Artisan Class

Although below peasants in the social scale, the artisans— tailors, silversmiths, goldsmiths, carpenters, and other crafts-workers—were highly regarded. Artisans had to go through a long instructive apprenticeship before they were recognized as skilled craftsworkers. Many artisans lived in market towns and worked for themselves, making their products in buildings that served as both home and shop. Artisans were also employed in small factories managed by enterprising townspeople. Some artisans lived in castle towns, working part time for the daimyo in exchange for a small salary. While often underpaid by the lord, an artisan found a more profitable market for wares among townspeople and visitors.

The artisans of Tokugawa times took great pride in their work. They were industrious, patient, and skillful. They turned out brocaded silk, samurai swords, highly polished lacquerware, useful and ornamental pottery, painted fans, cast-iron cookware, ivory fobs or ornaments called netsuke, folding screens, fine carved furniture, and other products that still command admiration.

The Merchant Class

Merchants in Tokugawa Japan were held in low esteem by the warriors. According to the Confucian thought underlying the social system, a person who produced nothing was little better than a parasite. Merchants made a living buying and selling goods that were produced by others. In addition, the proud samurai scorned merchants as people who schemed and sought favor from others to accumulate material goods. To the warrior, honor and self-respect were more worthy aims to pursue in life than wealth. Some samurai showed contempt for merchants and for money by refusing to count their change after making a purchase.

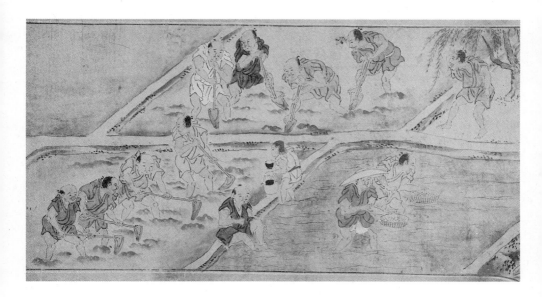

TOKUGAWA SOCIETY. Art depicts three classes of Tokugawa Society. Peasants working in the field are shown on a 17th century painted screen. An artisan (below left) is pictured crafting a sword. The figure (below right) is dressed as a samurai, complete with his swords. How did each class view the others in Tokugawa Japan?

99

Merchants were constantly reminded of their low rank in the social order. The government made a practice of excluding them from official positions, and they were forbidden by law to enjoy certain comforts and luxuries. If merchants became too showy in their dress or manner of living or offended a feudal lord, their wealth could be confiscated. Shrewd merchants, however, managed to get around such regulations. Some even managed to find a place for their children in the ranks of the military class. For a fee, samurai families would adopt the sons of merchants. Merchants often dressed, ate, and lived well and many became patrons of the arts. Sometimes they were able to use their money to gain favor with a poor daimyo or even with a member of the Bakufu. A saying of the time was, "If he has money, even a fool can become a master."

The Military Class

The military class dominated Tokugawa society—the shogun, the daimyo, and the samurai. (See page 44.) Technically the term *samurai* included the shogun and the daimyo, who were also sword-bearing members of the military class. As feudalism developed, common usage limited the term *samurai* to warriors below the status of daimyo who lived on salaries and pensions. Between 1700 and 1870, the population of the military class changed very little. With their families and retainers, the members of the military class totaled about two million, or about 6 percent of the population.

Behavior Patterns in Japanese Life

Neo–Confucian and Bushido requirements affected the habits, customs, and attitudes of all Japanese. Children were taught how to behave in all possible situations. They learned how to act toward their superiors in the family and in society at large. They learned what to expect from people of social classes lower than themselves. Differences in social rank were indicated in the spoken word. Pronouns and verbs changed, depending on whether the person being addressed was a superior, inferior, or equal. The same was true for the custom of bowing, which accompanied the acts of greeting, thanking, or saying farewell. The depth of the bow indicated whether the person receiving the bow was higher, lower, or equal in rank to the person making the bow. All these customs had existed in earlier periods, but during the Tokugawa era, Japanese patterns of behavior became more precise, and the obligation to observe them became stricter than before.

Customs and habits in any society are not easily discarded. Long after Japan's third military dynasty had come to an end, Tokugawa manners and customs persisted. Even today, the behavior of many Japanese people reveals strong traces of their feudal heritage.

The Samurai Problem

The peace that settled on Japan after the battle of Sekigahara created a difficult situation for both the Bakufu and the samurai. With no battles to fight, the samurai no longer had a purpose in life. Moreover the Tokugawa had greatly reduced the number of fiefs, taking many for themselves and giving others to favorite vassals. Thousands of samurai who previously had received income from such fiefs were left without a means of support. Most of the warriors were illiterate and thus unqualified for administrative positions in the feudal government. They were forbidden by law to farm, or at least discouraged from doing so. A warrior could become a merchant or trader only by giving up the status of a samurai. Few were willing to give up their high social class or to lower themselves to a class they traditionally looked down on. The most fortunate samurai were able to stay on with their lords or secure employment policing the many fiefs.

Thousands of samurai, however, found themselves with no masters, no income, and nothing to do. These became known as **ronin**—masterless samurai. Some of these ronin swallowed their pride and turned to trading or to farming when they saw that the government was ignoring this infraction of the law. Other ronin became street rowdies and vagrants, and some even became thieves.

One way the government tried to help the unemployed samurai was by stressing the importance of education. In one of his edicts, Ieyasu stated that learning and military arts should be equally pursued. As a consequence, many samurai found employment as teachers of the martial arts. Other samurai, having acquired an education, became officers in the Bakufu and in local feudal governments. Some samurai engaged in intellectual and artistic pursuits. Indeed the leading scholars, writers, poets, and artists of Tokugawa Japan were sword-bearing samurai. It was also samurai who pursued Dutch learning in Japan. (See page 93.) By the end of the Tokugawa period, the samurai still proudly carried their swords as a symbol of social status. Their military importance, however, had long given way to their practical skills.

Social Discontent in Tokugawa Japan

Despite the efforts of the shogunate to maintain a rigid social order, many Japanese were discontented with their social status and managed to change it. Dissatisfied peasants, artisans, and merchants evaded the law whenever they could. Many samurai who were tired of being poor and hungry, and discouraged by the lack of opportunities to advance, gave up their rank to become merchants. Some turned to the many new occupations that were opening up because of developments in agriculture, manufacturing, and business. The result was a changing social structure without action from the shogunate.

As conditions changed, the shogunate became willing to overlook certain violations of its regulations. But it was unwilling to modify the system and thus facilitate social mobility. The cardinal principle of Tokugawa rule was to maintain an unchanging social structure that would not allow a person's ambitions to threaten the status quo. This determination to resist change helped keep the shogunate alive for more than 200 years. In the end, however, this resistance to change brought about its downfall.

Check Your Understanding

1. **a.** Explain what is meant by the Japanese samurai mentality. **b.** How did samurai attitudes affect the status of women in Tokugawa Japan?
2. Compare the status of women in samurai families with women's status in merchant and peasant families.
3. What was the largest class by far in Tokugawa Japan?
4. What class was considered the lowest of all classes by the samurai?
5. **a.** What class dominated Tokugawa society? **b.** What conditions brought about changes in this class?
6. **Thinking Critically:** How did Neo–Confucian thought and the code of Bushido influence Japanese patterns of behavior and foster the rigidity of the social structure?

3. Economic Growth During the Early Tokugawa Age

With the peace of the Tokugawa era came a new prosperity. For the first time many peasants became prosperous, rich merchants grew even wealthier, and cities increased in size and importance. But prosperity created problems. For many people prices rose faster than income, and to make up the difference these people borrowed from moneylenders, usually at a very high rate of interest. The hardest hit group was the warrior class, the daimyo and samurai upon whom the feudal structure rested. Because they were unable to adjust satisfactorily to the changing economic system, the very base of Tokugawa rule was badly shaken.

Improvements in Peasant Life

During the Tokugawa period, many peasants experienced new prosperity. On fiefs where supervision was lax, the peasants often concealed part of their crop and gave the lords less than their share. Sometimes peasants acquired the right to till additional land and neglected to report the change to the proper authorities. Some peasants acquired fairly large estates and employed their less fortunate neighbors. Moreover, many of the peasants who found life on the farm too difficult ignored travel restrictions and moved to the castle towns and market cities. There they found work as servants, laborers, or artisans. Some even became merchants. A few peasants built local factories, turning out such products as cloth, paper, sugar, and Japanese rice wine. Such local businesspeople were respected by their fellow villagers, and even enjoyed some influence with the local feudal lords. Although the average peasant had to struggle to make ends meet, by the end of Tokugawa times the number of rich farmers had increased.

Merchant Benefits

As a result of the policies of the Bakufu, Japanese merchants benefited even more than the peasants from the new order. The merchants were generally taxed lightly, because the governing warrior class held merchants in such low esteem. Many of these merchants used their higher earnings to expand their businesses. Merchants also played an important role in the agricultural economy of the times. The rice the feudal lords received as income was bulky and difficult to transport. It was also awkward to use in settling accounts. Therefore, the rice was shipped to Osaka or Edo merchants who paid cash for the rice or granted the feudal lords bills of exchange that were honored by other merchants. The merchants then sold the rice for a price that was considerably higher than its purchase value. Merchant families used their growing wealth to establish factories, retail stores, and even department stores—the first in the world. In these ways many Japanese merchants were able to accumulate large fortunes.

The Rise of Prosperous Cities

Most of Japan's rich merchants lived in Edo, Osaka, or Kyoto, the three major trading centers. These cities more than rivaled London, Paris, and Amsterdam in area and population. The Dutch merchants from Deshima were greatly impressed by the tremendous quantity and variety of goods on display in shops and stores. A member of the Dutch trading mission of 1691, in writing about Kyoto as the chief mercantile town in the Empire said:

> Here they refine copper, coin money, print books, weave the richest stuffs [cloth] with gold and silver flowers. The best and scarcest dyes, the most artful carvings, all sorts of musical instruments, pictures, japaned [lacquered] cabinets, all sorts of things . . . are made here in the utmost perfection. . . . In short, there is nothing can be thought of, but what may be found at Kyoto, and nothing, however neatly made, can be imported from abroad but what some artisan in this capital will undertake to imitate. . . . There are but few houses in all the chief streets, where there is not something to be sold. For my part I could not help admiring how they can have customers enough for such an immense quantity of goods. [Engelbert Kaempfer, *The History of Japan*, trans. by J. G. Scheuchzer]

During the Tokugawa period, Edo became increasingly important as a political, economic, and artistic center and surpassed Kyoto as the greatest city in Japan. The shogun's capital was alive with thousands of officials and attendants. Moreover, to meet the requirements of the sankin kotai system, the great daimyo maintained palaces in Edo that were attended by highly select samurai. Understandably, each lord sought to outshine all of the others in splendor. Artisans also flocked to Edo from the smaller towns and rural villages, hoping to gain a share of the great wealth that was being spent there. Many an enterprising merchant amassed a fortune catering to the needs of Edo's people.

Hard Times for the Warrior Class

Taking into account their social rank, many members of the daimyo-samurai class did not fare at all well during Tokugawa times. Daimyo were obligated to pay the salaries of their samurai and to meet the requirements of the sankin kotai system, which became for them a double burden. Although some of the samurai were vassals with lands of their own, most others had to live on a salary. A poor rice crop, low prices on the rice market, or widespread tax evasion by peasants on the lords' domains could make it difficult for the daimyo to pay these salaries. An even greater expense stemmed from the lords' obligations to the Bakufu under the sankin kotai system. As a result, many daimyo found themselves falling hopelessly into debt.

As for the samurai, most of them lived on salaries based on the cost of living at the beginning of the Tokugawa period. Although prices rose during the 1600's, these salaries were not increased. Many daimyo, caught between rising prices and a fairly set income, were even forced to cut the already inadequate payments to their samurai. Too proud to admit their poverty, many samurai joined their overlords in seeking loans to meet their expenses.

About a century after the founding of the shogunate, many fiefs were in deep financial trouble. Lords and vassals alike were heavily in debt to rice brokers and merchant moneylenders. For many daimyo, the annual payments on their loans were greater than their annual incomes. Even members of the ruling Tokugawa family sometimes found it necessary to go to rich merchants for financial relief.

Leaders Tackle Economic Problems

The samurai administrators of Japan tried to understand the changing economic situation. The sankin kotai system brought together in Edo some of the leading men of Japan. Consequently they were able to meet and hold discussions that focused on their common problems, and to exchange ideas about how best to solve them. These gatherings even benefited the Bakufu. The fiefs served as a sort of testing ground for the Tokugawa, providing both new ideas and talented administrators. But it is doubtful that these men could have found the time to adapt the feudal government to the new conditions. Japan, which had been secluded for centuries, was beginning to feel the pressures of the outside world.

Check Your Understanding

1. How did the economic position of many peasants improve during Tokugawa times?
2. In what ways did merchants benefit from the improved economic times?
3. Why did the warrior class fall on hard times?
4. What efforts did the Bakufu make to adapt to Japan's changing economic conditions?
5. ***Thinking Critically:*** How did the sankin kotai system benefit the shogunate but serve as a disadvantage to the daimyo and samurai? What effect did the sankin kotai system have on Edo?

4. Development of a New Culture for Townspeople

Edo and Osaka became cultural centers as well as commercial centers during Tokugawa times. When they were not devoting their time to making money, the townspeople were looking for ways to spend it. The recreation and entertainment that appealed to the court nobility and to the samurai did not always suit the robust tastes of the townspeople. The townspeople were much less interested in improving their minds and in developing artistic skills than in enjoying themselves. Because they were less concerned with the past than with life about them, people in the cities, from the late seventeenth century on, turned to new forms of entertainment.

The Puppet Theater

The puppet play, known as **bunraku,** came into vogue in Osaka. The foremost writer of this type of drama was Chikamatsu. Strikingly lifelike, the actors in these plays were puppets about three quarters the size of humans. The puppets were manipulated on the stage by a team of three puppeteers whose expert performance depended upon long practice and split-second teamwork. To keep from being a distraction to the audience, the puppeteers wore black robes and hoods. But during presentations the audience was usually so intent on watching the puppets that the puppeteers were not even noticed. In a wing of the stage a narrator recited the story of the play.

Bunraku attained great popularity. Both children and adults attended the puppet theater. Although troupes were established in other cities, none ever rivaled the one in Osaka. The Osaka troupe has been designated a "national cultural treasure."

The Kabuki Theater

Kabuki had its origins in the puppet play and the Nō drama of Ashikaga days. Kabuki was presented in specially constructed theaters in the great cities. The stage, unusually long and deep, was well suited for these elegant spectacles. Many clever devices were used to heighten the dramatic action. Trapdoors enabled actors to disappear from sight in an instant, while wires could transport them, if need be, through the air. Revolving platforms permitted rapid changes of setting. But the most eye-catching feature was the hanamichi flower path—a long elevated runway extending from the stage to the rear of the theater. Actors made their entrances and exits, and delivered their orations, upon the hanamichi.

All roles, both male and female, in kabuki were played by men. Actors specializing in feminine roles were trained from childhood to walk, talk, and behave like women. The brightly colored costumes of kabuki players are in the styles of the Tokugawa period or earlier. Like the settings themselves, the essence of kabuki dazzles the eye and leaves nothing to the imagination. Everything is artfully exaggerated. Color, sound, speech, and dramatic action combine to make an overpowering assault upon the senses and emotions.

The repertoire of kabuki was practically completed by the late 1700's. Chikamatsu, who wrote many puppet plays, was also the foremost kabuki playwright. The favorite theme for both bunraku and kabuki was that of conflict between duty and per-

A Tokugawa artist captured a performance of the bunraku (puppet theater). A favorite entertainment of Tokugawa times, the bunraku required great skill and dexterity from the masters who manipulated the strings.

107

KABUKI. Dating from the late 1500's, kabuki became one of Japan's most popular art forms. Above, a scroll painting depicted an early performance featuring an actress named Okuni. After authorities banned women from the stage, men played both male and female roles. Fans snapped up prints (right) of favorite actors. Modern performances (below) continue to draw large audiences. Why do you think this is so?

sonal desires, with duty usually winning out in the end. Many of the plays are based upon tales and legends of early feudal Japan. The deeds of the heroes and villains in the wars between the Taira and Minamoto have been favorites year after year.

The Tale of the Forty-Seven Ronin, perhaps the national epic of Japan, is a favorite drama that is sometimes performed in the bunraku and kabuki theaters. The story is based on an incident that occurred in Edo just as the 1700's were beginning. Lord Asano inadvertently behaved improperly at court because Lord Kira intentionally had given him bad advice. Asano committed seppuku because he had disgraced himself. Asano's samurai, now without a master, became ronin. Forty-seven of these ronin secretly vowed vengeance against Lord Kira. To lull him into a false sense of security, however, the ronin pretended indifference to their late lord's humiliation. Then without warning, the ronin attacked Kira's mansion and killed him.

The shogun and many others at court sympathized with the ronin. The ronin, however, had broken the Tokugawa peace. Rather than punishing them, the shogun allowed them to commit seppuku. For the Japanese people the story of the 47 ronin symbolizes loyalty, courage, and fearlessness in the face of death.

Sensational contemporary events and scandals were also made into kabuki dramas. Occasionally, too, playwrights poked thinly disguised fun at pompous government officials. For variety's sake, examples of each type of play traditionally have been presented during a single performance, which still lasts five hours or more.

Woodblock Prints

A new form of art blossomed in the 1700's. With the growth of large cities even the less prosperous townspeople craved tasteful ways of decorating their homes. The ornate silk screens, costly ceramics, and fine paintings that adorned the residences of the wealthy were beyond their means. Moreover, these costly works of art were not meaningful to people with simple ways. The answer to their need was the woodblock print. Gay and colorful, such a print could be purchased for a few copper coins. What was especially appealing about woodblock prints was that they dealt with the "passing world," with life as it drifted by before one's very eyes.

The great Japanese woodblock printers of the 1700's and 1800's were men of the world, familiar with the richly diverse life of Edo, Osaka, and Kyoto. They knew the crowded streets

Carving the block from which the print will be made, this modern-day woodblock artisan is using methods dating back to Tokugawa times. The subject is a geisha in the elaborate wig and robes of her profession.

and shops, the popular eating houses, the busy markets, the public bath houses, and the bustling wharves and depicted these in their art. The woodblock artists also depicted the kabuki theater and its actors, famous beauties and women about town, and the famous wrestling champions. Often the owner of a restaurant or an inn would commission an artist's work to be used as an advertisement.

A woodblock print was produced by a team of three. The artist, considered the most important member of the team, painted the original sketch and determined the choice of colors. In the second stage an engraver took over. Using the sketch as a guide, the engraver cut the woodblocks, destroying the painting itself in the process. In the final stage the printer added the color by using a succession of overlays. While the engraver and printer were as important to the final product as the artist, the final product was always inscribed with the seal of the artist.

The Tokugawa woodblock artists traveled far and wide. Some of their finest work pictures the beautiful scenery of the Japanese archipelago—Mt. Fuji in all seasons, the rolling sea and the offshore pine-clad islands, dashing waterfalls, misty lakes, and meandering rivers. The series of "Fifty-Three Stopping Places on the Tokaido," by the great Hiroshige, has won recognition throughout the world. (The Tokaido, the main highway of Tokugawa times, connected Edo with Kyoto.) Hokusai is famed for his sketches of Mt. Fuji and the sea, while Utamaro's willowy women are popular everywhere.

The Haiku

The **haiku,** the unique 17-syllable Japanese poem, was developed during Tokugawa times. It was an abbreviation of the tanka, a form that had flourished in earlier centuries. (See page 48.) The final two lines of this older Japanese verse, composed of seven syllables each, were dropped. What remained was a poem of only three lines. The number of syllables in each line followed a fixed sequence of 5–7–5. Limited to a mere six or seven words, the haiku is the shortest verse form in the world.

The haiku was perfected by members of the rural-based samurai class, and was not directly related to the new urban culture. The great haiku poets were people of serious and sensitive mind and mood, who fixed their eyes upon nature. They expressed their awe and appreciation of the natural world in brief verse, often with a tinge of sadness. The haiku, although simple in form, can also be remarkably subtle in its meaning.

Basho, a samurai of the seventeenth century, is considered by the Japanese to be the greatest of all writers of haiku. The following haiku by Basho is known by many Japanese:

Furu-ike ya	An ancient pond.
Kawazu tobikomu	A frog leaps;
Mizu-no-oto	Splash!

This poem may be taken as a simple description of a common natural scene. Readers looking for more subtle meanings may see in it a commentary upon the impermanence of life. For such readers, human existence is like the ripples in the water caused by a diving frog.

Basho has been *admired* by composers of haiku. But Issa, a poet born in the eighteenth century, has been *loved*. Having suffered much in life, he wrote deeply reflective poetry. His verses are marked by compassion and understanding and show his ability to find humor and beauty in even the most commonplace of things:

Yare-utsu-na	Oh, don't mistreat
Hae ga te wo suru	the fly! He wrings his hands!
Ashi wo suru	He wrings his feet!

The haiku has endured as the principal form of Japanese poetry. Haiku is studied in all Japanese schools today. Haiku verses are regularly published in almost every newspaper and magazine in the country. Each year a national poetry contest is held, in which the theme is set by the emperor. Many of the poems submitted are haiku. Haiku poetry now has followers all over the world.

Check Your Understanding

1. How is bunraku different from kabuki?
2. Why were woodblock prints so popular?
3. **a.** What are haiku? **b.** How do they differ from tanka?
4. *Thinking Critically:* Why do you think so many of the traditional forms of art and drama remain popular with people in Japan today?

5. The End of Seclusion

In the mid-nineteenth century the ancient policy of seclusion finally was abandoned. Seclusion had led to a serious technological and military gap between Japan and the West, a fact that became painfully evident when a naval squadron from the United States anchored in Edo Bay in 1853. When the commander of the fleet delivered a request for a treaty between the United States and Japan, the Tokugawa officials realized they had to grant it.

The presence of unwanted foreigners in Japanese ports sparked the hostility smoldering against the Tokugawa. Two emotions fueled a rebellion against the Bakufu—hatred of the foreigners and loyalty to the emperor. After a short struggle the Tokugawa forces were defeated. When the shogun surrendered his title, two and a half centuries of Tokugawa rule came to an end.

Western Pressure

In the centuries since the establishment of the Tokugawa Shogunate, European influence in Asia and the Pacific had increased enormously. By the mid-1800's India and much of

Southeast Asia had come under the domination of European nations, and in East Asia even giant China was compelled to grant concessions to the foreigners. The sight of Western ships in Japanese coastal waters became commonplace, and requests from Westerners for permission to take on water and supplies grew ever more frequent. Although such requests were flatly rejected, the Westerners did not give up and go away, as Japanese officials wished they would. On one pretext or another, the Westerners tried to enter Japan.

Perry's Naval Expedition

In 1853 the United States sent a naval expedition to Japan under the command of Commodore Matthew C. Perry. Government officials assumed that a display of strength would persuade the Japanese to enter into discussions leading to a treaty. Perry, therefore, was given a squadron of the steam-powered warships that were then just coming into use. Perry's orders, however, made it clear that he was to use force only in self-defense. Perry's primary aim was to negotiate a treaty for the protection of American sailors shipwrecked in Japanese waters.

From time to time American whaling vessels in the North Pacific had been wrecked off the shores of Japan, and the survivors who came ashore had been mistreated. With the help of the Dutch at Deshima, the survivors eventually made their way back to the United States, where they complained bitterly about their treatment at the hands of the Japanese. Aroused by these accounts, shipowners urged the United States government to take steps to ensure better treatment for shipwrecked sailors. Perry's instructions also contained a request that Japan open ports where ships from the United States could take on supplies. With a look to the future, the government also directed Perry to make arrangements for coaling stations in the western Pacific and Japan for use by proposed trans-Pacific shipping lines. Finally, Perry was to seek new opportunities for trade.

The arrival of the American squadron in Edo Bay in July 1853 aroused a furor. The American warships, painted black and belching smoke from their funnels, terrified the Japanese. When Perry rejected orders to sail away, the Tokugawa officials did not dare to use force and, uneasily, agreed to hold discussions. The Commodore presented a letter from the President of the United States that outlined the United States requests. Then, promising to return for an answer within a year, and with a larger fleet, Perry sailed for China.

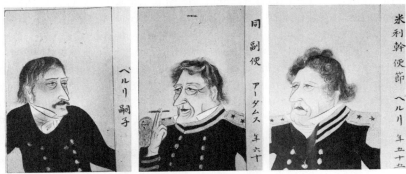

PERRY'S NAVAL EXPEDITION. An enterprising Westerner translated the notes made on a print of Commodore Perry's ship. Other prints showed Commodore Perry himself (right), his brother Oliver (center), and Commander Henry Adams (left).

The Treaty of Kanagawa

When the squadron returned to Japan in early 1854, Perry learned that the shogunate was ready to discuss a treaty. The Tokugawa authorities were convinced that no other course made sense. "If we try to drive them [the Americans] away," the shogun's advisers agreed,

> they will immediately commence hostilities, and then we shall be obliged to fight. If we once get into a dispute, we shall have an enemy to fight who will not be easily disposed of. He does not care how long a time he will have to spend over it, but he will come with several tens of thousands of men of war and surround our shores completely. He will capture our junks and blockade our ports and deprive us

of all hope of protecting our coasts. However large a number of his ships we might destroy, he is so accustomed to that sort of thing, that he would not care in the least. . . . In time the country would be put to an immense expense, and the people be plunged into misery. Rather than allow this, as we are not the equals of foreigners in the mechanical arts, let us have relations with foreign countries, learn their drills and tactics . . . and it will not be too late then to declare war. [Watanabe Shujiro, *Japan, 1853–1864 or Genji Yume Monogatari*, Ernest M. Satow, translator]

After much fanfare and negotiation, the Treaty of Kanagawa was signed in March 1854. In this first Japanese–American treaty the shogunate made only limited concessions. Proper treatment was promised for shipwrecked sailors. Permission was granted for American ships to take on supplies and to conduct limited trade with Japan, but only at two out-of-the-way ports. The United States was given permission to station a consul in Japan to look after matters involving Americans and American trade. Finally, the Japanese government agreed to extend to the United States any additional rights that they might later give to other Western nations. These concessions were the first significant cracks in Japan's wall of seclusion.

Growing Foreign Influence

Although comparatively minor, the shogunate's compromises had a serious effect on Japan's future. Soon after Perry's treaty was signed, England, Holland, and Russia reached similar agreements with Japan. Then in 1858 the first American consul to Japan, Townsend Harris, negotiated a new Japanese–United States commercial treaty. Again, the major European powers followed the lead of the United States and reached new agreements with Japan. Japan now had opened a number of its major ports to foreign trade. It had agreed not to prosecute foreigners accused of crimes, but to allow them to be tried in a court established by consular officials of the nation of which the accused were citizens. Japan no longer had control over tariffs. These duties were to be fixed by agreement between the Bakufu and the countries concerned.

Exposed Weaknesses

The Bakufu tried to blunt the effect of the new treaties by delaying their implementation. But there was no stopping the growing foreign influence. The trade agreements of the 1850's and 1860's shattered Japan's policy of national seclusion.

115

The new treaties forced the Japanese to accept an inferior status, making them "unequal treaties" in Japanese eyes. Every year it had become more evident that the Bakufu could not protect the country against foreign pressures. The government also displayed internal weakness by making serious political blunders. For instance, the Bakufu had taken the unprecedented step of asking the imperial leaders for their approval of the American treaty. Then the Bakufu asked the imperial leaders for advice in a dispute over succession to the shogunate, an issue that should have been decided within the Tokugawa house. The Bakufu had become so inept in its dealings with foreigners that it also began asking advice from officials of the various han.

Leaders with loyalist leanings were quick to take advantage of these shortcomings. Almost from the beginning of Tokugawa times there had been **loyalists** who called for reverence to the emperor and who regarded the shogun as a usurper of imperial power. When the Bakufu was reduced to seeking advice and support from outside the Tokugawa organization, the cause of the loyalists was greatly strengthened. As foreign influence grew stronger in Japan, the slogan "Expel the barbarians!" was added to the loyalists' cry of "Revere the emperor!" Left unsaid, but in the minds of many, was a parallel thought "Down with the shogunate!"

Undermining the Bakufu

Major resistance to Bakufu rule came from Satsuma and Choshu, two of the largest tozama fiefs in the land. (See map, page 91.) Bitter rivals in the drive for power, the two fiefs were united in their hatred for the Tokugawa and the foreigners. In the early 1860's Choshu had fired on Western ships. The samurai of both fiefs had attacked Westerners living in Japan. Both made strong demands for the immediate expulsion of all foreigners from Japanese soil. Such actions not only won favor for Choshu and Satsuma among anti-Western elements in Japan but also served to embarrass the shogunate.

At first, it appeared that Satsuma and Choshu had blundered in provoking the Western powers. Both fiefs were attacked by punitive foreign expeditions and their military weakness was exposed. But the leaders of the fiefs learned an important lesson from their foes. The recognition of the superiority of Western military training and technology led them to strengthen their own military power. Satsuma started building a modern navy, while Choshu concentrated on improving its land forces. Choshu adopted the radical new idea of mixed units made up of samurai and commoners using Western rifles and trained in Western methods of warfare. The units were led by samurai who were opponents of the Bakufu and by foreigners.

The End of Tokugawa Rule

Many fiefholders were unhappy with the government in the hands of the Tokugawa, but they found it difficult to reach an understanding among themselves. The Tokugawa had encouraged jealousies and rivalries, knowing that dissensions among the daimyo would prevent them from joining together to overthrow the government. After Satsuma and Choshu had emerged as leaders of the loyalists, each sought to win approval for its own plans and to discredit the other.

Gradually, Satsuma and Choshu moved into an uneasy alliance. Soon several small fiefs joined them in the military coalition. Armed with a questionable but impressive "imperial rescript [decree]," the allies seized the emperor's palace in Kyoto and announced the restoration of imperial rule. Scattered resistance from supporters of the Tokugawa was easily put down by the rebel armies. In May 1868, the last of the Tokugawa shoguns surrendered Edo to the loyalist forces and renounced his title. The seat of the new imperial government was moved from Kyoto to Edo, henceforth to be called Tokyo, "the Eastern Capital." In 1869 the young emperor took up his residence in the castle built by Ieyasu. The stage was set for the rise of modern Japan.

Check Your Understanding

1. How did foreign pressures end Japan's policy of seclusion from the outer world?
2. What were the objectives of Perry's mission to Japan?
3. What were the terms of the Treaty of Kanagawa?
4. Why did many Japanese resent the Treaty of Kanagawa and other treaties like it?
5. *Thinking Critically:* How did the unequal treaties eventually lead to the downfall of the Tokugawa Bakufu?

■ **Chapter Summary**

Section 1. Ieyasu's victory at Sekigahara marked the end of the turbulent period of feudal warfare that Japan had suffered for several hundred years and the beginning of the Tokugawa Shogunate. Under Ieyasu and his immediate successors the proud and semi-independent daimyo were brought under control by enlarging and strengthening the sankin kotai begun by Hideyoshi and by relocating potential rivals through the redistribution of fiefs belonging to the tozama. While retaining military and political control of Japan, Ieyasu and his successors retained the emperor and his imperial court. But Tokugawa officials opposed the spread of Christianity. Closely tied to the shogunate's anti-Christian attitude was the distrust of all foreigners and the implementation of a policy of seclusion. For 200 years the Dutch and the Chinese were the only major traders to enter Japan. Some "Dutch learning" allowed for some new information to enter Japan, but the total effect of the seclusion policy deprived Japan of almost all cultural and commercial contacts with other foreign nations.

Section 2. Under the Tokugawa, Japanese society was legally frozen into four classes: samurai, peasants, artisans, and merchants. Children were born into the class of their parents. The social responsibilities of each class were fixed by law and were highly influenced by the two philosophies of Neo-Confucianism and Buddhism and the code of behavior known as Bushido. Tokugawa Japan was an extremely male-directed society. The Tokugawa resistance to change kept control in their hands, but eventually discontent with Tokugawa rigidity brought an end to Tokugawa rule.

Section 3. Japan experienced both social change and economic growth. Internal trade flourished as a result of peace and Tokugawa policies. Towns grew into cities where townspeople developed a lively new culture. Whereas the city merchants grew rich from the sale of goods in the Tokugawa economy, the lot of the samurai worsened in peacetime. Some became masterless ronin. Others turned to new occupations or to scholarship.

Some people in other classes managed to improve their lives. Peasants improved their lot by cheating on their lords, or by acquiring the rights to additional acreage. Some peasants moved to the cities, where they became artisans or merchants. The average peasant, however, still struggled to make ends meet. Merchants benefited most of all from economic prosperity in the cities, using their growing wealth to establish new businesses.

Section 4. Edo and Osaka became cultural as well as commercial centers, and a new culture developed around the increasing numbers of townspeople whose interests were different from the samurai. Bunraku and kabuki were two types of theater entertainment that developed. Woodblock prints depicted scenes of Tokugawa life, and the haiku, an offshoot of the tanka, became a favorite form of poetry.

Section 5. After 200 years, Japan's military regime began to lose its control over the people. Disgruntled samurai began to intrigue against the shogunate. The Bakufu was boldly criticized and held accountable for Japan's problems, chief of which was its seclusion from the outside world. When the United States finally broke through the wall of seclusion with the Treaty of Kanagawa, other countries also negotiated treaties. The Japanese regarded these treaties as "unequal" because they imposed an inferior status on the Japanese. Discontent with the unequal treaties stirred rebellion. Uniting under the slogan *Revere the emperor; expel the barbarians!*, foes of the Tokugawa struck for power. In 1868 the Tokugawa dynasty came to an end, and the age of modern Japan began.

■ **Vocabulary Review**

Define: centralized government, fief, buffer zone, han, tozama, sankin kotai, seclusion laws, ronin, bunraku, kabuki, haiku, loyalist

■ **Places to Locate**

Locate: Pacific Ocean, Edo, Nagasaki, Kyushu, Deshima, Choshu, Osaka

■ **People to Know**

Identify: Tokugawa Ieyasu, Confucius, Zhuxi, Chikamatsu, Hiroshige, Hokusai, Utamaro, Basho, Issa, Matthew C. Perry, Townsend Harris

■ **Thinking Critically**

1. How did Tokugawa feudalism differ from Ashikaga feudalism? How did Ieyasu control the daimyo?

2. How did the Bakufu seek to regulate the activities of each class within the social structure and prevent movement from one class to another? Why did this policy meet with failure?

3. How did the rigidity of Japan's social structure, especially for the samurai and the daimyo, affect Japan's economy?

4. How did the forms of entertainment and culture that developed during Tokugawa times differ from the forms that developed during Ashikaga times?

5. What effects did the seclusion policy of the Tokugawa Bakufu have on Japan? Considering these effects, was the seclusion policy in Japan's best interests? Why or why not?

■ Extending and Applying Your Knowledge

1. Japan's isolation from its neighbors during the Tokugawa period did not bar the Japanese from travel within the islands. The main artery of travel was the Tokaido, a highway that ran along the eastern seacoast from Edo to Kyoto. Along this highway flowed all the bustling life of Tokugawa Japan. The flavor and vividness of life along the Tokaido and much of Japan's history is captured in the book *Japanese Inn: Reconstruction of the Past* by Oliver Statler. Using this book, write a report about the Tokaido.

2. Using encyclopedias and other reference works, research the kimono as a style of dress that is distinctive of Japan. Find out the symbolism of the designs that decorate the kimonos and what they indicate about the wearer of the kimono. Share your findings with the class in either a written or oral report. Use drawings to illustrate your report, if possible.

5

The Modernization of Japan

The emperor of Japan was only 15 years old at the time of the Imperial Restoration of 1868. He took no active part in overthrowing the Tokugawa Shogunate, nor did he play a conspicuous part in political affairs for some years to come. His personal name was Mutsuhito. Shortly after the overthrow of the Tokugawa, Mutsuhito, in keeping with custom, adopted the term Meiji, meaning "Enlightened Government," as the name of his reign. The Meiji emperor, as he was called, was the sovereign of Japan from 1868 to 1912. The Meiji era, which marked Japan's transition to a modern state, was studded with brilliant achievements.

The accomplishments of the Meiji era must be credited to the young samurai who had planned and carried out the Imperial Restoration. These energetic young leaders found themselves faced with two major challenges. The first was to bring Japan into the modern world as quickly as possible. The second was to gain Western recognition of Japan as an equal with other nations. The achievement of these goals, they knew, would require vast changes in every area of Japanese life. One of the chief marvels of the Meiji era was the willingness of the Japanese people to accept the necessity for changes and to carry them out.

Within half a century after the Restoration, Japan had been transformed. Feudalism had been abolished, modern industry established, and decisive steps taken toward a new system of government. By the end of the Meiji era, the island nation had taken its place among the great nations of the world.

1. Modernization of the Japanese Government

During the hostilities leading to the downfall of the Tokugawa, the emperor issued an edict on April 6, 1868, since known as the **Charter Oath.** At the time of the edict, the end of Tokugawa rule was imminent. Prepared by the leaders of the revolt, the Charter Oath established guidelines for the new government to follow. The Charter Oath had five main points:

1. Deliberative assemblies shall be established, and all matters shall be decided by public opinion.

2. The whole nation shall unite so that the administration of affairs of state may be carried out.

3. The people shall be given the opportunity to pursue callings of their choice.

4. Unworthy customs and practices of the past shall be discarded, and justice shall be based on the principles of nature.

5. Wisdom and knowledge shall be sought all over the world in order to promote the welfare of the Empire.

This statement of less than 100 words foreshadowed a major upheaval in Japanese life.

The dignity and character of the Meiji emperor were symbols of Japan's new age. Although the emperor had little contact with the government or his people, he nonetheless left a distinctive mark on the era that bore his name.

The Meiji Era

1868	The Imperial Restoration
1871	Abolition of feudalism
1873	Establishment of universal military conscription
1877	Satsuma Rebellion
1889	Proclamation of Meiji Constitution
1894–1895	Sino–Japanese War
1902	Anglo–Japanese Alliance
1904–1905	Russo–Japanese War
1908	Gentlemen's Agreement
1910	Annexation of Korea
1912–1925	Taisho Period
1914	Declaration of war against Germany
1915	Twenty–One Demands
1918	Rice Riots
1920	Admittance to the League of Nations

Leaders of the New Regime

From the outset the government and military commands of Meiji Japan were dominated by the small group of men, members of the imperial court or of the samurai class, who had engineered the overthrow of the Bakufu. Thus the men in control were from Satsuma and Choshu or were their allies. Finding themselves in complete control of the situation, the new leaders saw no reason to share power with the many feudal lords. Instead they decided to erect a strong central government exercising authority throughout the islands. Because there was no organized opposition, they divided up the highest offices in the new government among themselves and their supporters. Enjoying the confidence of the Meiji emperor, these political **oligarchs,** members of a small ruling group, dominated Japan during the entire Meiji era.

The men who took their place at the helm of the Meiji state were young, having an average age of about 32. Ambitious and open-minded, they were not bound by tradition or set in their thinking. Many of them had studied the ways of the West before the uprising, and all of them were deeply devoted to their coun-

123

try and the emperor. Winning power in 1868, this remarkable group of men guided the Japanese government for many years. As some of these leaders died or were assassinated, others from the group of able and well-trained administrators developed under the Tokugawa system of government took their places with a minimum of difficulty.

The nation thus enjoyed unusual political stability during a most critical era in its history. The Meiji leaders were fortunate in many ways when they took their first steps into the modern age. Japan was a small country, which meant that they could make known any change and put it into effect in a short time. Their people were culturally united, sharing common traditions and customs and speaking the same language. It was also important that the leaders were samurai. Not only were the leaders trained administrators, but once they seized power, the great mass of people would not dare question the decisions of their leaders. Accustomed as the peasants and townspeople were to rule by warriors, they generally went about their business while the new leaders developed the new political system. The policies of the oligarchs met with some opposition, principally from envious and resentful samurai who were not part of the leadership. By 1877, however, the Meiji oligarchs had crushed all remnants of resistance and opposition.

Guidance from the West

The leaders of the Meiji government both feared and admired the industrial and military might of Western nations. With few exceptions they were eager to transform their country into a powerful and respected nation, and shrewd enough to know that the key to this goal was modernization. Realizing that they lacked the knowledge and experience needed to carry out their plans, the leaders of the Meiji government quietly dropped their "expel the barbarian" slogan and sought assistance from the West.

For many years specialists from Europe and the United States were employed by the Meiji government as advisers to the heads of governmental agencies and departments. In selecting these advisers, the Meiji leaders sought out the ablest experts in the West. In building a modern national army, French, and later German, military officers were employed. English officers were hired to help in creating a modern navy. French and German experts were put to work to reform law codes and courts.

S IDELIGHT TO HISTORY

Japanese Calendars

At various times in the past, the Japanese have adopted different systems of dating and recording history. Today the Japanese have three systems of dating that are in common use.

The first system of dating is based on Japanese mythology. According to Japanese mythology, Jimmu— descendant of the Sun Goddess and first emperor of Japan—was enthroned on February 11, 660 B.C. Many Japanese date the years beginning with this event. According to the mythology-based system of dating, 1990 is the year 2650 (660 + 1990).

The Japanese borrowed the second system from the Chinese. Emperors, on ascending the throne, adopted a name for the era during which they would reign. Emperor Hirohito, who was Japan's emperor from 1926 to 1989, adopted Showa, meaning "Shining Peace," as the name of his reign. 1926 was thus the year Showa 1. His reign ended in the year Showa 64. His son and successor Akihito chose Heisei, meaning "Achieving Peace," as the name of his reign. The rest of 1989 became Heisei 1.

Japan borrowed its third calendar system from the West, adopting the Gregorian calendar on January 1, 1873. Since then, year dates in Japan have conformed to those of the West.

The imperial government placed great emphasis on education. At first specialists from the United States were brought in to help establish a system of compulsory elementary education. Later the Americans were replaced with Europeans. The Western advisers did their work well. Before the nineteenth century came to a close, the foundations of a modern state in Japan had been firmly laid down.

The Meiji leaders also visited the United States and Europe. Shortly after the Imperial Restoration, high-ranking officers of the new regime began to visit the modern states they both feared and envied. They attended sessions of parliaments and inspected mints, harbor works, and factories. They visited schools, banks, and libraries. Very little in the countries of the West was not of interest to them, and when they finally returned home, they were much the wiser for their travels. Furthermore, they understood much better the magnitude of the tasks that faced their nation. Since this tradition of official travel overseas persisted for many years, most of Japan's leaders after 1868 had firsthand knowledge of the West.

End of the Feudal System

The Meiji government, despite the samurai origin of many of its leaders, acted resolutely to uproot the old feudal class system. They considered the system an obstacle to modernization. They also believed that the existence of the han governments prevented the development of a truly centralized civil government. The oligarchs' first moves, therefore, were designed to reduce the feudal han to civil provinces under the direct control of the authorities in Tokyo. The daimyo voluntarily agreed to surrender their traditional rights and privileges. Although they were well compensated by the state for their losses, their deep patriotism cannot be denied. The oligarchs also eliminated the samurai class, reducing the former warriors to the status of commoners but permitting them for a while to wear their cherished swords. Until 1876 the Meiji government paid the former samurai part of the salaries they customarily had received from their overlords. When this obligation proved too heavy a financial burden, the ex-samurai were given a lump-sum payment and were then expected to fend for themselves.

The step that truly signaled the end of feudalism, however, was the introduction in 1873 of a system of universal military conscription. No longer was it the exclusive right of the samurai to bear arms in battle. Now all Japanese men, peasants and townspeople included, were subject to call for military training. This step freed the central government from dependence on the daimyo, over whose armies the government had never exercised effective control.

The Satsuma Rebellion

The deepest discontent against the central government developed in the province of Satsuma, a leader in the Restoration. Several of the Meiji oligarchs came from this region, but many Satsuma samurai bitterly opposed the reform programs initiated in Tokyo. They also had less hesitation in voicing their resentment than samurai in other areas. After all, the new government was made up of their former companions, many of whom had been of relatively low rank. The critical attitude of the Satsuma samurai

True to the stern feudal code upheld by Saigo and his followers, these wives and daughters of rebel samurai took up arms to defend their homes in Kyushu against the government forces.

was all the more dangerous because it centered about General Saigo Takamori (sah-EE-goh tak-kah-MORH-ee). Saigo, a model samurai and hero of the Imperial Restoration, was immensely popular in Japan. After serving in the Meiji government for several years, he resigned as a protest against its policies of modernization. Returning to Satsuma, he awaited an opportunity to restore the feudal way of life.

The Satsuma Rebellion erupted in early 1877 and was the most formidable threat the leaders of the Meiji government had to face. With thousands of former samurai under his command, Saigo set out to march on Tokyo. But he was halted before he could leave the island of Kyushu. Reinforcements were hurriedly mustered by the Meiji government and the entire national army was thrown against the rebels. Nonetheless, nine months of fighting were required to stamp out the uprising. Saigo remained true to the samurai tradition and committed suicide rather than be captured. Even in death this heroic warrior was held in high esteem, and his loyalty to the emperor was never questioned.

In putting down the rebellion, the government forces had suffered very heavy casualties. But the Meiji leaders with their use of force had demonstrated that the imperial government could not be toppled by a local uprising. As a result, rebellions, which had broken out sporadically in the past, no longer would trouble the Japanese government.

The Movement for Constitutional Government

Since the early years of the Meiji era the oligarchs had given much thought to the type of state and government they needed to construct. Although most of them believed a **constitutional government** was essential for a modern society, they disagreed on the specific form it should take. After more than a decade of thought and discussion, they realized that action could not be postponed much longer. In 1881 the emperor was persuaded to issue an edict promising the introduction of constitutional government by 1890.

A notable element in the movement to achieve constitutional government was the shift from military to political agitation. After the death of General Saigo, foes of the Meiji oligarchy no longer were content to denounce the military. Instead they demanded liberal political reforms. The chief threat to the Meiji leaders came from Okuma Shigenobu and Itagaki Taisuke, men who used newspapers and public lectures to reach the public. Taking their cue from the practice of politics in western European countries, they used ideas for weapons. How deeply their **liberalism** was mixed with political opportunism is unknown. Whatever the depth, their agitation inspired the oligarchs with a greater sense of urgency.

The ultimate responsibility for the preparation of Japan's first **constitution** was entrusted to the oligarch Ito Hirobumi (EE-toh hih-roh-BOO-mee). Although he already had some ideas

In 1889 the Meiji emperor presented Japan's first constitution. Present were members of the Imperial Court and the foreign diplomatic corps. This contemporary print documents the high point of the imposing ceremony.

IMPERIAL GOVERNMENT DURING THE MEIJI ERA

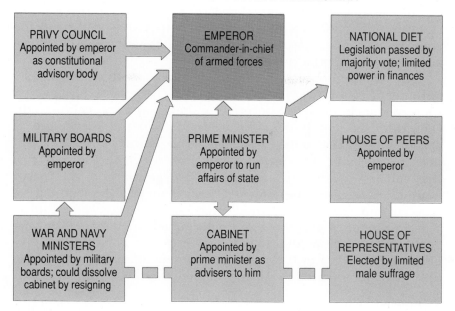

FLOW OF AUTHORITY. The actual power of government during the Meiji era was in the hands of the oligarchs who "governed from behind the screen" by serving at different times as members of the Privy Council, the Cabinet, the Military Boards, and as Prime Minister. In time, the oligarchs had served in so many different positions of government that they became known as the genro, or "elder statesmen." The solid-line arrows show direct access to the emperor. The dashed lines indicate the flow of communication between elected and appointed officials.

about the matter, Ito recognized the need for consultation with experts. Accompanied by his advisers, Ito departed for Europe to study the various political systems at firsthand. There Ito sought counsel from scholars and heads of state. One notable expert was Otto von Bismarck, the Chancellor of the German Empire. On Ito's return, Ito and his staff met in secret and drafted the constitution. In 1889, the emperor proclaimed the completed document to the nation. The Meiji Constitution was handed down to the people as a gift from His Imperial Majesty, and there was no opportunity for discussion or amendment of its provisions.

The New Constitution's Importance

The new constitution vested the highest authority in the emperor, whose position was justified by reference to the ancient myths of Shinto. In practice, however, the emperor had little real power. The actual power of the government was in the hands of the officials who had direct access to the emperor. Any member of the government with direct access to the emperor could claim to speak for him. Whether or not they had spoken to the emperor, their statements gave these high officials the moral authority of imperial approval.

The constitution also provided for a bicameral, or two-house, parliament called the National Diet. The Diet's powers, however, were extremely limited. The prime minister and the cabinet officers, who did not have to be selected from the Diet, were in theory responsible only to the emperor. During the Meiji era, however, actual ruling power was concentrated in the hands of the emperor's advisers—especially the **genro** and the **privy council,** whose members formed the oligarchy. The tradition of "government from behind the screen" was still very much alive. The privy council and the genro determined the budget. The Diet could only block additions to it. While the constitution proclaimed the rights of the people, the interests of the state came first, a major restriction on full implementation of these rights.

Power of the Military

The constitution designated the emperor commander-in-chief of the armed forces. As a result the ministers of the army and the navy had direct access to him. These two powerful officials, unlike other cabinet officers, could bypass the prime minister and plead the interests of the military services directly with the emperor. Later, the constitution provided that a general and an admiral, respectively, hold these important posts. Thus the ministers of the army and the navy could bring about the downfall of a cabinet that proposed actions they thought detrimental to the military's interests by resigning from it. The army and navy could also prevent the formation of a cabinet that might prove unfriendly to their interests by refusing to release a general and an admiral to serve in a cabinet. The power of the army and the navy had tragic consequences for the Japanese people by fostering the growth of militarism and ultimately plunging the nation into World War II.

Parliamentary government began in 1890. Several hastily organized political parties competed for seats in the National Diet. But only a small number of wealthy male taxpayers had the right to vote. Not until 1925 was universal **suffrage** granted to all males. Women in Japan did not receive the right to vote until after World War II. From the outset of parliamentary government, it was clear that the state was supreme and that the constitution of 1889 helped to perpetuate oligarchical rule.

1. How did the Charter Oath help to move Japan toward modernization?
2. How did the Meiji government perpetuate "government from behind the screen"?
3. Why did the oligarchy end feudalism?
4. How did the Japanese go about preparing a constitution?
5. *Thinking Critically:* Compare the emperor's position and power in theory and in practice under the Meiji constitution. Who held the real power in the Meiji government?

2. Japan's Rapid Industrialization

The oligarchs of the Meiji state were well aware that Japanese industry had to achieve modernization rapidly to become the equal of the Western powers. The attitude of the Meiji oligarchs toward modernization, however, combined pride in the country with recognition of its shortcomings.

Steps to Industrialization

Promoting rapid industrial growth in a primarily agricultural economy was a monumental task. Meiji leaders concluded that the state had to become actively involved in encouraging and directing economic activity. The lack of trained technicians was an especially critical problem. The government, therefore, founded technical schools and introduced the teaching of modern science. It employed foreign engineers as teachers and advisers in the new schools and factories. It also sent students to Europe and the United States for higher education and specialized training. Fortunately, because many private academies and Buddhist temple schools had been established in Tokugawa times, a large part of the population was already literate.

During the early Meiji period the Japanese were reluctant to build factories. Having little capital and lacking practical experience, they preferred to invest in more familiar types of businesses such as banking and domestic trade. The government itself, therefore, had to show the way. During the 1870's the state built and operated a number of small factories devoted to the production of military supplies and light **consumer goods.**

The first Japanese industry to be modernized during the Meiji era was textile production. Taking advantage of the large supply of inexpensive female labor, the Japanese set up mechanized factories such as this one.

In time state iron foundries, textile mills, and cement and glass works were operating on a paying basis. The government also helped to establish the first railroad and telegraph lines, and it subsidized the merchant marine. Through this direct participation in the nation's economic development, the government strongly influenced the form and direction of industrialization in modern Japan.

During the 1880's and 1890's private **capital** began to flow into industrial enterprises. The Satsuma Rebellion had strained the government's finances. When prices steadily increased and the nation seemed threatened with runaway **inflation**, the government adopted a program of financial retrenchment. The state sold some of its factories on liberal credit terms to far-seeing business investors. Still other investors took the initiative in setting up new plants and mills. During these years the foundations were laid for what rapidly grew into the country's greatest business enterprises. Known as the **zaibatsu** (ZY-bah-tsoo), such gigantic firms as Mitsui and Mitsubishi, important firms in present-day Japan, began to penetrate various sectors of the national economy.

Textile Production

Nations striving to modernize their economies often turn to the manufacture of cloth. Relatively speaking, textile mills did not require a heavy outlay of capital, and the workers, usually poorly paid women, were easily trained. This was Japan's experience. By 1890 Japan not only was producing enough cotton cloth for its own needs but had a surplus for export. This favorable balance was reached despite the need to import the raw cotton. From the 1890's until the 1960's, the textile industry was a mainstay of the Japanese economy. The manufacture of silk for export also increased very rapidly. For many years, exported silk was Japan's chief source of foreign exchange.

Financing Industrialization

Meiji leaders quickly learned that the costs of industrialization were staggering. Complicated and expensive machinery and technical equipment had to be imported from the West. On the other hand, government tax revenues were limited, a common condition in countries having an agricultural economy. Despite its financial plight, the Meiji regime was determined not to borrow money from the Western powers. It was not so much that the government feared to go into debt. The oligarchs did not want to give any foreign power the slightest pretext for intervening in Japanese affairs. Most of the funds needed for modernization programs, therefore, were raised within the country. People were asked to purchase government bonds, and loans were negotiated with domestic banks.

Japanese peasants paid much of the price of their country's industrialization. It seems doubtful that any other group in the population bore as heavy a burden of taxation as the peasants. Even though the government attempted to improve the efficiency of farming, the peasants paid dearly for whatever benefits they received.

After the Imperial Restoration, the Meiji regime gradually overhauled the land and tax system. The peasants obtained legal possession of the land that they and their ancestors had tilled for generations. For a brief while peasants turned over part of their crop in lieu of taxes. Consequently the income of the state varied from year to year as the size of the crop varied. Needing a more stable financial base, the central government decided to levy taxes based on the value of the land. This procedure meant not only a sharp increase in the tax that peasants had to pay but also that the assessment would remain the same whether or not the harvest was bountiful.

In the 1880's the peasants felt the full impact of this new tax system. Often unable to pay their taxes, farmers were compelled either to borrow money at high interest or to sell their

The cities of Japan first felt the effects of modernization, but the new ways soon reached the countryside. In this print, life appears to be standing still, but a telegraph wire can be seen linking the rural setting with the outside world.

land to wealthy landowners. Once the peasants lost their land, they became **tenant farmers,** renting the plots they tilled. They also found themselves paying extremely high rents. Tenant farming under trying conditions persisted until the end of World War II.

Cheap Labor

When the shogunate was overthrown, the population of Japan numbered a little more than 30 million. By 1900 it had soared to about 46 million. The expansion of the national economy, a great increase in agricultural productivity, and improvements in medical facilities and public sanitation help to explain this population increase. As the growing number of people living in rural areas and competing for tillable land forced land rentals upward, many young people sought work in the large cities.

Japanese industry benefited from the overcrowded countryside, which was a major source of cheap labor. The textile manufacturers especially were active in recruiting young women from peasant homes in which there were too many mouths to feed. Provided with board and room, usually in company dormitories, these young workers were paid very low wages. By paying labor low wages, factory owners managed to keep production costs low. Even as late as 1914 women made up more than 60 percent of the industrial labor force in Japan.

Japan's Foreign Trade

One of the sharpest breaks with the Tokugawa heritage made by Meiji Japan was in the area of foreign trade. Modernization could not be achieved without a great expansion of foreign trade. But Japan had little to export in the way of manufactured goods, agricultural commodities, or raw materials. Silk, a product in great demand in Europe and the United States, ranked for years near the top of Japan's export list. Neither silk nor cotton textiles, however, could earn enough foreign exchange to pay for the country's mounting volume of imports. Until 1914, therefore, imports regularly exceeded exports, giving Japan an unfavorable **balance of trade.**

Despite the progress made toward modernization during the Meiji period, much remained to be done in building a modern industrial state. By 1894 when Japan went to war with China, it still produced little iron and steel, and only small amounts of coal. Japan had no electrical or chemical industry of importance. Not much more than 2,000 miles of railroad had been laid, and the shipbuilding industry was still in its infancy. The greatest progress had been made in the area of **light industry.** Although Japan had acquired useful knowledge and experience, it was still struggling to industrialize to full capacity.

Check Your Understanding

1. What steps did the Japanese oligarchs take to industrialize the country as rapidly as possible?
2. Why did the Meiji hesitate to seek loans from foreign countries?
3. Where did they get the help they needed for their modernization programs?
4. How did the peasants fare in Japan's efforts to build an industrial economy?
5. *Thinking Critically:* Why did Japan have an unfavorable balance of trade during most of the Meiji period? Was this a disadvantage for Japan's industrialization? Why or why not?

3. Japan's Rise as a Major Power

Noting the surge of Western **imperialism** in the late nineteenth century, the leaders of Meiji Japan were worried about possible threats to their country's independence. They wished at all costs to avoid wars with the stronger Western powers. Such conflicts might destroy their national independence and set back plans for economic development. Throughout the early Meiji period, Japan's leaders made every effort to settle by diplomacy any dispute between their country and the West. This diplomatic policy was successful until Japan came into conflict with the West in the Russo-Japanese War of 1904–1905. To exclude Western imperialism from nearby areas, an encroachment that would endanger their country, the Meiji leaders decided on preventive action. They began to annex these areas, and, as a result, Japan itself became an imperialist nation.

The Problem of the "Unequal Treaties"

In the years immediately after Commodore Perry's arrival in Japan, the shogunate concluded treaties with several Western states. (See pages 113–115.) Though the main purpose of the treaties was to establish diplomatic and commercial relations, two features included in all the agreements greatly troubled the Japanese. First was the provision of **extraterritoriality** granted to Western residents in Japan. In effect, this privilege meant that in criminal cases foreigners would be tried in courts established by their own consular officials and in accordance with their own national laws. Foreigners were thus removed from Japanese jurisdiction. The second objection concerned the limitations that were imposed on Japan's tariff autonomy—Japanese tariffs were fixed by treaty and not solely by the nation's own decisions. At the time, these two restrictions were common to agreements imposed on Asian governments by states of Western Europe and by the United States.

Following the Meiji Restoration the oligarchs had sought to eliminate restrictions upon their country's sovereign rights. During 1871–1873 Prince Iwakura, the head of the Meiji government, led an imposing mission to the nations of the West for this purpose. But everywhere the prince went he was told that the time was not ripe for treaty revision. The Western governments insisted that Japan would have to modernize its laws and judicial practices before any changes could even be discussed. Japan, therefore, undertook the task of formulating new law codes in line with those of the Western powers.

Revision of the "Unequal Treaties"

By the early 1880's, the Japanese believed that the conditions for treaty revision had been fulfilled. But when Japan's leaders again raised the issue with the Western powers, they discovered that no Western nation was willing to surrender its special privileges. In reaction, the furious Japanese turned their backs on things Western, including missionary Christianity, which had made many converts since the Restoration. Many Japanese Christians now rejected their Christian faith. How sensitive the Japanese were to any signs of inequality became evident in 1889, when the foreign minister of Japan attempted to negotiate a revision of the treaties. When it was learned that the proposed revision did not completely eliminate extraterritoriality and the restrictions on tariff autonomy, an attempt was made on the foreign minister's life.

The "unequal treaties" were finally terminated. In 1894 an agreement was worked out with Great Britain whereby extraterritoriality was to be abolished five years later. Starting in 1899, tariff autonomy also would gradually be restored to Japan, the final restrictions to be eliminated in 1911. The other Western nations adopted the same pattern. Thus Japan, having lived with the "unequal treaties" for a half century, became the first Asian state to get rid of them.

Japanese Imperialism

Soon after the Meiji Restoration, Japanese leaders took the first steps in what became a policy of imperialism. Ringing Japan were several islands and island groups whose strategic importance was quickly recognized by the Meiji leaders. (See page 3.) The Japanese feared that their country would be in peril if any of these islands fell to an imperialist power. In 1875 the Japanese government annexed the Bonin Group, which lay 500 miles to the south of Tokyo Bay. In the same year Japan reached an agreement with Russia over islands in the northwest Pacific. Japan surrendered its claims to part of the large island of Sakhalin. Russia, in turn, gave up its claims to the southern Kurile Islands. Okinawa, an island monarchy south of Japan claimed by both Russia and China, was annexed outright by the Japanese Empire in 1879. (See map, page 138.)

Japanese Influence in Korea

For centuries the "Hermit Kingdom" of Korea had maintained close ties with China. During the Tokugawa period, contact be-

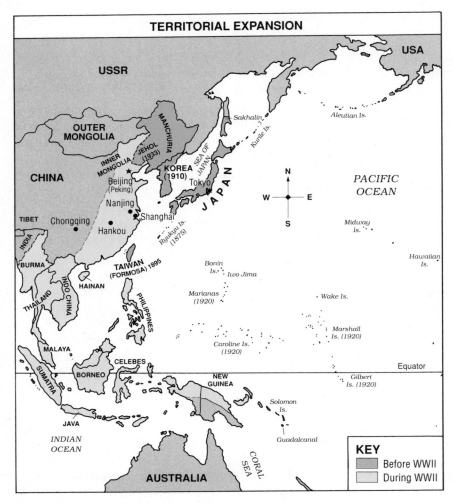

TERRITORIAL EXPANSION

KEY
- Before WWII
- During WWII

MOVEMENT: JAPANESE EXPANSION, 1890–1942. Between 1894 and 1905, the Japanese fought a war with China and a war with Russia. Between 1895 and 1942, the Japanese rapidly expanded their empire in the Pacific. Only defeat in World War II stopped Japanese expansion. What territory had Japan annexed as a result of these three wars?

tween Japan and Korea was strictly regulated. But after the Imperial Restoration, when the Japanese became concerned about their country's security, Korea was regarded as "a dagger pointed at the heart of Japan." The Meiji oligarchs, realizing that China's influence in Korea might decrease, were terrified by the thought that this neighbor might be taken over by a Western imperialist power. Japan brought an end to Korean isolation in 1876. Having negotiated a treaty calling for diplomatic and commercial relations, the Japanese sought to foster reforms in the Korean government and court. The Japanese believed that their country would benefit from a strong and independent Korea. Understandably, the Chinese were alarmed by the possibility that the Japanese might seek outright control of Korea. The growing tension and conflicting interests between the two countries led to the Sino–Japanese War in 1894–1895.

The Sino–Japanese War

In its first modern war, the reforms undertaken since the Imperial Restoration gave Japan a tremendous advantage over China. Major advantages were the unity and morale of the Japanese people. Giving their full support to the government, the Japanese were ready to make whatever sacrifices were necessary for victory. Japan's decisive victories on land and sea came as a surprise to those nations that had expected China to win. In less than a year, the Chinese Empire was forced to sue for peace. The international prestige of Japan rose sharply following this military triumph.

By the signing of the Treaty of Shimonoseki, which ended the Sino–Japanese War, the Japanese obtained the large island of Taiwan off the Chinese coast, the nearby Pescadores Islands, and the great promontory of south Manchuria known as the Liaodong (lee-OW-DOONG) Peninsula. Japan also was awarded an **indemnity** of several hundred million dollars in gold and valuable trade concessions. The delighted Japanese believed that these rewards made their sacrifices seem worthwhile. Unfortunately the Japanese also came to believe that future wars would yield equally rich returns. When these high hopes were not realized in the wars fought in the early twentieth century, resentment was aroused in the Japanese against the countries that had denied Japan its "just" rewards.

Japan's victory over China, however, was soured by one development. When it became known that Japan was to receive the Liaodong Peninsula, with its important naval base at Port Arthur, France, Russia, and Germany notified Japan of their disapproval. In the face of this action, which was called the "Tripartite Intervention," Japan had to back down. Japan withdrew its hopes of securing the Liaodong Peninsula and instead received an additional indemnity from China. In an odd twist of events the Russians, who were largely responsible for thwarting Japan, a few years later obtained a lease of Port Arthur from the Chinese Empire.

Japanese artists often recorded historic events. This oil painting shows a Japanese fleet, commanded by Admiral Togo, destroying a Russian fleet in the Sea of Japan in May 1905. After the battle, Admiral Togo became a great naval hero.

Rivalry with Russia

Korea, whose sovereignty had been limited by its close relationships with the Chinese Empire, became completely independent as a result of the Sino–Japanese War. But Korea's independence brought no joy to Japan, which found itself confronted with Russia as a new rival for primary influence in Korea. Having first won a foothold at Port Arthur, the Russians next entrenched themselves in Manchuria. Then they turned their eyes to Korea, just across the Manchurian border. The Japanese tried in vain to persuade the Russian czar to withdraw his troops from Manchuria.

To prepare for a possible war with Russia, the Meiji government and Great Britain in 1902 concluded a treaty called the Anglo–Japanese Alliance. According to the alliance both parties pledged to remain neutral if the other had to defend its East Asian interests in war. The two countries also agreed to come to the aid of the other if a third power entered the picture. Thus the alliance assured Japan that France would not side with Russia in a war with Japan. The Japanese believed they had a chance for victory if they had to fight only the Russians. The Anglo–Japanese Alliance, twice renewed, remained in effect for the next 20 years. It was the first treaty in which a Western power treated an Asian country as a diplomatic equal.

The Russo–Japanese War

Believing that delay might work to Russia's advantage, Japan in early 1904 launched a surprise attack on Port Arthur that badly damaged the Russian fleet based there. As was the case in the Sino–Japanese War, the Western nations expected Japan to be defeated. The Japanese, however, demonstrated again their bravery and skill in the fighting on land and sea. They drove the Russians out of Korea and southern Manchuria, and after a long siege captured the fortress of Port Arthur. In May 1905, the Japanese Navy, commanded by Admiral Tojo, in one of the great sea battles of modern times, destroyed some 30 Russian vessels in the waters off southwestern Japan.

Despite victories on land and sea, Japan was unable to defeat the Russians. After more than a year of war, Japan was short of funds and sorely needed peace. Defeats in East Asia and revolutionary unrest at home made peace equally necessary for Russia. After consulting both nations, President Theodore Roosevelt of the United States offered his services as **mediator** in the interests of peace. At Roosevelt's invitation, Japanese and Russian diplomats met for discussions in Portsmouth, New Hampshire. The Treaty of Portsmouth was concluded in September 1905. Roosevelt later received the Nobel Peace Prize for his efforts in bringing the war to a peaceful conclusion.

The Treaty of Portsmouth transferred to Japan Russia's lease on Port Arthur and Russian concessions in southern Manchuria. Japan also received the southern half of Sakhalin Island and Russia's promise not to meddle in Korean affairs. But a major disappointment for the Japanese was the failure to secure an indemnity from Russia to make up for the heavy costs of the war incurred by the Japanese.

Japan–United States Relations

Political and economic relations between the United States and Japan were cordial for many years after the Perry expedition of 1853. American advisers helped the Meiji government improve agriculture and education, and American missionaries were allowed to preach Christianity in Japan. In 1884 the Meiji government began permitting peasants and urban workers to emigrate. During the next 20 years, a small but steady stream of Japanese emigrants went to Hawaii. From there, many of them emigrated to California where they quickly acquired a reputation as efficient and hard-working immigrants.

The very success of the Japanese immigrants, however, aroused American resentment against them. In 1905 agitation

While President Theodore Roosevelt had no jurisdiction in local matters, he used his negotiating skills to ease the tensions in both San Francisco and Japan with the "Gentlemen's Agreement."

in California against the Japanese reached a danger point when citizens demanded that immigration from Japan be curbed. Soon after, the city of San Francisco enacted legislation calling for segregation of Japanese, Chinese, and Korean schoolchildren. The Japanese government lodged strong protests in Washington, D.C., against this discrimination, but President Roosevelt, while personally distressed over the situation, had no power to interfere in matters of local jurisdiction.

The tensions between the United States and Japan eased for a while in 1907. Under the Immigration Act of 1907, Japanese immigrants to the United States from countries other than Japan were to be excluded from the United States. San Francisco, in turn, revoked its segregation law. Equally important was the signing of the "Gentlemen's Agreement" in 1908, under which the Japanese government itself agreed to restrict the emigration of Japanese laborers to the United States. Merchants, students, professionals, and picture brides—wives of men already living in the United States, often wed by proxy following an exchange of photographs—were not affected by the agreement. Although ill will against the Japanese persisted in California, the "Gentlemen's Agreement" remained in effect until 1924.

The Annexation of Korea

The defeat of Russia in 1904–1905 gave the Japanese a free hand in Korea. No power was seriously interested in blocking Japanese penetration of Korea. In 1907 the Meiji government established a **protectorate** over Korea. Military leaders in Japan soon began to urge the outright annexation of Korea, arguing that this step was essential to Japan's security. Merchants also came to look upon Korea as a valuable market. Reacting to these pressures, in 1910 Japan swept aside the fiction of Korean independence and annexed Korea, which remained a part of the Japanese Empire until the end of World War II in 1945.

142

Check Your Understanding

1. **a.** Why did the Japanese consider the "unequal treaties" to be a problem? **b.** How was the problem solved?
2. Why did the Japanese undertake a policy of imperialism?
3. **a.** How did Japan's policies in Korea lead to the Sino–Japanese War? **b.** What was the outcome of this war?
4. **a.** How did Japan's rivalry with Russia develop? **b.** Why was Japan disappointed in the outcome of its war with Russia?
5. **a.** Why did Japan's relations with the United States become strained? **b.** How did the "Gentlemen's Agreement" ease this strain?
6. *Thinking Critically:* Compare Western interest in Japan's actions at the time of the Tripartite Intervention with Western interest at the time of Japan's annexation of Korea. Why do you think Western attitudes toward Japan had changed between 1895 and 1910?

4. Japan's Role in World War I

The outbreak of war in Europe in 1914 was viewed by the Japanese government as a "golden opportunity." Since the energies of all the Western powers except the United States were concentrated upon the hostilities, Japan was free to further its interests in East Asia. The four years of conflict saw Japan emerge as the chief power in East Asia and the western Pacific.

War Against Germany

Japan had no serious grievances against the German Empire. Nevertheless, after weighing the opportunities afforded by the war, Japan announced its decision to side with its ally, Great Britain. Although Japan sent no troops to the war fronts in Europe, it quickly seized the weakly defended German holdings and bases in China and in the Pacific. These remained under Japanese control for the duration of hostilities. Japanese naval vessels also protected Allied convoys in the Indian Ocean and the Mediterranean Sea from attack by German submarines and raiders. In other respects Japan remained aloof from the war in Europe.

Japan in China

In 1912, when the last Chinese emperor abdicated, his regime was replaced by a republican government. Had it not been for the strong hand of General Yuan Shikai (YOO-AHN SHUR-KY), the President, the country might well have disintegrated. The opportunity to profit from the troubled situation in China soon proved too attractive for Japan to resist. During World War I, the long-continued imperialist aggressions of the Western powers in China were surpassed by those of Japan.

In January 1915, the government of President Yuan was stunned when Japan presented a long list of demands for special rights and privileges called the "Twenty–One Demands." These demands were delivered with the warning that information about them be kept secret. If accepted, these demands would have made the Republic of China a Japanese protectorate. They called for sweeping concessions in many vital areas of Chinese life—political, military, economic, and financial. When China revealed the nature of these demands, a great hue and cry was raised by many Americans as well as by the Japanese who opposed their government's policies. As a result, the demands were scaled down and incorporated in treaties signed later in the year.

Japanese Gains in World War I

Within a year after the opening of World War I, Japan had made impressive gains at the expense of Germany, a country with which it was at war, and of China, with which it was at peace. Japan's concern was to make sure that these gains would be considered legitimate at the end of the conflict. An opportunity for Japan to obtain the needed pledges of legitimacy came in 1917. When hard-pressed Britain called upon its Asian ally for naval support, Japan set a price for its aid. After some hard bargaining a deal was arranged. In a series of secret treaties, Japan was promised British, French, Italian, and Russian support for its claims to the former German concessions in China and to islands in the Pacific north of the equator that formerly had been part of the German Empire.

During this long conflict, the European powers cut back trade with Asia to concentrate on the production of military supplies. Japan made the most of this opportunity to expand its overseas commerce. Customers in Asia and elsewhere,

144

unable to purchase goods from Western countries, turned to Japan. War materials were also produced, both for the Japanese armed forces and for the Allied Powers. As a result, established industries expanded, new ones were founded, and business profits soared. As late as 1914, Japan's imports were greater than its exports, and the nation was heavily in debt to foreign nations. By 1919, however, both situations were reversed.

Growing Unrest

Japan eventually had to pay for its great boom in wartime industry. Poor peasants drifted to the large cities in greater numbers than ever before, and the number of factory workers rose sharply. Even though the income of workers increased each year, the higher wages were more than offset by the steady rise in the cost of living. Growing unrest among the factory workers led to an increased number of industrial strikes, most of which were sparked by demands for more pay. Strikes continued to break out after the end of the war, despite the fact that trade unions were forbidden by law to strike.

Unrest stemming from rising prices came to a head in the "Rice Riots." In August 1918, housewives in a small fishing village, indignant over the soaring cost of rice, staged a public demonstration. Their protest led to similar actions in other communities. Within a short time angry citizens were attacking the profiteering rice dealers. When shops were set afire and clashes broke out in many large cities, the government sent troops to restore law and order. Emergency measures were taken to lower the price of rice but these steps were not immediately put into effect. Grumbling continued for months after World War I had come to a close.

The Paris Peace Conference

As a member of the "Big Five" in the Peace Conference, Japanese national pride was inflated by the country's participation, together with Britain, France, Italy, and the United States. At the peace talks, however, the Japanese delegates played a minor role. They had little interest in the reshuffling of European boundaries, the disposal of German colonies in Africa, and the breakup of the Turkish Empire. Their attention was focused on the Pacific and East Asia.

Germany's Pacific islands north of the equator came under Japanese control. The Mariana, Caroline, and Marshall islands were turned over to Japan as **mandates** under the League of Nations. The mandate was a disappointment to the Japanese, who had hoped for outright ownership. They were also disappointed in the disposition of the former German base at Jiaozhou Bay in China because they had wanted it transferred to them. Because of the strong objections of China, the status of the base was referred to China and Japan for settlement. This issue disturbed relations between the two countries until Japan surrendered Jiaozhou Bay to China in 1922.

President Woodrow Wilson's great dream during the war and at the Versailles Conference was the creation of a League of Nations. The purpose of this body was to promote "international cooperation and ensure the fulfillment of accepted international obligations and to provide safeguards against war." The proposed League of Nations was strongly supported by the Japanese delegates. Although the Japanese failed in their attempt to have written into the League's covenant, or charter, a clause calling for racial equality of nations, Japan backed the new international organization. As one of the "Big Five," Japan was granted a permanent seat in the League's Council.

By the end of World War I, Japan was by far the most powerful nation in Asia. This was a major change from Japan's status just 50 years before, at the time of the Imperial Restoration. Japan's rapid rise to power was made possible not only by its modernization efforts, but also by the collapse of the Chinese Empire and the overthrow of the czarist regime in Russia. Before Russia was torn by civil war, it had been a major power in northeast Asia. Following the Bolsheviks' establishment of the Union of Soviet Socialist Republics, popularly called the Soviet Union, it took many years for the Soviet Union to restore industrial production to prewar levels. Thus with China and the Soviet Union in serious difficulty, Japan's power in East Asia was left unchallenged.

Check Your Understanding

1. Why did the Japanese government join the Allied Powers after the outbreak of World War I in Europe?
2. What was Japan's policy toward China during this period?
3. *Thinking Critically:* Compare the status of Japan before the outbreak of World War I with its status at the end of the conflict. How had Japan managed to achieve its postwar status?

CHAPTER REVIEW

■ Chapter Summary

Section 1. The Imperial, or Meiji, Restoration was led by a small group of young samurai and court nobles. Determined to uproot the feudal system and establish a modern centralized state, they reduced the samurai class to commoners and instituted universal military conscription to free the government from dependence on the daimyo. Inevitably the break with feudalism aroused strong opposition, particularly among former samurai devoted to the traditional feudal way of life. The defenders of the feudal order, however, failed to overthrow the Meiji government. Thereafter the oligarchs were able to consolidate their power and begin taking steps toward constitutional government.

Taking guidance from the West, the oligarchs drafted a constitution that was handed down in 1889 as a gift from His Imperial Majesty. The constitution provided for a National Diet and voting by a small qualified male electorate. It concentrated power, however, in the hands of the oligarchy. The highest authority was vested in the emperor. But in practice he was only a figurehead, maintaining the old tradition of "government from behind the screen." The most powerful figures of the cabinet were the ministers of the army and navy.

Section 2. The Meiji leaders viewed industrialization as the key to modernization. With state support many economic innovations were introduced. Though progress was slow, within a generation Japan had succeeded in laying down the foundations of a completely modern industrial system, with emphasis on light industry. The peasants, however, paid the heaviest price for modernization when the overhaul of the tax system resulted in many peasants becoming tenant farmers. Many peasants also left the crowded countryside for the cities, where they became a source of cheap labor. But Japan had to import many more products than it exported, giving it an unfavorable balance of trade.

Section 3. Japan's zeal in modernizing was matched by its determination to preserve its independence and become a major power in Asia. A major goal of the Meiji oligarchy was to be treated as an equal of the Western powers through the elimination of the privileges of extraterritoriality and restoration of Japan's tariff autonomy. This goal led to attempts to renegotiate the "unequal treaties" that were signed during the final days of the Tokugawa Shogunate. The final elimination of the unequal treaties was accomplished in 1911.

Another major goal was to prevent the encroachment of Western imperialism. To secure this goal, Japan took the first steps at establishing its own imperialist policy, fighting a war with China in 1894 and with Russia in 1904. These wars greatly expanded the territory over which Japan had influence, including Korea. In 1902 Japan signed an alliance with Great Britain that was the first treaty in which an Asian country was treated as the equal of a Western power.

Relations with the United States became strained over Japanese immigration. But the strain eased in 1908 when Japan agreed to limit immigration to the United States with the signing of the "Gentlemen's Agreement."

Section 4. World War I accelerated Japan's rise to a place among the great powers. Entering the war on the side of the Allies, Japan furthered its imperialistic interests in China and the Pacific region at Germany's expense, receiving at the war's end former German territory as League of Nations mandates. The war also helped Japan to strengthen its industry and foreign trade. The balance of trade became highly favorable and many Western nations were in debt to Japan. The supreme recognition of Japan's prestige was its inclusion as one of the "Big Five" powers that dominated the Paris Peace Conference.

■ Vocabulary Review

Define: Charter Oath, oligarch, constitutional government, liberalism, constitution, genro, privy council, suffrage, consumer goods, capital, inflation, zaibatzu, tenant farmer, balance of trade, light industry, imperialism, extraterritoriality, indemnity, mediator, protectorate, mandate

■ Places to Locate

Locate: Bonin Islands, Russia, Sakhalin Island, Kurile Islands, China, Korea, Taiwan, Caroline Islands, Hawaiian Islands, Ryukyu Islands, Manchuria, Marianas

■ People to Know

Identify: Mutsuhito, Saigo Takamori, Ito Hirobumi, Theodore Roosevelt, Admiral Tojo, Yuan Shikai

■ Thinking Critically

1. Why was Japan so successful in modernizing its economy and its society?
2. Use evidence from the textbook to support or to refute the statement: *The Meiji constitution paid only lip service to democratic government.*
3. Discuss the advantages and the disadvantages of the Meiji government's close connections with industry. Could Japan's rapid industrialization during this period have been possible without these ties? Why or why not?
4. How did World War I facilitate Japanese imperialist policies?

■ Extending and Applying Your Knowledge

1. The bewildering but exciting days of change faced by the Japanese of the Meiji era are reflected in *Botchan*, written by Soseki Natsume, one of modern Japan's great novelists. Read and report on the book, which was reprinted in 1968 by the Charles E. Tuttle Company, Inc. (Rutland, Vermont).
2. Prepare a chart of important events in Japanese history using the mythology-based method of dating and the emperor-based method of dating adapted from the Chinese.

6

Japan on the March

For a decade after World War I, Japan cooperated with the other great powers in seeking to create a peaceful world order. But by 1931 when Japan expanded into Manchuria, this attitude of cooperation had been replaced by a policy of aggressively pursuing national interests without regard for world opinion. Essentially embittered by what it considered discriminatory actions on the part of the Western powers and hit hard by the worldwide economic depression, Japan set out to create a co-prosperity sphere in East and Southeast Asia. The Japanese intended to use the region's raw materials for their expanding industries and sell the finished products to the region's people.

During the early 1930's, the entire world was in the middle of a severe depression. No nation was free from grave political and economic problems. But other nations sought peaceful solutions to their problems. The Japanese leaders rejected their peaceful alternatives—cooperation with China's revolutionary government and a vigorous pursuit of foreign trade. Instead, government by responsible citizens gave way to rule by ambitious militarists and expansionists.

The tragic outcome of Japan's aggressive policies was a long and bloody involvement in World War II, or the "Great Pacific War," as the global conflict was called in Japan. Not only did the war result in Japan's total defeat, it also destroyed 75 years of hard work and sacrifice. Rarely in modern times has any nation paid so staggering a price for misguided policies.

1. New Domestic Crises After World War I

During the 1920's many Japanese expressed a growing impatience with the **authoritarianism** of the Meiji oligarchs and developed a lively interest in Western political thought which was demonstrated in newspapers and magazines. **Democracy, socialism, communism,** and **anarchism** attracted significant followers among the disenchanted of all classes. Confronted with demands from **liberals** and **radicals** for political and social reforms during the 1920's, **conservatives** were compelled to stay in the background. They thought it wise not to suppress the agitation for change that arose.

A New Generation of Leaders

In 1918 Hara Kei (HAR-rah KAY-ee) was named prime minister by the genro. Being named to this position was due primarily to his leadership of a political party. The appointment was a notable event because it marked the real beginning of parliamentary government in Japan. Known as the "commoner prime minister," Hara was the first prime minister named by the oligarchs as head of the Japanese government who was not an oligarch, an admiral, or a general. He was also the first prime minister to form a cabinet following the established principles of parliamentary government.

During the Meiji era, the oligarchs had become known as "elder statesmen," or genro. All of the genro had participated in the Imperial Restoration and had eventually become prime ministers themselves. The genro were not provided for in Japan's constitution, but in their unofficial capacity as advisers to the emperor, they were the ultimate guardians of state policy. The most important right claimed by the ruling oligarchs was the naming of the prime minister, a decision that received official approval through appointment by the emperor.

In 1922, General Yamagata Aritomo (yah-mah-GAT-tah ah-rih-TOH-moh), the architect of the modern Japanese army and a member of the genro, died. After Yamagata's death, the only surviving member of the genro was Prince Saionji (SY-ohn-jee). Yamagata's death magnified the influence of Saionji who lived until 1940.

Agitation for Reform

Many opponents of the existing regime sought to channel discontent into political organizations. Among these were the so-called proletarian parties that generally advocated some form

Imperial Japan

1912–1925	Taisho era
1918–1931	Liberal era
1921–1922	Washington Conference and the Nine–Power Treaty
1923	Great Earthquake
1925	Universal male suffrage
1929	Tanaka Memorandum
1931	Mukden Incident
1933	Withdrawal from the League of Nations
1936	Army mutiny
1936–1937	Anti–Comintern Pact
1937	Marco Polo Bridge Incident
1940	Tripartite Pact
1941	Attack on Pearl Harbor
1942	Offensive taken by Allies
1945	Atomic bombs on Hiroshima and Nagasaki

of socialism. Although they never united collectively and were never strong individually, they had the support of many factory workers, a scattering of peasants, and a considerable number of university professors and students. What these various groups lacked in the way of widespread support, they made up for by sheer energy. Never missing an opportunity to advance their ideas, their agitation for change and reform electrified the political atmosphere in Japan.

Labor unrest, which had risen sharply during World War I, continued after the coming of peace. Low wages, poor working conditions, and the high cost of living made it easy to organize discontented workers. The new **trade unions** then began to exert pressure upon both the government and factory owners for improvements in working conditions. These trade unions also gave their political support to the proletarian political parties, which fought for reform in government and society. Unfortunately for their hopes, the reform parties were bitterly divided on questions of political aims and methods. As a result, their agitation was comparatively ineffective.

During the 1920's and early 1930's many Japanese took part in political activity for the first time. These men are joining a march on Tokyo to protest the effects of the Great Depression.

Social and political unrest was also evident in other areas of Japanese life. Some of the reformers, for example, concentrated their efforts in behalf of the peasants. They encouraged the peasants to get involved in political activities and to participate in various self-help and mutual aid organizations. During these years Kagawa Toyohiko, one of modern Japan's best-known converts to Christianity, was very active in establishing peasant cooperatives. At this time too a campaign was started to give suffrage to Japanese women, a right they did not receive until after World War II.

Rebellion Among Youths

Many young men and women, exposed to the new ideas and fashions of the West, rebelled against the ways of their parents. Cherished traditions and customs were rejected as being old-fashioned. Western styles and customs in dress and behavior became increasingly popular. Men adopting the new fashions were called nonconformists and dubbed "mobo" (modern boy). Women who scorned tradition were known as "moga" (modern girl). Many of these young people questioned family authority, arranged marriages, and the long-standing custom of separate social lives for men and women. Most of the older Japanese were shocked by what was to them the improper behavior of teenagers and young adults.

Revolt against traditional authority was coupled with shouts for reform. The campuses of the imperial universities were centers of radical political movements. The state was particularly disturbed by this trend because many of the future leaders of Japanese government and business life graduated from these highly respected institutions. Some university professors and students did not hesitate to criticize loudly the conduct of government and to make demands for sweeping political change. These intellectuals founded clubs, established newspapers, and held forums for political discussion and debate. Some of these intellectuals, like the workers, were fervent backers of democracy, socialism, and even communism.

Bolshevik Influence

Not long after the 1917 Bolshevik Revolution in Russia, the influence of Communist ideas was beginning to be felt in Japan. The early Japanese followers of the Communist cause, mainly intellectuals, organized the Communist Party of Japan in 1922. From the outset this party was beset with problems that slowed any political headway. The leaders of the movement were a quarrelsome group and did not always see eye to eye on matters of political strategy. The very radical nature of the Party was perhaps its chief handicap. Its insistence that the "emperor system" be abolished was too much for most of the Japanese people to accept.

The police regarded the Communists with great suspicion, from time to time showing their antagonism by carrying out bruising raids that shattered the Party's ranks. By 1923, most of the important Communists were in prison. The Party barely survived. But over the next few years the energetic Communists succeeded in rebuilding their political organization. Then, in 1928 and 1929, the Party again was smashed by police raids and arrests. Dead for all political purposes, the Communist Party in Japan was not revived until after World War II had ended.

Effects of Reform

For the most part, the Japanese state tolerated, even if it did not approve of, the various reform campaigns. The government leaders were confident of their ability to control the political situation. In 1925, a law established universal male suffrage, increasing the number of eligible voters from 3.5 million to 14 million. But the great majority of these new voters were conser-

S IDELIGHT TO HISTORY

The Bolshevik Revolution in Russia

The Bolshevik Revolution of 1917 in Russia was the climax of long years of opposition to the czar's autocratic government. For years peasants had been agitating for land reform. Intellectuals had been discussing such revolutionary theories as Marxism and anarchism. Workers sought better working and living conditions. The middle class wanted more rights of self-government.

When workers revolted in 1905, the czar granted them a legislature and other reforms, but it was soon clear that he had not done enough to quiet the agitation. Even those who had supported Russia's entry into World War I in 1914 found the czar's wartime government hopelessly inefficient. The army at the front lacked military supplies and was poorly led. Food distribution was inefficient. Angry workers finally staged food riots and strikes, and the revolution quickly spread to other levels of society. The czar abdicated and was replaced by a provisional government composed of moderates and socialists.

The provisional government attempted to continue the war while reforming the governmental system. But the twofold task was simply too much for an inexperienced administration, and it failed. In November the weakened and divided regime was overthrown by radicals called Bolsheviks, who established the Communist government that still exists today. V. I. Lenin, the Bolshevik leader, declared that the temporary dictatorship would lead to a classless society in the future.

Russia was in a state of civil war for four years. The Bolsheviks, or Reds, fought bloody wars with other Russians, known as the Whites, who received aid from Allied troops after World War I. The Whites, however, were never unified, and the foreign troops soon withdrew from the struggle. Finally the Bolsheviks won out, and by the beginning of 1922 the new Communist regime was well established. The nation's name was changed to the Union of Soviet Socialist Republics.

vative peasants. They took a dim view of radical workers and intellectuals. They preferred to support the government and the long-established political parties. As a result, reformers and revolutionaries never amounted to more than a small minority of Japan's population.

The Taisho Era

Following the death of the Meiji emperor, his son Yoshihito succeeded him to the throne. Known as the Taisho (TEY-sho) Emperor, the new ruler reigned from 1912 to 1925. This Taisho Era will always be remembered as the time when Japan suffered one of the worst catastrophes in its history. On September 1, 1923, the Tokyo metropolitan area was rocked by a series of earthquake shocks. The resulting fires left much of the region in ashes, while the number of dead was counted to be at least 150,000.

The Japanese lost little time in repairing the considerable damage caused by the Great Earthquake. They immediately set about removing the debris and then built new homes, schools, factories, and stores as rapidly as possible. Ironically, the nation's industry actually benefited from the calamity. As new plants, mills, and factories were constructed, they were equipped with the most up-to-date machinery of the times. Industrial production thus became more efficient than it ever had been, enabling the Japanese to compete more successfully than before in the markets of the world.

Check Your Understanding

1. How did political leadership in Japan change after World War I?
2. How did many of the Japanese workers, peasants, and students show their discontent with authoritarianism?
3. Why did the Communist Party make little headway in postwar Japan?
4. What were the effects of reform efforts on Japanese life?
5. *Thinking Critically:* Explain how the passing of the genro affected Japan's politics following World War I.

2. Japan's Pursuit of a Militant Foreign Policy

During World War I Japan became the dominant power in East Asia. After the war the Japanese clearly showed that they intended to preserve and strengthen that position by making bold incursions on the Asian mainland to enlarge their empire and to secure raw materials and new markets. Attempts by the United States and other Western nations to check Japan's ambitions only made Japan more determined.

Menacing Moves in Siberia

World War I was in its last days when the Japanese first began to alarm the victorious Allies. After the Bolsheviks seized power in Russia in November 1917, the new Communist leaders made peace with Germany and withdrew from the war. (See page 154.) The Allies had landed expeditionary forces on the Black Sea, at Archangel in the north, and at Vladivostok in eastern Siberia. In doing so they hoped to overthrow the Communist government by supporting the White armies fighting the Bolshevik Red armies. (See page 155.) The Allies had agreed to limit the size of their respective forces in Siberia. The Japanese leaders, however, believed that sending troops to Siberia was an opportunity for enlarging Japan's holdings on the Asian mainland. Accordingly they sent to Siberia more troops than had been agreed on, and before long the Japanese were carrying on military operations far into the interior of Asia.

By early 1920 the other Allied nations had abandoned their blockade of Russia and withdrawn their military forces. The Japanese troops remained, however, and continued to fight the Bolsheviks and other local armies that opposed Japanese plans to expand their military operation. Meanwhile, the Japanese public, objecting to high taxes to maintain large military forces in peacetime, demanded an end to military operations abroad. Nonetheless the Japanese encroachments on Russian territory continued until 1922. Several years later, Japan and the new Soviet Union finally negotiated a treaty.

Exploitation of Korea

Japan's annexation of Korea in 1910 had met with resistance from the Koreans for many years. When the Koreans refused to cooperate with their new rulers, the Japanese retaliated with repressive measures. Korean resistance came to a peak in May 1919 with the Mansei Revolt. At this time the people of Korea launched a peaceful demonstration nationwide in support of independence. The Japanese suppressed the demonstration so brutally that similar protests were never again attempted by the Koreans.

In the 1920's the Japanese moved ahead rapidly with programs to develop Korea. In the process they left little doubt that their objective was to enrich themselves at the expense of the Hermit Kingdom. Japanese companies took over the best farming lands and their agricultural output, including some of the world's finest rice. They constructed new industries, railroad lines, and hydroelectric plants. Thousands of Japanese, moreover, were given good-paying positions in the colonial government. Japan's leaders stationed an army permanently in Korea to keep the Korean people in check. By the end of the 1920's the Hermit Kingdom had become an integral part of the Japanese Empire.

The Washington Naval Conference

While extending its hold on the Asian mainland, Japan was also strengthening its navy. To the Western powers, it seemed that Japan was determined to have the greatest fleet in the world. To forestall a costly naval race and advance peace and security in the Pacific, the United States called a meeting of the great powers. In 1921–1922, representatives of seven Western nations, Japan, and China gathered in Washington, D. C. The Washington Naval Conference produced several important results:

1. France, Great Britain, Japan, and the United States bound themselves to respect the integrity of each other's island possessions in the Pacific. This Four–Power Treaty replaced the 1902 Anglo–Japanese Alliance. (See page 140.)
2. The four powers listed above plus Belgium, China, Italy, the Netherlands, and Portugal signed the Nine–Power Treaty, which was an "open door" pact to respect the sovereignty, independence, and administrative integrity of China during peacetime and its neutrality in time of war.
3. In the Shandong Treaty, Japan agreed to return to China the German-held territory it had occupied in World War I and to modify the Twenty–One Demands made on China in 1915. (See page 144.)
4. In the Five–Power Treaty, Britain, the United States, Japan, France, and Italy agreed to limit future construction of battleships and aircraft carriers to a ratio of 5:5:3:1:1, respectively. No battleship was to exceed 35,000 tons or mount larger than 16-inch guns. No aircraft carrier was to exceed 135,000 tons.

Makeshift tents housed many unemployed Japanese during the Great Depression. What other nations were hard hit by the Great Depression?

Resentment Toward the West

At the end of 1922 the Western nations were confident that the "problem" of Japan was nearing settlement. The attitude in Japan, however, was quite different. Few Japanese were satisfied with the results of the Washington Naval Conference. The Western nations felt that Japan needed a fleet only in the Pacific and that the naval quotas were fair. But some Japanese looked on the naval quotas as an indication that the Western nations still regarded their country as inferior.

The Japanese resentment toward the West was increased in 1924 when the United States Congress passed a new immigration law. This law deliberately discriminated against Japanese and all other Asians by limiting the number of Asian immigrants to a few hundred each year. In Japan's case, there was good cause for bitterness because the new law was a violation of the "Gentlemen's Agreement." (See page 142.) While the Japanese acknowledged the sovereign right of the United States to choose any immigration policy it wanted, they argued correctly that the law was racist.

The worsening economic conditions of the late 1920's also had an adverse effect on relations between Japan and the West.

The decline in trade that accompanied the world depression of 1929 hit Japan especially hard because the country was critically dependent upon its overseas commerce. To pay for its necessary imports, Japan had to export manufactured goods, but the Western nations began raising tariff walls to protect their own industries against foreign competition. The Japanese charged that such policies were discriminatory. Thus by the beginning of the 1930's, Japanese–Western relations had become extremely strained.

Discontent with the Government

Japan's leaders wrestled desperately with the depression and the problems of foreign policy. But no matter what was done, the step taken was angrily criticized by one group or another. Government leaders were held responsible for the widespread unemployment. Many charged that businesspeople were reaping huge profits while the workers and the peasants were suffering. They also accused the government of neglecting the nation's interests in China and of bowing to the discriminatory policies of the Western nations. Everything, it seemed, was the fault of the government.

Discontent with the national leadership proved to be a boon to Japanese **ultra-nationalists**. Assuming that Japan alone among the nations of the world had to cope with desperate problems, these narrow-minded militants proposed simple solutions that they claimed were sure to be successful. These ultra-nationalists were winning increasing public support while confidence in the national government was beginning to reach an all-time low. The stage was set for the military domination of Japan.

Check Your Understanding

1. What moves did the Japanese make in Siberia and Korea to strengthen their position in Asia?
2. What major agreements were reached at the Washington Conference?
3. Why did the Japanese become increasingly resentful toward the West?
4. *Thinking Critically:* How did the Great Depression affect Japan? Why did it help the cause of Japanese ultra-nationalists?

3. All-Out War in Manchuria

Japan's military leaders proposed territorial expansion at China's expense as a solution to their country's problems. Manchuria, a rich and sparsely populated region, especially excited their greed. With fertile lands and rich deposits of coal and iron ore, the area would prove invaluable to the overpopulated and economically depressed archipelago. Manchuria might also provide an important market for Japan's exports. With such thoughts in mind, some hotheaded officers of the Japanese army prepared to defy world opinion and their own government. The means chosen was a daring attempt to gain control of China's northeastern storehouse.

Disagreement over China

The leaders of Japan disagreed on the kind of foreign policy they should pursue with China. Under the leadership of Dr. Sun Yat-sen (SOON YAT-SEN) and, after his death, of Chiang Kai-shek (JYAHNG KY-shek), the Nationalist Party, or Guomindang (GWOH-min-DAHNG), was reorganized. The new Chinese leadership seemed destined to unify a China ripped apart by warlords and exploited by imperialist powers.

Some groups in the Japanese government feared that the increasingly confident Guomindang would abolish Japan's special rights and privileges obtained over the years in China. They favored the use of force, if necessary, to uphold Japan's interest on the mainland. But others counseled the government to proceed cautiously. Believing that the nationalist revolution sooner or later would succeed, they urged cooperation with China. These **moderates** held that Japanese interests, in the long run, would be better served by a policy of friendship toward their mainland neighbor.

In the summer of 1927 Prime Minister Tanaka Giichi summoned many high-ranking officials to a conference in Tokyo to discuss East Asian affairs. Two years later the Chinese government published a startling document alleged to contain the conclusions reached at the Tokyo meeting. "The way to gain actual rights in Manchuria and Mongolia," the document stated,

> is to use this region as a base and under the pretext of trade and commerce penetrate the rest of China. Armed by the rights already secured we shall seize the resources all over the country. Having China's entire resources at our disposal we shall proceed to conquer India, the [East Indies] Archipelago, Asia Minor, Central Asia, and even Europe.

But to get control of Manchuria and Mongolia is the first step if the Yamato race wishes to distinguish itself on continental Asia. [Quoted in Arthur Tiedemann, *Modern Japan*, revised edition.]

The Japanese government denounced the so-called "Tanaka Memorandum" as a Chinese forgery and indignantly denied the drafting of a "plan for world conquest." The extreme proposals were certainly not in keeping with the moderate foreign policy advocated by Prime Minister Tanaka. No proof of the authenticity of the document has ever been uncovered. Yet, when Japanese military forces began their aggressive campaigns on the Asian mainland in the 1930's, it was charged that the "plan" was being put into effect.

The Mukden Incident

One of the many groups dissatisfied with Japan's China policy was a small core of officers in the Kwantung Army, the force stationed in that part of Manchuria under lease to Japan. Concerned by the efforts of Chiang Kai-shek to reestablish the Chinese central government's control in Manchuria, these officers advocated firm action to uphold their country's treaty rights in the region, which included the right to protect the tracks of the South Manchuria Railroad for about 700 miles. Several different plans for blocking the Guomindang were considered by high-ranking army commanders. One was finally put into effect on the night of September 18, 1931.

Claiming that troops of a Manchurian warlord had attempted to derail an express train just outside of Mukden, now called Shenyang, Japanese garrison forces swiftly moved into action. A bomb, which actually did little damage, had been planted on the tracks by Japanese conspirators. Since the forces of General Chiang were too weak to risk war with Japan, and the Manchurian warlord's forces were no match for the Kwantung Army, the entire region was soon overrun.

Political and military leaders in Japan were stunned by the Mukden Incident. The units of the Kwantung Army, in attacking the troops of the Manchurian warlord, clearly committed an act of aggression against China. Moreover, by taking it upon themselves to determine their nation's foreign policy, the army officers showed their contempt for the imperial officials in Tokyo. Aware that its control over the military was critically affected, the civilian government struggled desperately to recover its authority and prestige.

Prime Minister Hamaguchi Yuko was the most prominent victim of the militant nationalist movement. Wounded on November 15, 1930, he was an invalid until his death on August 25, 1931. This picture was taken shortly before he died.

A Campaign Against Moderates

Some of Japan's moderate civilian leaders opposed an overly risky foreign policy. Consequently they became very unpopular with the radicals. Taking advantage of the unrest and outbursts of violence that stemmed from the Great Depression, young officers and ultra-nationalists denounced the moderates as corrupt and cowardly. Hoping to bring about a change in leadership, the ultra-nationalists engaged in intrigues and conspiracies. When Prime Minister Hamaguchi Yuko failed to demand **naval parity** with Britain and the United States at the London Naval Conference of 1930, hotheaded Japanese ultra-nationalists became outraged and assassinated him on his return to Japan. Hamaguchi's death proved to be a warning of **terrorism** yet to come.

Many moderates in the government, the armed forces, and business were dismayed by the reckless talk of the Japanese ultra-nationalists. These moderates recognized that Japan's problems could not be solved by imperialist adventures. They opposed the demands for sweeping changes in the nation's government and economy. Increasingly these moderates were denounced as "enemies of the state," and in 1932 they became victims of terrorism. Several veteran political leaders, high-ranking military officers, and leaders of industry were assassinated or wounded by nationalist fanatics. Thus the supporters of moderate policies were intimidated and gradually silenced.

Criticism Against Aggression

Unwilling to admit that it had lost control of the army, the imperial government found it difficult to explain to the rest of the world the developments in Manchuria. Western nations, and

163

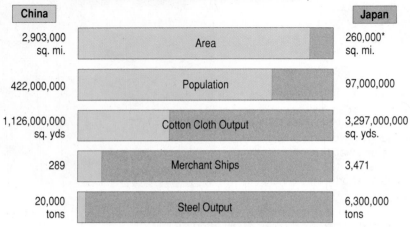

RESOURCES: JAPANESE EMPIRE vs. CHINA, 1937

China		Japan
2,903,000 sq. mi.	Area	260,000* sq. mi.
422,000,000	Population	97,000,000
1,126,000,000 sq. yds	Cotton Cloth Output	3,297,000,000 sq. yds.
289	Merchant Ships	3,471
20,000 tons	Steel Output	6,300,000 tons

*Area includes all territory under Japanese control

COMPARING RESOURCES: In land, population, and natural resources China was far richer than Japan, but the island empire's industrial strength outweighed these advantages.

especially the United States, were angry. The American Secretary of State, Henry Stimson, received repeated assurances that the Kwantung Army would be restrained, but the Japanese troops continued to advance. Stimson tried to persuade the European powers to take a firm stand against Japanese aggression. When they refused, he announced that the United States would not recognize any government in Manchuria controlled by Japan.

Soon after Stimson's action, Nationalist China turned to the League of Nations for support in its efforts to undo Japan's aggression. After careful study of the circumstances, the League's five-nation team of investigators, which was called the Lytton Commission, submitted its report. Accepting the Commission's findings, the League of Nations held Japan guilty of an act of aggression. To protest this action, Japan withdrew from the League in 1933. But the international body had not taken any positive action to stop the aggression, and respect for the League began to decline rapidly as a result.

The Puppet State of Manchukuo

The three northeastern provinces of China conquered by Japan in 1931–1932 were an imperial prize of incalculable value, with an area larger than the Japanese archipelago. Indeed the three provinces were far larger than any European country except the Soviet Union. At the time of the Japanese occupation, Manchuria's population, mainly Chinese, was estimated at about 30

Japan's warlike stance and militaristic attitude alarmed much of the world in the 1930's. While Emperor Hirohito had no military power, the appearance of his approval for all military actions was important, and he frequently reviewed the troops. Hirohito is shown here on a white horse, wearing a general's uniform.

million. Although endowed with vast stretches of fertile land and rich sources of raw materials, especially coal and iron ore, Manchuria was an underdeveloped area. Recognizing the economic importance of their new imperial domain, the Japanese tended to overlook the manner of Manchuria's acquisition.

The Japanese attempted to foster the myth that the events following the Mukden Incident represented a revolt of the local inhabitants against Chinese rule. Since the overwhelming portion of the population was Chinese, this claim was not very convincing. Nevertheless, the Japanese proceeded to set up a puppet state named Manchukuo (mahn-CHOO-gwoh), the "Country of the Manchus." Continuing the fiction, in 1934 the Japanese brought Pu Yi (POO YEE), the last of the Manchu emperors of China, out of retirement and installed him as ruler of Manchukuo. No one was deceived. Until the puppet state fell in 1945, the Japanese were the real rulers.

Manchuria was transformed under Japanese rule. Investing heavily in the region, the Japanese built it into the most powerful economic and military base on the Asian mainland. In central Manchuria they constructed a tremendous coal, iron, and steel complex. Factories, hydroelectric plants, and new railroads were built, while huge tracts of arable land were opened for cultivation. Manchuria also became a prime market for goods manufactured in Japan. Japan also set up many military camps and garrisons. A steady stream of new recruits from the islands was trained in them for service in the imperial army. At Japan's peak of strength in the early 1940's, its forces in Manchuria numbered 750,000 men.

Unexpected Chinese Resistance

The seizure of Manchuria did not satisfy the appetites of the expansionists. Encouraged by the earlier failure of the Chinese Guomindang government to take a firm stand, Japanese troops began probing into Inner Mongolia and North China. Japan's aggressions soon whipped up a war fever in China where anti-Japanese feeling had been building up for years. After the Mukden Incident Japanese imperialism was denounced even more strongly, and the cries for war became louder. Then, on July 7, 1937, Japanese troops on maneuvers near Beijing clashed with Chinese soldiers. Who started the fighting is impossible to say, but the Marco Polo Bridge Incident, as the clash was called, was the spark needed to start the conflagration. From that point on China was to resist Japanese aggression on the mainland.

Japanese military leaders fully expected Chiang's forces to wilt before the highly disciplined Japanese army. As military operations were extended, however, it became evident that Chinese opposition would be extensive. It took three months of heavy fighting before the Japanese troops captured the great Chinese port of Shanghai. Similar opposition was found in other places where the two forces met.

When the Chinese Nationalist government failed to fall, Japan expanded the area of conflict. From the original battle scene near Beijing in North China, operations were extended southward to the frontier of French Indochina, in the northern part of present-day Vietnam. Japanese divisions also smashed their way westward into the Chinese interior, forcing the Nationalists to abandon first Nanjing, the capital at the time, and later Hankou, a metropolis in central China. Chiang's regime finally moved its headquarters to the city of Chongqing in the almost inaccessible southwestern part of the country. By 1939 Japan held all the large cities of eastern China, had captured the principal railways, and had blockaded the long coast. Despite these advances, however, final victory remained beyond the grasp of Japan. It was apparent that the Marco Polo Bridge Incident had been expanded into a long and bitter struggle.

1. **a.** What was the Mukden Incident? **b.** How did the League of Nations, the United States, and China each react to it?
2. How did terrorism affect opposition to expansion?
3. Why did Japan find Manchuria such a valuable prize?
4. *Thinking Critically:* Why was Chinese resistance to aggression a surprise to the Japanese? Why did the Chinese stiffen their resistance?

4. The March of Japan to Defeat

Despite their success on the mainland, many Japanese military leaders still hoped to avoid an all-out war with China. Some believed that the cost of such a struggle would be too great. Others viewed the Soviet Union as Japan's real enemy. They insisted that the "wrong war was being waged in the wrong place." Manchuria, they hoped, could serve as a base for a showdown with the Soviets. Still other Japanese leaders, especially some in the navy, looked with longing toward Southeast Asia. If a war had to be fought, they argued, the great resources of Southeast Asia were an attractive prize. Japan's ruling military regime, trying to balance these considerations of foreign policy, led the nation into a most fatal war.

Transformation into a Military State

After the Mukden Incident of 1931, Japan turned to **militarism**. Political rights were gradually curtailed, newspapers were censored, public meetings were carefully watched by the police, and citizens were arrested on such charges as "dangerous thinking." Political parties, which had shown signs of becoming strong during the 1920's, were afraid to advocate any policy that conflicted with military thinking. Becoming increasingly ineffective, all parties were finally merged in 1940 into the government-dominated Imperial Rule Assistance Association.

The industrial buildup of Japan also had a decidedly military focus. Beginning in the mid-1930's, Japan rapidly expanded its heavy industry. The production of coal and electric power rose sharply, but so did that of iron and steel, aluminum, motor vehicles, and aircraft. The levels achieved in the building of merchant and naval ships was quite impressive. All these advances, while not necessarily of a military nature, considerably strengthened Japan's capability to wage war. By 1940 Japan was manufacturing more high explosives than the United States. Moreover, during the 1930's the size and war potential of Japan's military forces steadily increased. All signs pointed to preparation for further aggression.

Rebellion Against Militarism

In February 1936, a part of Tokyo near the Imperial Palace became a battlefield when discontented units of the Imperial Guard rebelled against the leadership of the army and the government. In the process of carrying out their coup, the rebels killed or wounded several members of the court, the cabinet, and the army leadership. While the rebels had no clearly defined program, it seemed that they wanted to "restore" the authority of the emperor. The attempted coup had the sympathy of several high-ranking officers, but most officers were unwilling to tolerate rebellion in the military forces. Emperor Hirohito, for his part, was outraged over the killing of his close advisers. The rebellion was quickly suppressed by loyal troops and the ringleaders of the coup were severely punished.

A New Imperial System

Territorial additions during the 1930's gave the Japanese Empire a vast overseas realm. The very rise of the huge imperial domain also affected the entire world of East and Southeast Asia. Japanese nationalists were determined that their country would win the greatest benefits from the new international order they were establishing. Their framework was the program known as the Greater East Asia Co–Prosperity Sphere.

Japanese leaders tried to persuade the East Asian peoples, both conquered and free, that political and economic cooperation with Japan was in their best interests. As the economically most advanced nation in the region, Japan reserved for itself the responsibility of providing manufactured goods, technical services, and investment capital for other states in the Co–Prosperity Sphere. In turn, the "satellite states" were to produce mainly agricultural products and raw materials for Japan's factories. Outwardly it seemed that everyone would benefit from this arrangement. In practice, however, such areas as Korea, North China, Manchukuo, and Taiwan served as little more than colonies exploited for the welfare of the dominant Japanese.

Alliance with the Axis Powers

Many expansionists in Japan felt attracted to Nazi Germany and Fascist Italy, aggressive nations like their own. Since Japan, like Germany, opposed communism, the two countries formed the Anti–Comintern Pact in 1936. The following year they were joined by Italy. The Comintern, or Communist International, had been formed at a meeting in Russia in 1919 to promote "world revolution" by encouraging Communist Parties throughout the world to seize power. The parent and guiding light of the Comintern was the Communist Party that engineered the Russian (Bolshevik) Revolution of 1917. By signing the Anti–Comintern Pact, Japan, Germany, and Italy agreed to cooperate in checking the spread of international communism. In 1940 the three nations formed an even closer alliance in the Tripartite Pact. This alliance, commonly called the Rome–Berlin–Tokyo Axis, recognized the leadership of Germany and Italy in Europe and Japan in Asia. The three countries promised to come to each other's aid if attacked by another nation.

United States Reactions

The United States condemned Japan's encroachments in Manchuria and China as violations of the "Open Door" policy toward China. This policy, affirmed by the United States and other nations, called for the preservation of China as a nation and for equal and impartial commercial opportunity in China for all nations. Formulated at the turn of the century, the Open Door Policy was adopted as the only way to prevent a weak, divided China from being carved up into near-colonial "spheres of influence" by Japan and the Western nations. Japan's actions were sharply criticized by many Americans in private, in the press, and in Congress.

Thoroughly aroused by Japan's continuing aggressions in China and elsewhere in East Asia, the United States began taking commercial and diplomatic action against Japan. In 1940 the United States paved the way for economic embargoes against Japan by permitting its commercial treaty with the island empire to expire. It then stepped up the ban upon the export of war materials to Japan, hoping that a shortage of vital supplies would force the Japanese to use a little more restraint.

Eyes on Southeast Asia

In the spring of 1941 Japan signed a pact with the Soviet Union. Since each pledged not to go to war with the other, the status quo in northern Asia was ensured. Less fearful of attack by the Soviet Union, and in control of the valuable resources of Manchuria, Japan felt free to turn its attention to Southeast Asia. For years Japanese empire-builders had eyed this region, which was controlled by France, Britain, the Netherlands, and the United States. It was rich in raw materials, especially oil and rubber, and its conquest promised to solve many of Japan's economic problems. No great resistance was expected because France and the Netherlands had been overrun by Hitler's Nazi troops, and Britain was fighting for its very survival. Only the United States had the power to block Japan.

The United States wanted a pledge that Japan would not expand into Southeast Asia. Since the European powers that held possessions in that region were involved in World War II, their colonies were practically helpless in case of attack. The United States also wanted Japan to withdraw from China. For many months in 1941, discussions between representatives of the two governments were held in Washington and Tokyo. But even while the negotiations were being conducted, Japan was making plans to remove the danger of American interference.

Pearl Harbor

On December 7, 1941, while American officials were preparing for another meeting with Japanese representatives in Washington, word reached President Franklin D. Roosevelt that Japan had launched a surprise attack against American bases in the Pacific. The following day the President requested and received from Congress a declaration of war against Japan.

The Japanese naval-air operation, directed principally against Pearl Harbor, was executed masterfully. The attack fleet, built around a group of aircraft carriers, secretly left its base in the southern Kuriles and sailed unobserved across the ordinarily untraveled North Pacific. The utmost caution was taken to escape detection. Actually, the movements did not come as a complete surprise to American political and military leaders. The secret Japanese radio code had been broken by American intelligence, enabling the United States to learn much about Japan's plans. Unfortunately it was not possible to discover exactly when and where the Japanese would attack. One basic assumption had been that the attack would be opened in Southeast Asia. Thus, the assault on Pearl Harbor took American military leaders by surprise. The Japanese approached within several hundred miles of Pearl Harbor before launching their planes. The American base was caught off guard, and the raiders made a shambles of Pearl Harbor and other nearby installations. The Japanese destroyed or put out of action a large number of warships, including seven battleships. The United States Pacific fleet had been crippled. The Japanese, however, were deeply disappointed because the American aircraft carriers, given top priority as targets, were not in harbor.

The War in the Pacific

Japanese forces instantly followed up their strike at the United States and its allies. Within a few months Western power in Southeast Asia and the southwest Pacific was shattered, and the American base in Hawaii appeared to be marked for invasion. Japanese armies soon drove across Burma towards the frontier of India, while other Japanese forces occupied many of the islands north of Australia. Japan's military leaders had reason to be elated. Victory seemed assured if the Nazis crushed the Soviet Union and Britain in Europe. They doubted that the United States, without its European allies, could wage war against Japan in the Pacific and against Germany and Italy in Europe.

Actually American naval and air power soon brought the Japanese advance to a halt. In the crucial naval battles of the Coral Sea and Midway, the Japanese were dealt crippling blows to their seapower. In August 1942, United States Marines stormed ashore at Guadalcanal in the Southwest Pacific. After an agonizing struggle lasting many months this strategic island was taken. The American victory at Guadalcanal not only blocked the Japanese thrust towards Australia, but also furnished the United States a springboard for offensive campaigns against the Japanese in the South Pacific. By the first anniversary of the attack on Pearl Harbor, the initiative in the Pacific war shifted to the United States.

Japan on the Defensive

In battle after battle Japanese troops demonstrated their bravery. Stubbornly opposing island landings by American assault forces, they stubbornly fought to the death rather than surrender. The closing phase of many campaigns was the "banzai charge," a suicidal attack by the remnants of Japanese defense forces. Equally spectacular and tremendously destructive were the attacks on American shipping by kamikaze pilots who deliberately sought to crash their bomb-laden planes into American ships.

Japan's Superships

For several years during World War II, the Imperial Japanese Navy boasted the two most powerful battleships ever built. The *Yamato* and its companion ship, the *Musashi*, were constructed in great secrecy in the years following the Marco Polo Bridge Incident. They were designed to tilt the balance of naval power in Japan's favor in the event of conflict in the Pacific. More than 850 feet long and displacing almost 70,000 tons, these battleships were considered invincible. The most awesome feature of their armament was their nine 18-inch guns. Capable of hurling shells of more than a ton for 30 miles, they were the heaviest guns ever mounted on a ship.

Ironically, both the *Yamato* and *Musashi* were obsolete before they were completed, shortly after the outbreak of war in the Pacific. Japan's very success at Pearl Harbor demonstrated that the most formidable warship was the aircraft carrier. Neither of Japan's monster battleships brought their super-guns into action until the Second Battle of the Philippine Sea in the fall of 1944. In this epochal naval engagement, American pilots sank the *Musashi* and damaged the *Yamato*. In the spring of the following year, the *Yamato* sank off southeastern Japan while trying to carry out a suicidal strike against the American armada off Okinawa.

A third Japanese supership, the *Shinano*, was even larger than the *Yamato* and *Musashi*. Designed originally as a 72,000-ton battleship, it was converted into an aircraft carrier and completed in November 1944. Just 17 hours after it was launched, it was sunk by American submarine torpedoes off the coast of Japan.

Before hostilities began, some Japanese commanders, especially in the navy, had told war planners that victory must be achieved quickly through devastating strikes by Japan's sea and air power. Admiral Isoroku Yamamoto, who planned the Pearl Harbor attack, warned that after hostilities began Japan could command the seas for perhaps a year, but no longer. In a long, drawn-out struggle Japan would lack the industrial resources

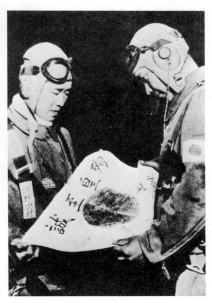

JAPAN AT WAR. In the early years of the war the Imperial Army seemed invincible. The triumphant soldiers are cheering a victory in the Philippines, certain that total defeat for the enemy is near.

In a desperate attempt to destroy enemy ships, kamikaze pilots patriotically carried Japanese flags when they flew suicide planes loaded with explosives into Allied ships.

Symbolic of the "turning of the tide" is this Japanese cruiser, destroyed in the Battle of Midway. After 1942 most of the victories were Allied.

Fire-bomb raids devasted this section of Tokyo. Survivors pick their way through the rubble to their shelters—shacks built of salvaged material.

to defeat the United States. This realistic outlook, however, was not shared by other Japanese commanders, especially in the army. Because they insisted on continuing the war long after the tide had clearly turned, the toll in death and destruction was greatly increased.

Causes of Japan's Defeat

At the outbreak of war, Americans had tended to underestimate the military capacity of the Japanese. The early victories won by Japan led to a more accurate appraisal. Thereafter the Japanese were never treated lightly. In every major campaign, careful preparations were made to assure American superiority in all areas.

Japanese military leaders were less quick to make an accurate estimate of American strength. They tended to discount the United States edge in science, industry, and technology. Convinced that the chief goal of the American way of life was to acquire material things, they held the United States in contempt. The Japanese leaders firmly believed that Americans would not make the sacrifices necessary for victory. In other words, the Japanese acknowledged industrial inferiority but claimed spiritual superiority. Morale, they believed, would be the decisive factor in the long run. The Japanese repeatedly stated their determination to fight for 100 years if that were necessary for victory. But the Japanese had badly miscalculated. The surprise attack on Pearl Harbor united the American people behind the war effort. Equally important, the vast industrial superiority of the United States soon proved to be decisive. In the final analysis, the war was won on the home front in American factories.

Victory was facilitated by the coordinated efforts of the Allied forces, although the United States played the largest role in the war effort. In the Southwest Pacific, General Douglas MacArthur adopted a policy of hopping from one important island to another, bypassing the islands in between. Troop landings were supported by naval units and military aircraft. The enemy on the invaded islands was destroyed or isolated. On the bypassed islands, Japanese forces were cut off from food and supplies.

The U.S. Army's greatest triumph was the liberation of the Philippines. Equally stirring was the drive of the U.S. Navy and U.S. Marines in the Central Pacific. In a series of daring and well-executed amphibious landings, these forces moved from the Gilbert Islands westward to Okinawa, splitting the Japanese Empire in two. The imperial forces in Southeast Asia and the southwest Pacific, already under attack by Allied troops and native resistance forces, thus were cut off from the homeland. Fatal blows were suffered by the Japanese fleet in attacks made by American carrier-based aircraft. American submarines took a terrible toll of enemy supply ships and merchant vessels. Gradually an even tighter blockade was imposed on the Japanese archipelago. During the final months of the war, fleets of huge B-29 bombers reduced the main military and industrial centers in Japan to smoldering ruins. But still the Japanese refused any thought of surrender.

Atomic Bombs on Japan

The summer of 1945 saw Japan, despite frightful losses in lives and resources, continuing the fight. Allied leaders were convinced that only an invasion of the Japanese islands promised final victory. The casualty estimate in such a military operation was one million for the American forces alone. "In all," President Harry S. Truman recalled, "it had been estimated that it would require until the late fall of 1946 to bring Japan to [its] knees. This was a formidable conception, and all of us realized fully that the fighting would be fierce and the losses heavy." These sober thoughts convinced the President that use of a new and terrible weapon was necessary and justifiable. "The final decision," he wrote,

> of where and when to use the atomic bomb was up to me.
> Let there be no mistake about it. I regarded the bomb as
> a military weapon and never had any doubt that it should

S IDELIGHT TO HISTORY

A-Bomb Targets

Why was Hiroshima, among the many cities in the Japanese islands, selected as the target for the first atomic bombing attack in history? The decision was carefully reached by U.S. military leaders. After agreeing to the use of the fateful weapon, President Truman specified that a *military* target be selected. Hiroshima, a large coastal city in Honshu, fitted this specification. It was an important army headquarters. It was the site of numerous war industries, and a major naval base and shipbuilding yards were located in the adjoining city of Kure. Hiroshima, moreover, had not as yet been extensively bombed by American aircraft.

When Japan refused to surrender after Hiroshima was destroyed, the United States decided to drop a second atomic bomb. The city of Kokura, in the heart of a vital iron, steel, and coal complex on the north coast of Kyushu, was chosen as the target. Because of a heavy smoke and cloud cover, the American bombing crew was unable to see its target clearly. Following orders, the crew then headed for its alternate target, the city of Nagasaki not too far away. Nagasaki, an important port with well-developed shipbuilding yards and military industries, was not destroyed as totally as Hiroshima because the explosion took place on the outskirts of the city. Nevertheless, the explosion set off fires that soon reduced much of the city to ashes.

be used. The top military advisers to the President recommended its use, and when I talked to [Prime Minister] Churchill he unhesitatingly told me that he favored the use of the atomic bomb if it might aid to end the war.   [Harry S. Truman, *Memoirs*, Vol I.]

On August 6, 1945, the city of Hiroshima, military headquarters of western Japan, was obliterated by an American atomic bomb. When the Japanese government refused to surrender, a second bomb was exploded three days later over the great seaport of Nagasaki.

On August 8, the Soviet Union declared war on Japan. The next day Soviet forces moved across the borders of the Soviet Union into Manchuria and Korea. The Soviet troops speedily overran Japanese positions. By going to war against Japan, the Soviet Union violated the neutrality pact concluded with Japan in the spring of 1941. The attack came as a result of a pledge made by Soviet leader Joseph Stalin at the Yalta Conference in February 1945. He promised the Allied leaders that the Soviet Union would move against Japan "about 90 days" after the end of war in Europe.

At noon on August 15 the Japanese people listened in silence to an unfamiliar voice on the radio. In an address to his subjects the emperor announced that he had decided to surrender to the Allied nations.

Check Your Understanding

1. What steps did Japan take to transform itself into a military state?
2. How did the rise of Japan's huge imperial domain affect the nations within its co-prosperity sphere?
3. How did Japan underestimate the ability of the United States to recover from the attack on Pearl Harbor as well as underestimate the moral fiber of most Americans?
4. *Thinking Critically:* Why did Japan become one of the Axis Powers? Was its neutrality pact with the Soviet Union a violation of the treaty that formed the Rome–Berlin–Tokyo Axis?

CHAPTER REVIEW

■ Chapter Summary

Section 1. In the decade following World War I, Japan underwent considerable change. Government reforms were introduced. New political parties, often of a radical nature, were founded. Factory workers and peasants were organized into unions. Many young people rebelled against the traditions and authority of their parents. But the Communist insistence on the abolition of the "emperor system" effectively killed its acceptance in Japan until after World War II. The Japanese quickly recovered from the Great Earthquake of September 1, 1923, which proved to be a benefit to Japan because in replacing damaged buildings and equipment Japan was able to modernize its economy and improve the efficiency of its industry.

Section 2. After World War I Japan showed that it intended to preserve and strengthen the dominant position in Asia that it had achieved during the war. Siberia became a target for its ambitions, as did Korea. The Washington Naval Conference attempted to curb Japan's rising naval strength by limiting ship tonnage. Rather than easing tensions, the conference increased them, especially in Japan which resented the position of inferiority forced on it. Adding to the resentment was the passage of a new immigration law in the United States that was clearly racist in its intent to exclude Japanese immigrants.

Section 3. In the ensuing decade ultra-nationalists and moderates clashed over Japan's foreign policy. Moderates wanted cooperation with a newly rejuvenated China, but ultra-nationalists—many of whom were in military positions—wanted to take advantage of China before it became too strong. Through the Mukden Incident, military leaders made inroads into Manchuria, eventually setting up the puppet state of Manchukuo. Terrorists unleashed a campaign against moderates and others who disagreed with Japan's military policies. After Japan withdrew from the League of Nations in 1933, its attacks on China increased, turning into a full-scale war by 1937 after the Marco Polo Bridge Incident.

Section 4. Japan's military ambitions brought it into the Axis camp. It then launched a surprise attack on the United States at Pearl Harbor in December 1941. By its attack, Japan hoped to land a blow from which the United States could not recover in time to stop the Japanese from securing for themselves the nations within their Greater East Asia Co–Prosperity Sphere. But the Japanese underestimated the capacity for recovery as well as the moral fiber of the American people. Their miscalculations led them to total defeat in World War II.

■ **Vocabulary Review**

Define: authoritarianism, democracy, socialism, communism, anarchism, liberal, radical, conservative, trade union, ultra-nationalist, moderate, naval parity, terrorism, militarism

■ Places to Locate

Locate: USSR, Inner Mongolia, Burma, Guadalcanal, Shanghai, Beijing, Nanjing, Hankou, Chongqing

■ People to Know

Identify: Hara Kei, Yamagata Aritomo, Prince Saionji, Kagawa Toyohiko, Yoshihito, Tanaka Giichi, Sun Yat-sen, Chiang Kai-shek, Hamaguchi Yuko, Henry Stimson, Pu Yi, Douglas MacArthur

■ Thinking Critically

1. Discuss the liberal and conservative influences in postwar Japan that were either pushing for or against reform, assessing the effectiveness of each in the area of creating lasting reforms.
2. Once militarism took over in Japan, was it inevitable that Japan aggressively pursue an overseas empire? Why or why not?
3. Japan's strategy in pursuit of an overseas empire seemed carefully planned. Explain its main steps and indicate why and where you think the strategy went wrong.
4. Why did Japan target the United States as the main enemy to be defeated in its plan to create a co-prosperity sphere in the Pacific?

■ Extending and Applying Your Knowledge

1. The changes in Japanese life that began during the Meiji period were accelerated in the twentieth century. To learn about the effects of these changes on the lives and thoughts of individual Japanese, read one of several autobiographies available in English such as *Facing Two Ways: The Story of My Life* by Baroness Shidzue Ishimoto and reprints of either *My Narrow Isle: The Story of a Modern Woman in Japan* or *The Broader Way: A Woman's Life in the New Japan* by Sumie Mishima.
2. Using reference books and one or more naval histories of World War II, give a report on the Battle of Midway, the Battle of the Coral Sea, or another of the major naval battles fought between the United States Navy and the Japanese fleet. Use maps to illustrate your report.

7

Postwar Japan

When the Great Pacific War ended in 1945, much of Japan lay in ruins. The physical challenge of rebuilding seemed an almost impossible task. Spiritual and intellectual challenges also faced the Japanese. Defeat in war shook the Japanese people's faith and confidence in the long-standing traditions of their heritage. The Japanese needed to find new ideals and ways of thought to lead them through the trying times ahead.

In 1952, with the signing of the Treaty of San Francisco, Japan once again became a fully independent nation. By 1972, just two decades after regaining its independence, Japan hosted the Winter Olympics in Sapporo, the largest city on the island of Hokkaido. Eight years previously it had hosted the Summer Olympics in Tokyo. Both events demonstrated the economic successes of Japan, which now boasted the world's third-largest economy, after the United States and the Soviet Union.

Many factors contributed to Japan's success in meeting its many challenges. The United States contributed to Japan's economic prosperity and helped it develop a solid democratic base after the war. But most of the credit for the nation's postwar resurgence belongs to the Japanese, who were hardworking, almost universally literate, and highly cooperative with one another. What the Japanese borrowed from the United States they skillfully adapted to their own needs and circumstances, as they had done for centuries. In the process they earned worldwide respect.

180

1. A Return to Peace

On September 2, 1945, a memorable ceremony took place aboard the battleship U.S.S. *Missouri,* anchored in Tokyo Bay. Representatives of the emperor met with officers of the Allied military command to sign the documents of **unconditional surrender**. Soon thereafter thousands of Allied troops landed in Japan. For the first time in its history, foreign soldiers occupied the country. For almost seven years, Japan's government was under the control of foreign military officials. During those years, United States officials were amazed at the cooperation of the Japanese people to the demands of the Occupation. Nevertheless, the Japanese looked forward to the time when they would again control their own national affairs.

Transforming Japan

When the Great Pacific War ended, Japan was completely under the control of the Allied nations. Technically all the Allied nations were responsible for bringing Japanese affairs back to normal. Actually the United States was in charge. In the United States, opinion about how the defeated nation should be treated was divided. The surprise attack on Pearl Harbor, the atrocious treatment of American prisoners of war, and the tales of inhu-

On September 2, 1945, Japanese officials came aboard the U.S.S. *Missouri* to sign the Instrument of Surrender. The war was officially over.

Postwar Japan

1945	Surrender to Allies
1947	Adoption of new constitution
1952	Treaty of San Francisco
	Mutual Security Pact
1956	Admittance of Japan to the United Nations
1960	First renewal of Mutual Security Pact
1964	Election of Prime Minister Sato
1970	Second renewal of Mutual Security Pact
1972	Return of Okinawa to Japan
	Renewal of Sino–Japanese diplomatic relations

man behavior by Japanese troops made some Americans demand that the Japanese be treated harshly. The opinions of other Americans prevailed, however, making it possible for the United States to lay the foundations for a firm and lasting peace in Japan.

President Harry Truman announced a twofold aim for the Japanese Occupation. The first aim was to transform Japan into a peaceful nation by rooting out the influences of militarism and dismantling the forces of war. The second aim was to build a strong democratic system of government in Japan.

The task of setting up the administrative machinery for the American plan fell to General Douglas MacArthur, the top Allied army commander in the Pacific, who was given the title of Supreme Commander for the Allied Powers, or SCAP. As the Occupation proceeded, the abbreviation *SCAP* came to be applied to the entire administrative structure surrounding MacArthur. MacArthur directed the Occupation for six years, carrying out his duties with zeal and dedication, until General Matthew Ridgeway replaced him in 1951. When MacArthur departed the archipelago, Japan was a remarkably transformed nation.

Rapid Demilitarization

The first order of business for SCAP was to erase all traces of Japanese militarism. Hundreds of Japanese military installations in Japan and Southeast Asia and on islands in the Pacific were dismantled, and tremendous quantities of war supplies were destroyed. All Japanese troops, as well as Japanese civilians living outside the archipelago, were returned to Japan. A major exception were the nearly 500,000 Japanese troops captured by the Soviets in Manchuria and North Korea. The Soviets evacuated these prisoners to Siberia where they confined them in prison camps for many years. Eventually the Soviets returned the survivors to Japan. The armed forces of Japan were dissolved, and civilian organizations of a nationalistic or militaristic character were disbanded. The domestic police forces of Japan were placed under major restrictions. By the spring of 1946, Japan was completely disarmed.

The process of demilitarization proceeded even after Japan was deprived of its ability to wage war. War trials for Japan's foremost military leaders continued through 1948, resulting in the execution of seven of the 25 defendants. One of the seven was General Tojo Hideki, wartime prime minister from 1941 to 1944. The remaining 18 leaders received long prison terms that were later shortened. On a broader scope, some 200,000 military, government, and business leaders who were involved in the war effort were denied the right to hold any office in government. Thus Japan's career military establishment was excluded from effective participation in the political process. The Occupation authorities also dissolved the ties between the state and the Shinto religion.

Loss of Japan's Overseas Empire

To punish Japan for its long record of aggression, the Allied nations deprived Japan of its overseas possessions. Manchuria was restored to China. At the same time, the Chinese Nationalists, or Guomindang, and the Chinese Communists were fighting one another for control of mainland China. Eventually the Communists won, forming the People's Republic of China on the mainland, and the Nationalists were forced to establish the Republic of China on the island of Taiwan. Japan's mandates in the central Pacific were occupied by American troops. Ever since, they have been administered by the United States as a United Nations trusteeship.

Soviet armies occupied the northern part of Korea and American forces occupied the southern part, roughly splitting Japan's former colony in two. When North Korean forces supported by the Soviet Union tried to move into the southern part, the United Nations intervened, beginning what the UN called a police action. Fought mainly by United States troops, it became popularly known in the United States as the Korean War.

Okinawa and the Bonin Islands, the islands on Japan's doorstep, also came under American control. In the following years, Okinawa became a keystone of the United States defense system in the western Pacific. In the final days of World War II, the Soviets took over the southern half of Sakhalin Island and the Kurile Islands and has never relinquished them. Japan has continued to dispute the Soviet Union's legal right to them.

Japan's New Constitution

Even while SCAP was doing away with the Japanese military state, it was attempting to build a new democratic government in its place. On May 3, 1947, a new constitution went into effect. Although technically an amendment to the Meiji Constitution of 1889, the new document was largely the work of Occupation forces. The first draft was written in the offices of SCAP and given to a committee of the National Diet. The committee made so few changes that the new constitution reads like an awkward translation from English.

In the new constitution sovereignty resided in the people. The emperor was merely the symbol of the state and of the unity of the people, much like the monarch of the United Kingdom. The constitution provided for a two-house National Diet. The lower house consisted of a House of Representatives chosen from several hundred electoral districts. The upper house of the Diet was the House of Councillors, who were chosen partly from **prefectures** and partly from the nation at large. Executive functions were to be performed by a prime minister, a member of the House of Representatives and the leader of the strongest political party in that body. The prime minister was assisted by a cabinet chosen from the membership of the House of Representatives. As in the United States, the national court system was completely independent of all legislative and executive offices and served as a check on their powers.

Labor and Industry's New Look

A major concern of SCAP was the future of Japanese industry and business. In addition to removing thousands of pro-war corporation officers and business leaders, SCAP attempted to destroy the zaibatsu. (See page 132.) These gigantic business and industrial corporations were held partly responsible for the growth of militarism in Japan. Consequently they were broken up, although in many instances they later regrouped in loose

Here Emperor Hirohito opens the first postwar session of the Diet. What were the primary goals of the Occupation?

coalitions. In a sense the zaibatsu continued to function, although without the centralized control that had characterized them in prewar days. Occupation officials eventually realized that great industrial complexes, adequately supervised, could do much to rebuild Japan. By early 1948 the policy of breaking up the zaibatsu had been quietly forgotten.

While attempting to break up the zaibatsus, SCAP sponsored reforms designed to ensure better working conditions and more power and rights for the workers. Encouraged by SCAP to organize, some 6.5 million factory workers, government employees, teachers, and members of the merchant marine were unionized by 1949 with millions more organized in the ensuing years. Workers' rights were guaranteed in a series of laws passed by the National Diet. Special laws were also passed to protect women and children, two groups of workers that had been greatly exploited by prewar industrialists.

Agricultural Reform

SCAP was determined to improve living conditions for peasants, who still made up a majority of Japan's postwar population. Many peasants were tenant farmers who leased their plots at high rents. Prompted by Occupation officials, the National Diet passed laws that required landlords of the larger farms to sell most of their land to the government at a very low price. Peas-

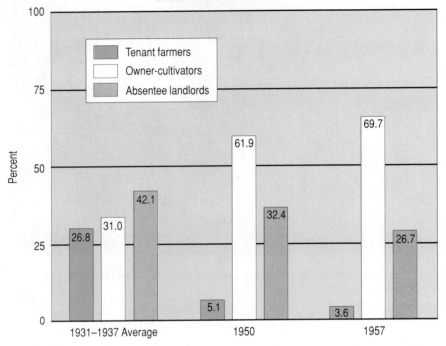

LAND REFORM IN JAPAN

LAND REFORM. The percentage of owner-cultivators in Japan increased dramatically as a result of land reforms passed by the National Diet. Compare the prewar percentages with those in 1950 and 1957. Which group showed the greatest increase?

ants were then given the opportunity to buy about 2.5 acres of land at the same low price and on liberal credit terms.

Practically overnight Japan became a land of small family-owned farms. The farmers were able to pay off their loans quickly because of the profit made from selling their products at inflated prices. Japan's peasants quickly became the greatest independent body of farmers in Asia.

The Status of Women

At the turn of the century, Lafcadio Hearn, a well-known Western writer on Japanese topics, lavished praise on Japanese womanhood. The "most wonderful aesthetic products of Japan," he wrote, "are not its ivories, nor its bronzes, nor its porcelains, nor its swords, nor any of its marvels in metal or lacquer—but its women." But for all their proverbial charm and loveliness, Japanese women had endured a less-than-equal social and legal status. Although improvements in their situation were introduced from Meiji times on, as late as 1945 women were still considered inferior to men and were discriminated against in countless ways.

Officials of SCAP were determined to improve women's place in Japanese society. With this goal in mind, they spurred many changes. In the new constitution women were granted all the rights previously enjoyed only by men. Most notably, women were given the right to vote. The National Diet also enacted laws protecting women's rights in marriage and divorce. In addition, new labor codes were enacted that accorded women in the workplace special protection. At least from a legal point of view, the position of women was changed for the better. From a practical point of view, further changes could come only from the development of new attitudes on the part of both men and women, a process that relied on the development of new traditions and education.

Postwar Education

As part of its program to eliminate militarism, SCAP directed a thorough overhaul of Japanese education. Before Japan's defeat, the nation's classrooms had been breeding grounds for militant nationalism. After World War II they became forums for fostering popular support for democracy. Courses of study were reorganized and new textbooks, especially in social studies, were written. Compulsory education was extended from six to nine years and included both sexes.

The Occupation also opened new doors for students who wanted to continue their education beyond high school. Acting on SCAP's suggestion, the Japanese government established a university in every prefecture that did not already have one. Private colleges were encouraged, and a great many junior colleges came into being. By the early 1970's Japan had some 850 colleges and universities. Almost 380 were four-year institutions, while the rest were junior colleges.

The End of the Occupation

After only two years of the Occupation, General MacArthur concluded that SCAP was outliving its usefulness. Beginning in late 1947, his organization increasingly left decisions to Japanese officials. At the urging of MacArthur, the United States undertook preparations for a treaty of peace and termination of the Occupation. These efforts were speeded up when the Korean War broke out in 1950 and American forces in Japan were shifted to the war front. In 1951 a treaty to end the war with Japan and the Occupation was drawn up and signed in San Francisco by Japan, the United States, and 47 other nations. Ratified in 1952, the Treaty of San Francisco fully restored the independence of Japan.

After the restoration of its independence, Japan continued to maintain the closest political, economic, and military relations with the United States.

Check Your Understanding

1. What basic aims did the United States seek in its treatment of postwar Japan?
2. How were all traces of militarism erased from Japan?
3. Name the nations that received parts of Japan's overseas empire and the parts each received.
4. Describe the basic structure of government provided by Japan's new constitution.
5. **a.** Why did SCAP try to destroy the zaibatsu?
   b. Why did it change its policies?
6. *Thinking Critically:* Which group in postwar Japan seems to have benefited most from SCAP's reforms? Which seems to have benefited the least? Use evidence from the text to support your conclusions.

2. Economic Growth in Postwar Japan

Japan showed the scars of war for years after its surrender. Many of its largest cities had been burned to the ground, housing was in critically short supply, transportation lines were badly damaged, and harbor and port facilities lay in ruins. The United States Congress furnished millions of dollars to help Japan through its most trying years. Nevertheless, the rebuilding of the shattered economy was largely done by the Japanese themselves. In a remarkably short time, they made Japan one of the world's foremost industrial countries.

Japan's Economic Outlook

Despite the extent of wartime destruction, the outlook for Japan was not without hope. The industrious and frugal Japanese were willing to work hard to reconstruct their land. Fearful that chaos

RECONSTRUCTION.

Japan's return to prosperity was amazingly swift. In 1945 a once-busy corner of the Ginza, Tokyo's famous shopping street (above), was the site of burned-out buildings and rubble. Later, new buildings had gone up in the same intersection (right) and the streets were filled with automobiles, many of them built in Japan. Reconstruction is now only a memory. Tokyo, with its many high-rise buildings, is one of the world's most modern cities.

would breed communism, the United States provided massive financial and technical aid to help spur Japan's economy. Since the United States provided military protection, the Japanese could channel funds normally needed for defense into projects to rebuild the economy. Unlike the emerging nations of Africa and Asia, Japan was familiar with modern scientific and technical methods. It had experienced business leaders, engineers, scientists, and technicians to provide the required leadership and know-how. Japan had one of the world's most highly developed and efficiently managed banking and financial systems to provide the funds needed for industrial expansion. Moreover, Japanese industry received an unexpected stimulus just about the time the country was ready to resume control of its own affairs. In 1950, when the Korean War started, Japanese firms were given profitable contracts for war material needed by the United Nations in that struggle. The nation's economy thus moved ahead at a constantly accelerating rate.

Emergence of a Market Economy

The economic system that began to take shape in Japan in the early 1950's was radically different from that of prewar days. The system of centralized control geared for military production that characterized the prewar days disappeared. In its place a competitive market system that emphasized the production of consumer goods appeared. Careful analysis was made of the needs of the consumers, whose purchasing power and living standards rose steadily. One indicator of the growing concern for domestic consumers was the sharply increased volume of domestic advertising. Before the war, Japanese businesses seldom bothered to advertise their wares in their own country. After the war, however, many companies began to earmark large sums of money for advertising in newspapers and magazines and on radio and television.

In building their new economy the Japanese people wisely took advantage of many of the scientific and technological advances that had been developed in the West during the preceding two decades. By adapting existing technology, the Japanese managed to escape heavy research and development costs. The transistor, for example, revolutionized the electronics industry. Originally an American invention, the transistor received little notice in the United States until Japanese firms began to make use of it in manufacturing radios, television sets, and other electronic devices. Since then the transistor's use has spread throughout the world.

Second only to the United States in motor-vehicle production, Japan relies on its automakers for a major share of its export trade. What new economic patterns emerged in Japan after World War II?

New industries that flourished in postwar Japan scarcely existed in prewar Japan. The new methods of production called for highly skilled workers and heavy investments of capital in modern equipment. By 1970 Japan had become a major producer of radios and television sets, hydroelectric equipment, automobiles, and petroleum products. The country also became one of the world's largest producers of steel. Its steel mills were as modern as any in the world. Japan also became the world's leader in shipbuilding.

New Production and Trade Patterns

In prewar days Japan was critically dependent on overseas commerce. Uneasiness about foreign markets and the desire to gain control of raw materials induced the nation's leaders to undertake military adventures abroad. In the postwar period, Japan expanded its foreign trade to an extent never dreamed of before. Moreover, the new approach rested upon firmer foundations than the old. In prewar times Japan's principal customers were the United States, China, and colonies and countries within the Japanese Empire. By 1965 Japan was trading with almost every nation in the world.

Japan's prewar exports consisted largely of textiles and a vast variety of inexpensive goods manufactured in the country's thousands of factories and small workshops. In the postwar era much of this changed. Though Japan continued to export such commodities, they made up but a small portion of the nation's

S IDELIGHT TO HISTORY

MITI

The Ministry of International Trade and Industry (MITI) is the government agency in Japan that is charged with responsibility for coordinating Japan's industrial policies. Japan, like the United States, has an economy based on capitalism. But unlike the United States, Japan's government is actively involved in pushing for the success of its private corporations and businesses. Through MITI, the government produces periodic master plans for economic development. In producing its master plans it studies all the industries that are important to Japan's economic well-being. It then ranks the industries from most important to least important, allocating assistance as needed. One industry that always ranks at or near the top is the producer of the nation's leading export—the automobile industry.

Depending on the goals of its latest master plan, MITI provides financial and technical assistance to private firms. With such assistance MITI encourages technological progress. An early example of MITI's technological assistance is its sponsorship of Japan's "Brain City," a research and development center that was started in the 1960's in the city of Tsukuba (SKOO-bah) about 40 miles outside Tokyo. By 1985, 46 government-run institutions and universities, along with some private firms, had opened their doors in Tsukuba, staffed by more than 7,000 scientists and technicians. The institutions carry on research and help develop futuristic technology in such fields as computer science, medicine, genetic engineering, and the use of robots and lasers.

MITI assists Japanese firms in the acquisition of funds and equipment by extending low-interest loans. It also sets a variety of guidelines for the nation's industries. It helps unprofitable industries become more profitable by steering them into new areas of manufacturing and by providing the capital to retool their machines and to retrain their workers. While MITI has little formal authority in the enforcement of its policies and guidelines, most Japanese firms follow them because they usually produce good results. The postwar Japanese "miracle" of economic growth is proof of those good results.

foreign trade. The Japanese now supplied their world customers with locomotives, trucks, and other kinds of heavy industrial equipment, machine tools, generators of all types and sizes, and high-quality, precision-made commodities. In the United States, for example, such Japanese automobiles as the Toyota and Nissan had by the mid–1970's captured a large share of the small-car market.

Although Japan's population increased by more than 50 percent between the Meiji Restoration and the beginning of World War I, the nation's farms were producing enough to be able to feed the people. After World War I, however, large quantities of foodstuffs had to be imported, mainly from within the expanding empire. By the outbreak of World War II, the Japanese people depended on outside sources for approximately 25 percent of their food supplies. This fact helps to explain why Japan's export trade, which paid for the nation's food imports, was considered to be of such vital importance.

Japan's prewar leaders believed that the country's best interests demanded self-sufficiency in the production of food. When self-sufficiency could not be attained within the archipelago, its fulfillment was sought in the Greater East Asia Co–Prosperity Sphere. Since the war, however, Japan's exports have been high enough to pay for all its food needs.

Japan's farmers have also managed to increase their productivity, inspired by land reforms that enabled them to purchase their own land and generously supported by government subsidies. By applying the skills and knowledge of modern science to farming, Japanese farmers have been able to achieve some of the world's highest crop yields per acre, particularly of rice, a staple of the Japanese diet. By the 1960's Japan was producing more rice than it could consume.

Check Your Understanding

1. What factors gave Japan an advantage in rebuilding its economy?
2. Explain how agriculture and food production affected Japan's imports and exports.
3. How did changes in the life of the Japanese consumer affect business practices?
4. **Thinking Critically:** Compare Japan's postwar market economy with its prewar economy, emphasizing similarities as well as differences.

3. Postwar Social Patterns

By the late 1960's Japan had emerged as the third-greatest industrial nation in the world, surpassed only by the United States and the Soviet Union. The country seemed to reflect a glow of prosperity. But prosperity itself created new difficulties. Not all the Japanese had fared well in the country's rising fortunes. Moreover, Japan had not fully come to terms with its own recent history, nor had it found a new sense of national identity to replace the one destroyed by defeat. Despite the highly visible evidence of great achievement, an underlying sense of uneasiness was ever present as the country moved forward into the 1970's.

Population Patterns

Ten years after the surrender, most Japanese people were enjoying good times. But living conditions for most farmers were still poorer than those of most city dwellers. For many years farmers saw the gap in living standards between themselves and city dwellers widen. As a result, many thousands of Japanese peasants moved to the city. Some who were reluctant to give up their farming plots commuted between a city job and a home in the country. In 1960 the Japanese government inaugurated an ambitious policy of reducing the number of people living off the land. The objectives of this policy were to narrow the gap in living standards and to provide workers for rapidly expanding industries in the cities. The exodus to the city increased sharply. In 1962, 45 percent of Japan's population was rural, but a decade later only 30 percent was rural. Those who remained on the land, however, saw their incomes rise rapidly.

The movement to the cities produced a serious housing shortage. Public utilities such as telephone, electric, water, and waste disposal systems were overtaxed. The urban transportation systems, though modern, could not handle the great mass of users. Tokyo, Osaka, and other large cities experienced enormous traffic jams. More schools, hospitals, libraries, and recreational facilities were needed. And the ravages of pollution were spoiling the environment. In Tokyo the smog was so bad that residents were often unable to see nearby Mount Fuji.

Migration to the cities by no means solved industry's labor shortage. The rapidly expanding economy required an ever-growing number of skilled workers and trained technicians. Every company had more openings than it could fill. To recruit needed engineers, scientists, and other professional personnel, the large corporations conducted talent searches on college campuses. And even though the colleges of the nation were turning out a million graduates a year, compared to a prewar figure of a quarter million, the demand for college graduates exceeded the supply.

With one of the highest **population densities** in the world, Japan would have remained heavily populated even if the growth rate remained low. During the Occupation period, the annual population increase was about 2 million. Knowing that a continuation of this rate of growth would hamper recovery, the Japanese government passed laws in 1948 and 1952 to encourage **family planning.** The number of births began to drop, and by the end of the 1950's the annual population increase was less than a million.

While the **birthrate** continued to be low, better diet and improved medical care enabled the Japanese to live longer. Thus, the percentage of young people in the total population declined while the percentage of the elderly increased. This age distribution trend contrasted sharply with age distribution in most other countries of the world.

Changing Living Patterns

As living conditions improved, Japanese patterns of living changed drastically. The diet was a good example. Among urban residents especially, such longtime favorites as fish, rice, and vegetables were supplemented by beef, milk, butter, and cheese.

One aspect of Tokyo's population problem was reflected in the throngs using commuter trains at rush hours. The national railway hired "pushers" to cope with the thousands of workers who had to be accommodated in already full cars.

After the war, Japanese royalty became more visible in social and cultural affairs. In the photo above, Emperor Hirohito (standing before the microphone) is shown speaking at the 1970 opening of the Osaka World Exposition. His son Akihito, who became emperor in 1989, stands at Hirohito's right.

Bread was eaten with meals as often as rice, while coffee supplanted tea as the nation's most popular beverage. The Japanese people enjoyed more luxuries than ever before. Many families acquired television sets, refrigerators, washing machines, vacuum cleaners, and toasters. This was becoming increasingly true in rural areas as well—even where the family lived in the traditional cottage of wood, paper, and straw.

Some of the most noticeable changes in Japanese society were in the field of recreation. In many cities and towns the long-familiar teahouse gave way to the neon-lighted ice cream parlor. The geishas—professional hostesses at traditionally male parties—met stiff competition in the less traditional night club. Kabuki was being crowded out by the movie theater, which in turn had to compete with television shows for an audience. The entire country became baseball fans—far more so than in the United States. Sumo (wrestling), judo, karate, and kendo (fencing) continued to draw fans, but more and more of the younger generation were drawn to golf, bowling, and tennis.

Formality in social relationships was greatly weakened in postwar Japan. Postwar youths showed less respect for the "wisdom and experience" of their elders. In prewar years, boys and girls were "segregated" from about the age of seven or eight until marriage. As coeducation increased, dating among teenagers became common. In postwar Japan the sight of a boy and a girl walking hand in hand was no longer considered scandalous.

WOMEN'S ROLES. Geishas take part in an annual festival at Osaka (right). This profession was one of few open to women in Japan before World War II. Today, most women who work outside the home are employed in production industries (bottom). A growing number of women are entering other fields, however, like this manager at an automobile plant (below left). Still, many women remain in the traditional role of wife and mother (below right).

Marriages were less frequently arranged by the families involved than was true in traditional Japan. Young married couples often took up housekeeping on their own instead of settling down in the parents' home.

The Changing Role of Women

For women changes in traditional behavior were difficult to accomplish. The vast majority of women continued to marry, raise families, and settle down to household routines. For the most part a housewife's social activity continued to be within the circle of other housewives because the Japanese man did not ordinarily include his wife in his social circle or in his after-work entertainment. But for women who wished to live in a less traditional way, the path was opening to new careers and new opportunities for service in big business and industry. Women won many political offices, but rarely at the highest levels. Although less emancipated than American women, Japanese women made a start toward the goal of achieving equality.

A New Nationalism

In the postwar years, the Japanese sought a new sense of national identity and purpose. The Japanese people wanted world esteem not only for their economic achievements, but also for the political influence they could exercise as a world power. But through the 1970's, the Japanese government continued to shy away from the responsibilities of a world leader. In general, it avoided a leading role in international affairs, and it continued to rely for its defense on the protective umbrella of American military power.

The quest for a new nationalism was evident in every aspect of Japanese life. Pride in Japan's heritage and national values was being restored. Traditional subjects such as Japanese mythology that were banned during the Occupation were again being taught in schools. Authors and artists who dealt with traditional Japan began enjoying new popularity. One writer, Yasunari Kawabata, won the Nobel Prize for literature in 1968. Kawabata had been writing since the 1920's. But people outside Japan did not have a chance to read translations of his novels, such as *Snow Country* and *A Thousand Cranes,* until the 1950's. Kawabata, noted for his delicate handling of Japanese traditions and his sensitive insights into Japanese attitudes, helped rekindle pride in the nation's traditions, customs, values, and heroes. In aiding developing nations in Asia, Africa, and Latin

The Todai-ji in the city of Nara, shown above, is visited by thousands of students and tourists each month. How do visits to national monuments, such as the Todai-ji, help Japanese students develop a sense of pride in their heritage?

America, the Japanese sought to create an image of themselves as a charitable country. Japan also prided itself on its scientific accomplishments. It gradually entered the field of space exploration by orbiting earth satellites. Japan also became a leader in developing peacetime uses of nuclear energy. Clearly the Japanese were eager to make their mark in the world by more than economic achievements.

Check Your Understanding

1. Why did the Japanese government encourage the migration of farmers and other rural people to the cities?
2. What problems were caused by migration to the cities?
3. In what ways did Japanese social customs change from the 1950's to the 1970's?
4. *Thinking Critically:* What were some of the effects of Japan's high population density?

4. Government in Postwar Japan

Political parties and leadership changed greatly in Japan during and after the Occupation. The old political organizations and their leaders were discredited by the nation's defeat. New political parties were formed, usually by officials and bureaucrats who were not well known during the war because the Occupation had removed from office the nation's familiar leadership. Most of the new political leaders were conservatives who had no love for either the authoritarian governments of the 1930's and 1940's or the wholesale reforms of the Occupation. In general, these new leaders tried to find a middle ground between the two extremes of tradition and social upheaval. In election after election their practical approach appealed to the Japanese people.

Conservative Government

Yoshida Shigeru (yoh-SHEE-dah shee-GAY-roo), leader of one of postwar Japan's major conservative parties, was prime minister for seven years (1946–1947; 1948–1954). A shrewd, tough politician, he supported many but not all of the Occupation reforms and stubbornly sought to slow the pace of change. After Japan's independence was restored, Yoshida contributed much to the country's economic recovery and the growth of national self-confidence. His peppery tongue and high-handed political tactics often offended people. Nevertheless, his program of upholding democratic government, encouraging **capitalism,** and cooperating with the United States in its opposition to communism was widely approved.

With the support of most of the Japanese people, Yoshida attempted to undo or alter some of the Occupation reforms. One of his major aims was to strengthen the power of the central government. To prevent the revival of authoritarianism, the Occupation forces had deliberately stripped the national government of many of its powers. Yoshida, and other conservative prime ministers who succeeded him, sought to recover much of this lost authority. In their eyes the weakness of the central government fostered inefficiency and encouraged the rise of political troublemakers.

Yoshida was only partially successful. Decentralization was far advanced by the time Japan recovered its independence, and the individual prefectures and communities were often unwilling to return to centralized control. The conservatives, however, recovered a great deal of control over the educational system from

PARLIAMENTARY GOVERNMENT IN JAPAN

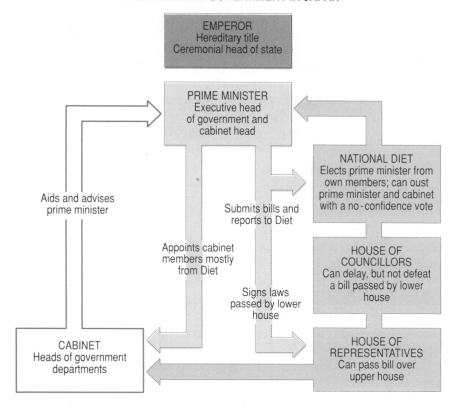

PARLIAMENTARY GOVERNMENT. In this type of government, legislative executive functions are vested in the prime minister, making him the working head of state and the leader of the National Diet. How can the prime minister be ousted?

the local governments. The conservatives also did away with local control of the police and succeeded in imposing restrictions upon labor unions. More important, the conservatives established themselves as an immovable force in national politics. To this day, conservatives control Japan's government.

The Socialists

Squelched before the war, Japan's Socialists rejoiced at the downfall of the military state. They approved the new, democratic constitution and enthusiastically supported most of the Occupation reforms. The main objection they had to the new order was the emphasis it placed on capitalism. Opposed to free enterprise, the Socialists wanted to bring Japan's large industries under public ownership and introduce new and broader programs of social welfare. They also opposed the government policy of siding with the United States and its friends and allies in the **cold war**. Most Socialists were opposed to the Mutual Security Pact concluded between the United States and Japan in 1952. (See pages 205–206.)

The Socialists represented many shades of opinion. Constantly quarreling among themselves, they often split into competing camps. Only the gravest crises could persuade them to settle their differences. Their chief fear was that Japan's conservatives would undermine and destroy the new democracy. In October 1955, the two dominant wings of the Socialist Party reached an accord. Though they were able to present a united front for a few years, their bickerings finally divided them into two separate parties.

The Liberal Democrats

When the Socialists closed ranks in 1955, they compelled the rival conservatives to do likewise. Yoshida's party, which called itself the Liberal Party, merged with the Democrats and various conservative splinter groups to form the Liberal Democratic Party. The Liberal Democrats often found it difficult to agree among themselves, but they managed to retain control of the government.

The united Liberal Democrats produced several outstanding prime ministers. Kishi Nobusuke (KEE-shee noh-BUS-kay) took office in 1957 and served for more than three years. During his administration the first clear signs of Japan's postwar economic miracle appeared. Sato Eisaku (SAH-toh ah-SAY-koo) assumed office in 1964 and was re-elected in 1968. Under Sato, the Liberal Democrats were unbeatable in national elections, even though their popular support slowly declined. In 1972 Sato announced his retirement. As his successor, the Liberal Democrats chose Tanaka Kakuei (tah-NAH-kah kah-KOO-ay), who had been a member of Sato's cabinet. Tanaka promised "powerful leadership to fit a new era."

Communism in Japan

Although the Communist Party enjoyed a brief period of popularity after the war, it soon became a negligible, if vocal, factor in domestic politics. Communism's greatest enemy was prosperity. As economic conditions improved in Japan, popular support for communism waned. The Japanese Communist Party, however, never gave up its hope for political power. It believed that a severe economic crisis would someday afford it an opportunity to take over the leadership of the nation.

Attitudes toward non-Japanese influences played an important role in the history of Japan's Communist Party. One of its major objectives in the postwar period was to weaken American influence in Japan and throughout East Asia. Communists tried to whip up anti-American feeling by every means possible. And because of their interest in the leadership of the Communist world, Japanese Communists kept a close watch on the power struggle between the Soviet Union and the People's Republic of China, or Communist China. Many Party members, as well as a significant portion of the general population, were impressed by Communist China's rapid rise to power. This caused a split in the Japanese Communist Party, although supporters of Soviet leadership outnumbered those attracted to China. The "Kremlin line" continued to dominate Japanese communism.

The Komeito Party

In 1964 a new political party called the Komeito, or the Clean Government, Party made its appearance in Japanese national elections. The Komeito Party was the political arm of the Soka Gakkai, or Value Creating Society, a religious sect that advocated the basic teachings of Nichiren Buddhism. (See page 66.) The doctrine of Soka Gakkai reflected a concern for the welfare of the poor and the uprooted. But as a solution to poverty's problems, the sect advocated self-help rather than socialist doctrines. The new sect attracted millions of Japanese who had been bypassed by the postwar prosperity.

The Komeito Party promised to sweep corruption out of government and to use political power for the benefit of the people. It also pledged to support the cause of peace, to defend the constitution, and to strive for the abolition of nuclear weapons. Impressed by this platform and by the party's success in avoiding scandal, more and more Japanese supported the Komeito Party. In the political campaign of 1968, the Komeito Party received more than 15 percent of the vote, coming in a close third among the various parties in terms of popular support. Although discounted by critics when it was first organized, the Komeito Party showed that it was now a serious force in Japanese political life.

Democracy as a Continuing Process

No country has established democracy by the wave of a "magic wand." In Japan, the Occupation had a better-than-average chance of rapidly creating a workable democratic system. One advantage was the Japanese experience with a modern tradition of constitutionalism, political parties, and elections. Two disadvantages, however, were Japanese traditions and the patterns of behavior that these traditions fostered. The Japanese were long accustomed to obeying authoritarian figures, both in the family and in the government. Many Japanese were used to deferring to a strong ruler. They were not accustomed to accepting responsibility for governing themselves. The development of a democratic system was directly influenced by the American Occupation of postwar Japan. But the development of democracy was an ongoing process. Increasingly Japanese democracy took on a Japanese form and quality.

Check Your Understanding

1. What policies were advocated by the conservatives?
2. What policies were advocated by the Socialists?
3. Why was the Japanese Communist Party unattractive to many Japanese voters?
4. How was the Komeito Party able to attract voters?
5. *Thinking Critically:* Why have the Liberal Democrats been able to dominate Japanese politics for so many years?

5. Gaining a Place in the World Community

During the years of American Occupation, Japan had little to do with the outside world. Most Japanese were so taken up with the pressing problems of daily survival that they paid little attention to the major developments of the postwar period. Japan, moreover, maintained no formal diplomatic relations with other countries and, in effect, had no foreign policy. Its foreign affairs were the responsibility of the Occupation government.

After the Occupation, Japan made a new start in the international community. As part of their task of building a new state, the Japanese re-established diplomatic relations with most of the governments of the world. In 1956 Japan became a member of the United Nations. By following a cautious policy in international affairs, Japan established itself as a respected member of the international community of nations.

Japan's Renouncement of War

Article Nine of Japan's 1947 constitution states the following about settling disputes by war:

Aspiring sincerely to an international peace based on justice and order, the Japanese people forever renounce war as a sovereign right of the nation and the threat or use of force as a means of settling international disputes.

In order to accomplish the aim of the preceding paragraph, land, sea, and air forces, as well as other war potential, will never be maintained. The right of belligerency of the state will not be recognized.

This **no-war clause** caused many disputes and problems. At the time, however, both Japanese and American officials thought it necessary and desirable. If the constitution banned war, Occupation officials reasoned, there could be no rebirth of Japanese militarism. For their part, the Japanese were content to leave their defense to the United States. Aside from having little real choice in the matter, they remembered all too well their tremendous losses in lives, resources, and world esteem under a militaristic regime. The Japanese had no desire to pursue that course again.

Conditions in East Asia after the Occupation caused Japan to remain dependent on American military strength for its security. Tremendous political upheavals had taken place. The cold war between the United States and the Soviet Union kept tensions high in East Asia. A Communist government had come to power in China. A divided Korea had become a battleground between Communist and United Nations forces. In the circumstances the Japanese government agreed with the United States that steps must be taken to ensure the security of the new democratically oriented Japan. On the same day in 1951 that the San Francisco Peace Treaty was completed, a United States–Japan Mutual Security Pact was also signed. The United States agreed to retain the major responsibility for defending Japan against aggression.

Opposition to the Mutual Security Pact

From the very beginning the Japanese–American defense treaty was controversial. A majority of Japanese reluctantly decided they had no better alternative. Still, to some Japanese the presence of American bases on their soil was a humiliating reminder of defeat and occupation. The Japanese were also afraid that the presence of these bases might draw their country into any war in which the United States became involved. The Socialists, especially, were determined to stir up opposition to the treaty.

The controversy over the military ties with the United States reached a climax when the Mutual Security Pact was revised in 1960. The new treaty, as negotiated by Prime Minister Kishi, changed or eliminated a number of the objectionable features of the earlier pact. But the Socialists, backed by the Communists, were opposed to any defense treaty, and launched a wave of demonstrations. They even tried to block ratification of the pact by throwing the National Diet into an uproar.

The crisis ended dramatically. A scheduled visit to Japan by President Dwight Eisenhower was canceled because demonstrations had become so intense that the Japanese government felt unable to ensure his safety. Kishi finally pushed ratification of the new pact through the Diet, but only at the expense of his political career. He had never enjoyed great personal popularity, and he handled the crisis in a way that antagonized many people and strengthened opposing factions within the Liberal Democratic Party. With his own party badly split, Kishi resigned from office.

Once the Mutual Security Pact was renewed, objections to it practically disappeared. Not until the late 1960's did Japanese opponents of the treaty resume their protests. In part, this reflected their resentment over the use of Japanese facilities by the United States in carrying on the Vietnam War. It was expected, when the Mutual Security Pact came up for renewal in 1970, that a replay of the demonstrations of 1960 might take place. But when the Sato government arranged for the pact to continue, only minor protests were heard.

Creation of Self–Defense Forces

The United States withdrew many of its troops from Japan and dispatched them to Korea when the Korean War began in 1950. Japan hastily organized a small army and naval units to replace the American forces. With the constitution forbidding the maintenance of "armed forces," the new military units were called **self-defense forces.** At a later time air units were also established. After the Korean War, the United States decided to maintain only a small American military force in Japan. The United States then began to steadily shift the primary responsibility for defense to the Japanese themselves. By 1972 Japan's land, sea, and air self-defense forces numbered more than 250,000. Not many countries in the world had a military establishment larger than Japan's.

Despite the steady buildup, the Japanese government insisted that its military forces were designed only for defense. It frequently pointed out that the constitution did not permit any other use of such forces. Many Japanese political leaders, notably Liberal Democrats, from time to time cautiously raised proposals to amend the no-war clause of the constitution. But abolishing the clause continued to meet with strong opposition. A majority of Japanese reluctantly preferred to rely for national security on their self-defense forces, and on the nuclear umbrella provided by the United States.

Japan's Foreign Policy

Under Prime Minister Sato Japan sought to play a more vigorous role in international affairs. Sato was well aware of restive feelings over Japan's reliance on the United States. But Sato declared that Japan's best interests lay in close cooperation between the two countries. After Richard Nixon became president in 1969, however, relations between Japan and the United States entered a new stage. Over the ensuing years, they were subjected to serious strain by what came to be known in Japan as the "Nixon shocks."

One of the "Nixon shocks" concerned policy toward the two Chinas. When a Communist government gained control of mainland China in 1949 as the People's Republic of China, the United States refused to recognize it. The American government continued to recognize Nationalist China, the regime of Chiang Kai-shek, based on Taiwan, as the only legitimate government of China. Japan followed this policy.

No basic change was made in either the American or Japanese position until President Nixon dramatically announced in 1971 that he would soon visit the People's Republic of China. His purpose would be to discuss normalizing relations between the United States and the Beijing government. Stunned, the Japanese government quickly protested the failure of the United States to consult with it in planning such a major foreign policy shift. President Nixon then met with Prime Minister Sato in January 1972 to restore the relationship of trust and cooperation that had been strained by the United States' announcement of its new China policy and also by a new trade policy.

American–Japanese Economic Relations

Since the days of the American Occupation, trade relations between Japan and the United States had been close and beneficial to both countries. By the early 1970's one third of Japan's exports went to the United States, and about one fourth of Japanese imports were American products. Few trading partners in the world carried on a greater exchange of goods in either volume or value.

After the mid–1960's, however, a significant shift occurred in the balance of American–Japanese trade. For the first time in years Japan sold to the United States more than it bought. By 1971 the **trade deficit** of the United States amounted to about $2.5 billion annually. The United States charged Japan with maintaining tariff barriers against goods from the United States and other countries. To cope with the problems facing American foreign trade in general, President Nixon raised tariffs on imports in 1971. Although other nations were affected, few stood to lose as heavily as Japan. Its protests led to new rounds of discussions with the United States.

Okinawa and the Bonin Islands

Okinawa was another issue in Japanese–American relations. The Ryukyu Islands (Nansei Shoto) and the Bonin Islands had been occupied by the United States in 1945. While the northern Ryukyu Islands were eventually restored to Japan, Okinawa in the south, as well as the Bonins, remained in American hands. After the war the United States built a military base on Okinawa that became a vital link in the American security system in the western Pacific. But the Japanese continued to resent American control of Okinawa and the Bonins. They did not protest when lands annexed since the Russo–Japanese War were taken from them, but they regarded Okinawa and the Bonin group as part of their traditional domain. The Japanese saw no reason why they should be deprived of lands that had not been acquired through imperialist expansion.

Prime Minister Sato well understood that the American bases on Okinawa were important for the defense of both Japan and the United States. However, his electorate loudly demanded the restoration of Okinawa to full Japanese control. Sato therefore had to plead Japan's case for the island. In 1968 he succeeded in obtaining the return of the Bonin group but not Okinawa. Then, as the Nixon administration began to "wind down" the war in Vietnam, the United States had less need for the military bases on Okinawa. In 1971 Japan at last secured an agreement that Okinawa would be restored to Japanese rule. Okinawa reverted to Japanese control in March 1972. The United States, however, continued to maintain military forces on the island.

Soviet–Japanese Relations

After World War II there was little reason to believe that Japan and the Soviet Union would ever become friends. The Soviets

Opposition to the security pact with the United States has led to occasional violence in Japanese cities. Above, Tokyo police used torrents of water in trying to break up anti-U.S. demonstrations.

refused to sign a peace treaty with the Japanese, and had no intention of giving up the islands that had been seized from Japan during the war. (See page 183.) Japan, on its part, adamantly refused to consider a separate treaty with the Soviet Union until that country agreed to surrender some of the islands that were disputed. Tensions gradually began to ease, however, and in 1956 the two countries did resume diplomatic and commercial relations. But they still did not sign a formal peace treaty.

The 1960's saw a steady improvement in Soviet–Japanese relations, partly because of the Soviet Union's widening split with Communist China. Hoping to win Japan to its side in the controversy, the Soviet Union began to trade more with Japan. Investment-minded Japanese business leaders were also invited to join in development projects in eastern Siberia. In 1972 Soviet and Japanese government officials agreed that they would negotiate a peace treaty and would also discuss the status of the disputed islands.

Japan's New China Policy

After 1949 many Japanese were eager to make friends with Communist China. Although the expansion of trade with the United States more than offset the loss of the China market, many Japanese still hoped to resume trade with the Communist Chinese. After all, mainland China had once been Japan's best customer.

But those Japanese who wanted more trade with mainland China made little headway. Because of American objections, the Japanese government limited business contacts with Communist China. Moreover, Japan was reluctant to endanger its flourishing trade with Nationalist China by expanding trade with Chiang Kai-shek's enemy. But the policies and actions of the Chinese Communists were themselves obstacles to trade. Several times, when it seemed that business deals with Communist China were about to be closed, the Japanese discovered that unacceptable strings had been attached. Gradually desire for business with the Communist Chinese waned.

In 1964 Communist China exploded its first atomic bomb, driving a sharp wedge between itself and Japan. It was a jolt to the Japanese to learn that their close neighbor had joined the exclusive club of nuclear powers. Many Japanese believed that their country's security could be maintained merely by proclaiming devotion to peace. Now they began to have doubts.

In 1971 the American move to open relations with Communist China compelled the Sato government to review its own China policy. Soon Japan and China exchanged informal diplomatic representatives. In 1972 Prime Minister Tanaka Kakuei visited Beijing. Japan and China then announced an agreement by which Japan recognized Communist China as the sole legal government of the Chinese mainland. The Chinese, for their part, withdrew their demand for war indemnities from Japan.

Relations with Korea

Japan's prewar colony of Korea was divided into North Korea, a Communist country with which Japan has had no formal relations, and South Korea. For years after the end of World War II, relations between Japan and South Korea were extremely cool. Underlying the strained relations was a disagreement over Japan's record as Korea's former overlord. From the Japanese point of view, Korea had benefited from being part of Japan's empire between 1910 and 1945. But the Koreans insisted that they had been mercilessly exploited by the Japanese for 35 years. The Koreans demanded reparations amounting to billions of dollars. The failure of the two countries to settle their differences chiefly hurt Korea, which was poor and desperately needed economic help from its wealthy neighbor.

By 1965 a settlement became possible when South Korea reduced its demands. Moreover, responding to American urging, Japan agreed to hold negotiations with the South Korean government. The treaties that resulted provided for the restoration of diplomatic relations between the two countries. Japan also agreed to make loans and to give economic aid to hard-pressed South Korea. This timely help contributed to the rapid economic expansion then getting under way in South Korea. Relations between Japan and South Korea continued to improve.

Southeast Asia

One of Japan's dreams was to play a major economic role in Southeast Asia. But the Japanese were aware that wounds left by their country's wartime militarism in that area had not yet healed. To create good will in Southeast Asia, therefore, Japan gave financial and technical aid to countries that were struggling to develop modern economies. It also paid reparations to those countries that had suffered from Japanese aggression. Moreover, no country was more active than Japan in the Asian Development Bank, an international organization founded to improve economic conditions in the underdeveloped lands of Asia.

Japan's commercial stake in Southeast Asia grew steadily. The countries of this region bought about a third of Japan's total exports. The Japanese hopes for even more trade with the area were stymied by the war in Vietnam.

Japan's Role in World Affairs

By 1972 Japan's recovery from defeat was more than complete. Prime Minister Sato spoke for many Japanese when he announced that Japan hoped for international influence equal to its economic power. But the Japanese had to show they were willing to match their desire for world leadership with a willingness to take on the responsibilities of a world power.

The Japanese were by no means united on this position in 1972. Many conservatives believed that the country needed to take a more active role in the keeping of world peace. They called for amendment of the no-war clause and a subsequent military buildup, a move that would be bitterly, perhaps violently, opposed by the Socialists and Communists. While the nation was united in its desire to be an influential world power, there was no agreement on how this role should be carried out.

Check Your Understanding

1. How did Article Nine of Japan's 1947 constitution affect its foreign relations with the United States?
2. Why were objections raised in the postwar years to Japan's Mutual Security Pact with the United States?
3. What effects did the "Nixon shocks" have on Japanese–American relations?
4. *Thinking Critically:* Compare Japan's prewar foreign relations to its postwar foreign relations with Korea, Southeast Asia, and the Soviet Union.

CHAPTER REVIEW

■ Chapter Summary

Section 1. As a defeated nation of World War II, Japan was occupied by United States military forces. The Occupation from 1945 to 1952, which was under the direction of General Douglas MacArthur, was intended to demilitarize Japan and to establish a democratic system of government. Both these aims were accomplished with Japanese acceptance of a new constitution that contained a no-war clause and that established a parliamentary system of government. The Occupation ended in 1952 with the ratification of the Treaty of San Francisco, which restored Japan to the status of an independent nation. Meanwhile many aspects of Japanese life had been changed through various reform measures, including universal suffrage for all Japanese adults, expansion of education, land reform for farmers, and better working conditions for workers in Japan's growing industrial sector.

Section 2. Japan made astounding economic gains in the 20 years following the end of the Occupation, transforming war-scarred cities into thriving industrial centers and producing a rice surplus from its efficiently run farms. Spurred by massive amounts of United States financial aid, the impetus of the Korean War, and the industrious, hardworking nature of the Japanese people, the nation's economy constantly accelerated and new patterns of foreign trade were established. By 1972 Japan was the world's third-largest industrial nation, ranking just behind the United States and the Soviet Union.

Section 3. The new prosperity created by Japan's economic achievements created new kinds of problems. To incorporate farmers into Japan's prosperity, the government began a program of attracting people from rural areas to the cities. The migration to the cities sorely taxed urban resources and produced a labor supply that needed training in high-tech skills. As living conditions gradually improved, many Japanese adopted ways of living that were different from the past. Formality in social relationships between men and women was reduced, and women began to find opportunities for work outside the home. An especially positive note was the development of a new sense of national identity and pride among the Japanese people.

Section 4. The establishment of parliamentary democracy saw the growth of a number of political parties. But most Japanese found themselves more comfortable with conservative politics than with the liberal politics of Socialists or the radical politics of Communists. Since the end of the Occupation, Japan's prime ministers have come from the Liberal Democratic Party. Through the years, democracy in Japan has taken on its own form and quality.

Section 5. For many years after World War II, Japan downplayed its role in foreign affairs, content mainly to concentrate on economic development. For its national defense Japan relied heavily on the United States, renewing the Mutual Security Pact twice, and generally following the lead of the United States in international affairs after being admitted to the United Nations in 1956. By the early 1970's, however, the Japanese were becoming more restive about their nation's foreign policy, especially after the "Nixon shocks." The return of Okinawa to Japanese control helped smooth relations with the United States after it recognized Communist China. Postwar Japan re-established diplomatic relations with South Korea, the Soviet Union, and with Communist China.

■ **Vocabulary Review**

Define: unconditional surrender, prefectures, population density, family planning, birthrate, capitalism, cold war, no-war clause, self-defense force, trade deficit.

■ **Places to Locate**

Locate: China, Taiwan, South Korea, North Korea, Sakhalin, Kurile Islands, Bonin Islands, Ryukyu Islands

■ People to Know

Identify: General Douglas MacArthur, General Matthew Ridgeway, General Tojo Hideki, Yoshida Shigeru, Kishi Nobusuke, Sato Eisaku, Richard Nixon

■ Thinking Critically

1. What were the new directions toward which the United States' Occupation pointed Japan?
2. Why was Japan's reliance on the United States for its defense during the postwar years a contributing factor to its economic growth?
3. A continuing characteristic of the Japanese people throughout their history has been their ability to adopt foreign ways and adapt them so they have a truly Japanese shape and form. Use evidence from your text to show how this has been true in the postwar years.
4. Why have the Socialist and Communist parties in Japan failed to attract enough votes to dominate the government?
5. Why do you think Japan's leaders have been reluctant to play a more important role in international affairs?

■ Extending and Applying Your Knowledge

1. Many of the differences in the political climates of prewar and postwar Japan can be traced to differences in the Meiji and 1947 constitutions. Compare and contrast these two important documents as the basis for a brief research report.
2. Hosting the Olympics is a considerable undertaking for any city or country. Use the *Readers' Guide to Periodical Literature* to research the changes that came to Sapporo in 1972 or Tokyo in 1964 because of the Olympics. Also find out the part the Olympics played in boosting Japan's economic growth in the postwar years.

8

Economic
Superpower

The funeral of Emperor Hirohito, which took place early in 1989, provided a poignant scene. In attendance was George Bush, President of the United States. In World War II as a fighter pilot in the United States Navy, he was shot down by a Japanese pilot but was safely rescued. Now with the memories of war tempered by time, George Bush, along with leaders from all over the world, was paying his respects to the man for whom his attacker had fought.

During the 1970's and 1980's Japan grew into an economic colossus. The presence of so many world leaders at Hirohito's funeral was a measure, not only of respect for Hirohito himself, but also for Japan's global economic might. The emergence of Japan as an economic powerhouse ranks among the greatest developments of the second half of the twentieth century. Once countries in need of capital to fund their economic development looked to the United States, Western Europe, or the Soviet Union for help. Now increasing numbers of countries are turning to Japan for help.

Japan's rapid rise to the status of an economic superpower has had its advantages. Japan has become a respected, though not always a popular, member of the international community of nations. Most of all, the country has become a prosperous society, but prosperity has brought with it new problems. Japan needs to meet the challenges of overcrowding, of combating pollution from industrialization and urbanization, of an aging population, and of changes in its values and social structure.

1. The Continued Popularity of the Liberal Democratic Party

It has often been said that Japan has a "one-and-a-half party system." The "one" is the Liberal Democratic Party (LDP), while the "half" is the Japan Socialist Party (JSP). The LDP has been in control of both houses of the National Diet since 1955. All prime ministers and cabinet officers have been members of the LDP. Over the years, various opposition parties have tried to form a **coalition** that would win enough seats in the House of Representatives to be able to form a government to lead the nation. But opposition parties have never come close to unseating the LDP because they have been unable to reach agreement among themselves on the terms of such a coalition. But in July 1989 the LDP suffered its first electoral setback in 34 years, and the leadership of the LDP had to regroup if it was to remain Japan's dominant party.

Opposition Parties

The nation's second largest party is the Japan Socialist Party (JSP). Its main support comes from organized labor, but it also has support among suburban and agricultural voters. The JSP advocates increased spending for social **welfare.** In foreign policy it favors an abolition of the Self–Defense Forces.

The Komeito is Japan's third largest party, drawing its primary support from the lower middle class. (See page 203.) The Komeito favors legislation to enhance the quality of life through social welfare. The Komeito has given mild support to the Mutual Security Treaty and to the Self–Defense Forces but advocates a foreign policy more independent of the United States.

The Democratic Socialist Party (DSP), formed in 1960, usually finishes fourth in elections to both houses of the Diet. Despite its socialist designation, the DSP frequently takes positions that are similar to those of the Liberal Democratic Party. The Japan Communist Party (JCP) is the smallest of the regular parties. Since its break with the Chinese Communists in 1965, the JCP has pursued an independent line. Like the Japan Socialist Party, the JCP supports a neutral stance in foreign policy and a severing of military ties with the United States.

Causes of LDP's Popularity

Division among opposition parties alone does not explain the continued popularity of the LDP. Many Japanese believe that the LDP deserves at least some credit for Japan's ongoing economic

---

TIMETABLE

Challenges Ahead

1955–	Continuing domination of the National Diet by the Liberal Democratic Party
1972–1974	Prime Minister Tanaka in office
1973	400 percent increase in price of oil
	Japan's shift to high-tech industries
1974–1977	Prime Minister Fukuda in office
1976	Beginnings of financial scandal in government
1977	Pronouncement of Fukuda Doctrine
1978	Sino–Japanese treaty of friendship
1982–1987	Prime Minister Nakasone in office
1987–1989	Prime Minister Takeshita in office
1989	Emperor Hirohito's death
	Akihito as emperor
1989	Prime Minister Uno in office
	Uno resigns; Prime Minister Kaifu in office

---

growth and prosperity. Others credit LDP's continuing flexibility in its policies and its lack of a specific party platform. Unlike various opposition parties, the LDP espouses a situational approach in its political philosophy, refraining from rigidly adhering to any long-term policy. As the demands and expectations of business and farming groups have changed over the years, the LDP has altered its policies to fit their needs. In global economic issues and in foreign affairs, the LDP takes a similar pragmatic approach. But overall, the top leadership of the LDP has cooperated closely with the United States.

Factions Within the LDP

One reason for the lack of rigid philosophy is the composition of the LDP's membership, which is made up of **factions.** Every LDP member of the National Diet belongs to a faction. Each faction has its own leader and campaign headquarters. At election time, candidates depend on their factions for money to support their campaigns. The factions obtain campaign contributions from big business and other groups. These contributors then expect the elected members of these factions to advance

217

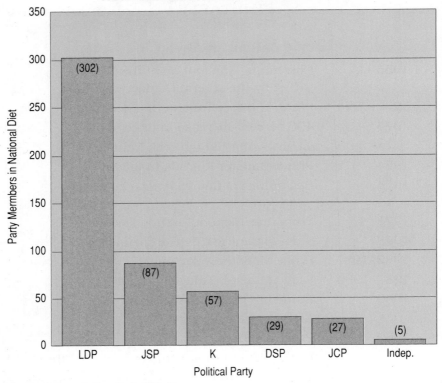

PARTY REPRESENTATION IN NATIONAL DIET

Party Members in National Diet

- LDP (302)
- JSP (87)
- K (57)
- DSP (29)
- JCP (27)
- Indep. (5)

Political Party

Source: *Statesman's Year–Book, 1988–89*

LDP DOMINANCE. The popularity of the Liberal Democratic Party is clearly seen in this graph. The graph also indicates the competition the Komeito offered the Japan Socialist Party in the parliamentary election of November 1987.

their interests in the Diet by approving and funding projects or by voting for legislation that furthers their interests.

At election time, faction members often run against one another for the same Diet seat. The aggressiveness, however, usually has little to do with political philosophy and is more of a competition for power. Once the Diet elections are over, the leader of the LDP faction that gains the most seats usually becomes president of the LDP and that person is then elected prime minister by the lower house.

The Tanaka Case

The Tanaka case illustrates the rule of factions. In 1972 Tanaka Kakuei became prime minister. (See page 202.) Tanaka, who made a fortune in the construction business, had two nicknames. Those who had experienced his enormous ambition called him "bulldozer." Those who experienced his use of power called him "Hideyoshi." Like the famous general of the past who rose to fame from a background of poverty and obscurity, Tanaka was the first person without a college degree to be named prime minister in the postwar period.

In 1974 Tanaka was forced to resign as prime minister amid allegations that he had made part of his fortune illegally and that as a Diet member he had engaged in financial irregularities. In 1976 Tanaka was accused of having accepted large payments from the Lockheed Corporation in the United States in return for using his influence to persuade All Nippon Airways to purchase Lockheed planes. He was later found guilty. Despite his legal difficulties, for several years Tanaka remained in control of his faction, which was the largest in the LDP. In that position he was able to act as a powerbroker, exercising enormous influence over the choice of a prime minister in the years between 1974 and 1982.

During the 1980's Tanaka's role as a powerbroker gradually waned. The decline in his power was probably due more to ill health than to his legal difficulties. Finally Takeshita Noboru (tah-KESH-tah noh-BOH-roo) successfully challenged Tanaka for the leadership of their faction and eventually became prime minister in 1987. But other accusations of corruption continued to plague the leadership of the LDP. Takeshita resigned in May 1989 after revelations of bribery and influence-peddling (the so-called Recruit Scandal) that involved as many as 15 top LDP politicians. Other revelations also troubled the tenure of Takeshita's successor, Uno Sousuke, who resigned in August 1989.

As the election for half the seats in the upper house of the Diet approached in July 1989, the LDP found itself in trouble. Farmers were especially angered by a lifting of some price supports and some of the restrictions on agricultural imports. A sales tax on consumer goods that went into effect in April 1989 upset many women voters, who outnumber men at the polls. Also many voters voted against the LDP rather than for an opposition party's policies because of the lingering effects of the scandals affecting the LDP leadership. With only two months as prime minister, Uno announced his resignation, plunging the LDP into an uncertain future and the greatest test of its dominance since 1955.

A New Mood

As the Japanese became more prosperous in the 1970's and 1980's, they began to insist that the government improve the quality of their lives with programs in social welfare and pollu-

Factory smokestacks that send pollutants into the air are the objects of voters' concerns in many industrialized nations worldwide. How did such concerns in Japan cause the LDP to respond to the voters?

tion control, better health care, and new recreation facilities. In foreign affairs as well, the national mood changed. The government had always maintained a close working relationship with the United States. But as World War II faded into memory and the economy continued to expand, the Japanese people began to insist on a more equal relationship with the United States. As the decade of the 1990's began, the LDP had again to respond to Japanese demands, regardless of faction. By being flexible and open to change, the LDP leadership in the past had always managed to maintain its party's popularity at the polls and undercut the opposition, which tends to adhere rigidly to stated policies.

The LDP's flexibility can be seen in its response to pollution. Japan's economic progress had created serious environmental problems. By the early 1970's many of the country's rivers and seas were contaminated, and air quality in urban centers was poor. When the public began to clamor for environmental protection, the LDP changed its policy of indifference to widening pollution and sponsored legislation regulating all sources of air and water pollution. In law and in court decisions, the principle was established that the polluter must compensate the victim. By the end of the decade, much progress in combating and controlling pollution had been made.

Check Your Understanding

1. What are the chief policies of each of the four main opposition parties in Japan?
2. Why is the Liberal Democratic Party facing its greatest challenge since 1955?
3. What contributes to the flexible political position of the Liberal Democratic Party?
4. How does the Tanaka case illustrate the "rule of factions"?
5. *Thinking Critically:* How has the LDP's practical approach affected the strength or weakness of democracy in Japan?

2. Japan's Emerging Role in International Affairs

To a large extent, the patterns set in the immediate postwar decades have continued to dominate Japan's relations with other nations. The development of a manufacturing sector that efficiently produced automotive and other products, the appearance of a competitive economic system that emphasized the marketing and production of consumer goods and their export to the world, and a favorable balance of trade made Japan into an economic giant. By renouncing war as an instrument of national policy, Japan was able to allocate most of its human and natural resources to peacetime pursuits. All in all Japan's growth has been spectacular enough to rank its economy third behind the United States and the Soviet Union.

In international relations, Japan gained a respected place in the world community as it mended the wounds left by its World War II aggressive militarism. By the early 1970's Japan began to participate more fully in international affairs, especially in the area of providing foreign aid to countries seeking to industrialize their economies. In 1989 at a major economic conference held in Europe, Japan indicated it was about ready to accept the responsibility for world leadership that is commensurate with its economic strength by promising large sums of economic aid to developing nations.

A New Shift in Economic Priorities

During the early 1970's Japan entered a new phase in its economic development and in its commercial relationships with the outside world. The price of oil and other raw materials in the 1960's had been low. In 1973 the Organization of Petroleum Exporting Countries (OPEC) engineered a 400 percent increase in the price of oil, producing an "oil shock" felt as intensely in Japan as in the rest of the world.

For Japan the oil shock brought to an end the period of rapid economic growth. But Japan quickly and effectively adapted to the higher oil prices. Government and business stressed energy conservation and increased their investment in producing electricity through the use of such alternative energy sources as nuclear power and waterpower. With the help of government planning and funding, Japanese businesses began to move away from iron and steel production, shipbuilding, and other heavy industries that required high inputs of energy. Instead Japanese companies began to enter such high technology fields as **robotics** and micro-electronics, including the manufacture of computers and other devices using transistorized parts. These industries used small inputs of raw materials and energy. They also utilized the highly educated and trained labor force that Japan had developed through its rigorous educational system. When a second round of oil shock occurred in 1978–1979, the impact on the Japanese economy was limited.

Trade Problems

The avalanche of Japanese products into global markets gave consumers a wider selection of products from which to choose. But manufacturers around the world felt the impact of competing goods. Some countries began to take steps designed to protect domestic manufacturers from competing with lower-priced, foreign-made goods. During the 1970's and 1980's various types of regulations aimed at limiting imports were placed on foreign-made goods. Taxes of various kinds were also levied on imports to bring their prices more in line with goods that were domestically produced.

Unable to reduce **protectionism** itself, the Japanese took several steps to avoid the effects of protectionism. For one thing, they opened new foreign markets in East and Southeast Asia so they would not be overly dependent on a few key markets, such as the United States and the nations of Western Europe. For another thing, Japan steadily expanded its foreign-aid program. In an effort to promote commercial opportunities for Japanese companies, the aid often came with the requirement that the country receiving the aid buy Japanese goods. A third step to counter protectionism in foreign countries was a policy of

TRADE WITH SELECTED COUNTRIES

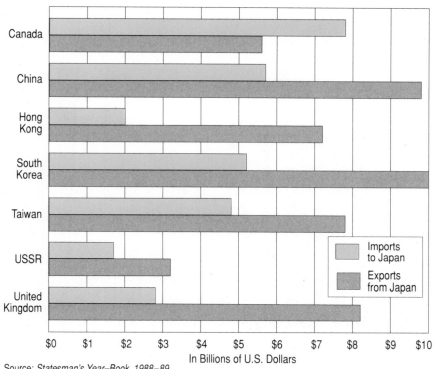

Source: *Statesman's Year–Book, 1988–89*

TRADE WITH THE UNITED STATES

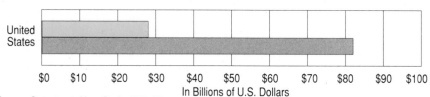

Source: *Statesman's Year–Book, 1988–89*

BALANCE OF TRADE. The graphs on this page show the favorable trade balance that Japan enjoys with selected nations of the world. With which country does it have the most favorable trade balance?

encouraging Japanese capitalists to invest extensively in foreign lands. Even if governments abroad restricted imports, companies manufacturing products within a country's borders would be able to sell these products without restrictions. As a result, during the 1970's and far more so during the 1980's, Japanese investments in mainland China, Taiwan, South Korea, Singapore, and other nations in East and Southeast Asia increased dramatically. Honda, Nissan, Toyota, and other Japanese com-

223

JAPAN'S TRADE BALANCE

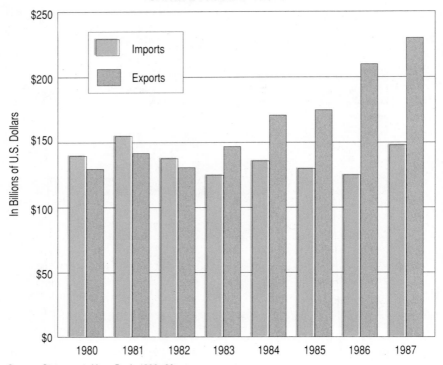

Source: *Statesman's Year–Book, 1988–89*
Information Please Almanac, 1989

TRADING SUCCESS. In 1970 Japan had $19.3 billion in exports. By 1984, its exports amounted to $170 billion. What were Japan's total exports by 1987? By how many billion had Japan's exports increased since 1984?

panies established manufacturing plants in the United States and other countries. Several Japanese banks opened branches in major cities around the world. In addition, cash-rich Japanese companies and individuals bought extensive real estate. The Japanese also became very active in the world's stock and bond markets.

From 1982 to 1987, Prime Minister Nakasone had to grapple with incessant complaints about the huge **trade surpluses** that Japan was building up with its trading partners, or conversely, the huge **trade deficits** that other nations had with Japan. (See graphs, pages 223 and 224.) Under enormous pressure from nations building up huge trade deficits with Japan, Nakasone urged the Japanese to buy more foreign goods. He also asked the Japanese to spend more on consumer goods, even if it meant saving less. He hoped that these moves would help to lower Japan's trade surpluses with other nations. The Japanese began to increase their purchases. But the increase hardly made a dent because of the Japanese marked preference for domestically produced goods.

Japanese–American Trade Relations

The United States was gravely concerned over its trade relations with Japan. While Japan exported enormous amounts of goods to the United States each year, it placed severe limits on the amount of imports from the United States. The outcome for Japan was a trade surplus and a favorable balance of trade with the United States. But for the United States the outcome was a trade deficit and an unfavorable balance of trade. (See graph, page 223.)

In an effort to help the United States, reduce its trade deficit, Japan took a leading role in driving down the value of the United States dollar on the world market. Lowering the value of the United States dollar made United State exports cheaper in foreign countries. It also increased the price of imports in the United States. Despite Nakasone's efforts and those of Takeshita and Uno succeeding him as prime ministers, the United States trade deficit with Japan remained huge. Americans argued that Japan could do more to open its markets to United States exports. The Japanese responded that they did all they could and were being made scapegoats for the shortcomings of the American economy.

Another complaint arose from the trade restrictions placed on United States businesses wanting to trade with Japan. Americans wanting to do business in Japan complained that the Japanese government erected barriers to trade by establishing quotas on such imports as beef, citrus fruit, and rice. They also complained about the Japanese preference for domestically produced goods over foreign-made goods. The Japanese countered with the argument that no country, including the United States, allows free access of all goods into its market. They also defended Japanese preferences for Japanese-made goods by pointing out the often inferior quality of foreign-made goods and their high prices. Furthermore they criticized the low level of knowledge that foreigners have about Japanese culture. They asked why so few foreigners speak Japanese. They said that it was foolish of foreigners to expect to conduct business successfully in a country without learning that country's language, its history, and its culture.

Pricing and Investment Concerns

Another area of trade that has caused concern is competition. Many Americans complained about Japan's pricing policies on exports. The same product that was sold at a relatively high price in Japan was often sold for a much lower price in the United States. This was possible because of certain tax advantages Japanese companies enjoyed at home as well as their pricing policies. That is, because of a protected domestic market, the Japanese could charge the full price in Japan and offer a lower price abroad. Americans argued that Japan's pricing policies caused business failures in the United States economy. The Japanese argued that the primary reason for their success in the American market was the high quality of their goods and their willingness to charge reasonable prices.

Some Americans were also quite troubled by what they considered a Japanese buying spree in the United States. They argued that Japanese economic power in the United States carried with it political influence. On the other hand, some Americans pointed out that Japanese investments provided jobs and helped reduce the United States budget deficit. These same Americans wondered why there was so much concern about the Japanese when Canadians, the British, and the Dutch had a much larger economic presence in the United States.

Japanese-American Defense Issues

Japan's defense has rested heavily on its Mutual Defense Treaty with the United States. Some Americans have argued that Japan has been relying too much on the United States to defend Japan and has not been doing enough to develop its own military capabilities. In support of their assertion, these Americans pointed to the more than 6 percent of its Gross National Product (GNP) the United States spent on defense, contrasting it with the 1 percent of GNP that Japan spent. But Japanese critics of this argument countered with the explanation that 1 percent of Japan's large GNP equaled a fairly large sum for a nation so much smaller than the United States.

People who wanted Japan to play a larger defense role have argued that United States budget deficits have been so high in part because military spending has been so high. They have insisted that it was only reasonable for Japan, an economic colossus, to pay more for its own defense. The United States government has repeatedly urged Japan to increase its defense budget and to play a larger role in the defense of East Asia. As the 1980's progressed, this demand grew increasingly insis-

JAPAN AND THE WORLD. Through trade and aid Japan develops world-wide markets for its products. Japan's main trading partner, the United States, imports large quantities of automobiles each year. A cargo ship unloads Japanese autos in Baltimore (below). Hoping to build future markets for its goods, Japan helps Third World countries develop their economies. A Japanese instructor demonstrates modern equipment to farmers in Kenya (above). In the Philippines, a Japanese engineer explains the workings of an engine (bottom).

tent, and led to Japan's defense expenditures in 1987 edging for the first time over the 1 percent figure.

In a related issue, a few Japanese began to voice misgivings about relying so heavily on the defense umbrella provided by the United States. Most Japanese, however, continued to be satisfied with the existing security arrangement with the United States. They continued to point out that their constitution forbids offensive military action. These same Japanese feared that rearmament might trigger a revival of militarism. In any case, raising defense spending might make many of Japan's neighbors uneasy and jeopardize economic relations with them.

Soviet–Japanese Relations

During the 1970's Soviet–Japanese relations worsened. Earlier in the decade, Japan had hoped that the Soviet Union would return southern Sakhalin Island and the Kuriles. But talks to this end brought no new developments. In 1979 the Soviets began a military buildup on the islands. They also expanded their naval presence in the Pacific. Coupled with the Soviet intervention in Afghanistan beginning in 1979 and the shooting down of a South Korean airliner over Soviet territory in 1983, these aggressive moves troubled the Japanese. Soviet–Japanese relations eased somewhat after 1985 and the coming to power of Mikhail Gorbachev (mih-KAYL GORH-bah-choff). Still the Japanese have insisted that a return of Sakhalin and the Kuriles is a precondition for better relations.

For his part, Gorbachev wanted to import Japanese technology and to obtain Japanese investments for oil and gas projects in Siberia. But with low energy prices prevailing since the early 1980's, Japan has shown little interest in such investments. Gorbachev also wanted to weaken the diplomatic and military ties that existed between the United States and Japan. Both the Soviet Union and Japan have vital interests in Asia, but both countries have a long history of mutual antagonism and suspicion. It remains to be seen if they can fashion a harmonious relationship that does not sacrifice those interests.

Sino–Japanese Relations

Japan's China policy has been formulated largely with economic considerations in mind. Before World War II, mainland China was Japan's most important customer and the site of sizable Japanese investments. When Japan and the People's Republic of China reestablished diplomatic relations in 1972, Japanese business leaders hoped for a resumption of close economic ties, seeing China as a massive market and a source of cheap labor and important natural resources. The new leaders who replaced Mao Zedong in 1976 planned to industrialize rapidly. They sought to encourage trade and to bring in foreign investment and technology. Encouraged by these new developments, Japanese investments increased dramatically, with Japan becoming the largest foreign investor in China.

In its China policy, Japan has tried to steer clear of controversial issues. This has not always been possible. Japan was able to avoid being drawn into the Sino–Soviet conflict, but Japan was forced to become involved in disputes between Chinese Communists and Chinese Nationalists. In 1978 Japan and the People's Republic of China signed a treaty of peace and friendship, formally ending the state of war that had existed between them since 1937. The Japanese were careful to assure the Soviet Union that the treaty was not an anti-Soviet alliance. It was more difficult for Tokyo to sidestep the dispute between the Chinese Communists on the mainland and the Chinese Nationalists of the Republic of China on the island of Taiwan. When Japan and Communist China established diplomatic relations in 1972, diplomatic ties between Taiwan and Japan were cut. Despite the absence of formal relations, however, Japan and Taiwan have continued to carry on a brisk, two-way trade.

Relations with South Korea

During the 1970's and 1980's the economic relationship between Japan and South Korea continued to expand. In addition to increasing trade, the Japanese have made extensive investments in South Korea, especially to take advantage of the low-cost labor that is available there. Diplomatic relations between South Korea and Japan, however, remain somewhat strained. Many South Koreans still harbor bitter memories of past Japanese excesses. They also have been concerned about Japan's large investments in their country. To allay such suspicions, Japan has increased its foreign aid to South Korea. Japan has viewed this foreign aid as vital to the peace and security of East Asia, because a war between North and South Korea would bring instability to the area and might possibly lead to a superpower confrontation.

Southeast Asia Relations

Japan's involvement in nations of Southeast Asia has in part been motivated by events in other parts of the world, such as the rise of protectionism in the United States and elsewhere.

In 1985 Prime Minister Nakasone visited France on his way to an international conference in West Germany. Here he is shown listening to welcoming ceremonies by French diplomats, other government officials, and businesspeople.

The Japanese also hoped to take advantage of the cheap labor that is available in Southeast Asia in order to offset the escalation of their own labor costs in Japan. The Japanese felt that setting up production facilities in resource-rich Southeast Asia would help to ensure a steady supply of raw materials for Japanese industry.

The people of Southeast Asia, however, claimed that the Japanese were indifferent to local problems. In addition, Southeast Asians have not forgotten past Japanese aggressions. Many in Southeast Asia have contended that Japan's large economic presence in their countries is really a form of imperialism and nothing more than a Greater East Asia Co–Prosperity Sphere in a new form.

When Prime Minister Tanaka visited Southeast Asia in 1974, he was greeted with anti-Japanese demonstrations. The Japanese responded with an expansion of foreign aid to the region and with the introduction of cultural exchanges. Some Japanese companies began making grants to local universities and charitable institutions. Then in 1977 Prime Minister Fukuda announced what has since come to be called the Fukuda Doctrine. In this statement Fukuda reemphasized Japan's renouncement of militarism and pledged to deal with the nations of Southeast Asia on a basis of equality.

When Prime Minister Nakasone visited Southeast Asia in 1983, he received a cordial reception. Since then, Japan has continued to expand its foreign aid to the region. Indeed Japan's 1989 budget made Japan the largest foreign-aid donor in the world, and much of this foreign aid went to Southeast Asia. While relations remain lukewarm, they have become more harmonious. The countries of the region have insisted that Japan still needs to do more for them, considering Japan's enormous wealth and their own great needs.

Japan's Future Status

In the 1990's, Japan is unlikely to become a world power, at least not in the traditional sense of the term. Superpower status requires four ingredients—a strong economy, a powerful military, an exportable vision of the future, and the will to lead. Of these four elements, Japan possesses only the first. Japan's enormous economic capacity allows it to influence worldwide events. Japan is content with its present military posture. It also does not possess a set of ideas about the future that other peoples find appealing and are willing to follow. People everywhere find the United States appealing because it stands for democracy and has shown that capitalism provides the base for a strong economy. Other people find appealing the Soviet Union and its advocacy of socialism as a step on the path to communism. Both the United States and the Soviet Union are considered world powers. The leaders of both nations are looked to as world leaders. Not so Japan. But all consider Japan an economic giant. For now, that assessment is enough for Japan.

Check Your Understanding

1. How did Japan respond to the oil shortages of the 1970's?
2. How did the nations of the world respond to Japan's growing trade surpluses?
3. What problems continue to plague Japan's relations with the United States?
4. What arguments are presented on both sides concerning Japan's reliance on United States military capabilities, including its nuclear umbrella?
5. *Thinking Critically:* What common threads seem to run through Japan's relations with the Soviet Union, mainland China, South Korea, and the nations of Southeast Asia?

3. Social Patterns in a Land of Affluence

The younger generation of Japanese today is the first in the nation's history to grow up in a land of affluence. Most of these young people have never known deprivation because their parents and grandparents, who created Japan's modern industrial state, made sure that the fruits of their efforts were widely shared. Nonetheless the younger generation of Japanese have their own challenges to meet. New social patterns will arise as they meet the challenges of caring for an aging population, responding to new family relationships as women move slowly into the mainstream of Japanese life, and inserting the air of creativity into the Japanese educational system. They will also have to grapple with challenges that as yet are only dimly perceived.

A High Standard of Living

The Japanese people presently have one of the world's highest **standards of living**. In 1988 the Japanese **per capita income** was one of the highest in the world. But the Japanese pay a price for their affluence, especially when it comes to food. Japanese farmers with their small plots of land produce food at a high cost. To protect the agricultural sector from foreign competition, the Japanese government has placed tariffs and quota restrictions on various food imports. These restrictions raise the price charged for imported food. Japanese farmers receive an equivalent price for similar goods produced on their own farms.

With recent increases in Japan's standard of living, more and more Japanese take their vacations abroad. In this photo Japanese tourists in Hawaii are shown learning how to perform the hula, a Hawaiian dance.

Food and other consumer products sold in Japan often cost three times as much as their counterparts in the United States. These items cost so much because they pass through several intermediaries before reaching the consumer. Frequently Japanese manufacturers charge high prices at home to offset the lower prices at which their goods are sold abroad. Japanese visitors to the United States are often surprised at the "bargain prices" displayed on Japanese imports. In fact many Japanese visitors stock up on Japanese-made products while in the United States and bring them back to their own country either for their own use or for resale to friends and relatives.

Farmers are no longer poorer than people living in the cities. Farm families usually have a higher income than the national average because of the government policy of keeping agricultural prices high. Moreover most farm families have two incomes. Often the wife takes care of the farm while the husband works at a full-time or seasonal job in a nearby town or city. Sometimes the job is located at some distance from the farm. Then the husband lives apart from his family, sometimes only during the workweek and sometimes for months at a time.

Living Patterns

Another price of Japanese affluence is the high cost of owning a home. Most younger Japanese are finding that they cannot afford to own a home and probably never will. Houses have become too expensive because land, particularly in urban areas, carries with it an astronomical price—the result of too little land and too many people.

In Tokyo, for example, there are approximately 4 million housing units that average only 500 square feet in size. A piece of land in Tokyo that is no larger than a human footprint may cost the equivalent of $8,000 in United States currency. Japan is 76 percent urban, with more than 60 percent of Japan's urbanites concentrated in the Tokyo, Osaka, Nagoya, and Kitakyushu **metropolitan areas.** Japan's expensive land and housing is an outgrowth of its average population density, which is about 840 people per square mile. This makes for extremely crowded living conditions.

Living quarters in Japan are almost always small, even in the huge look-alike apartment complexes built by the government to ease the housing shortage. Many Japanese are able to afford only the cheaper homes or apartments located on the outskirts of a city or even in the countryside. Consequently daily commutes of two hours and more each way are common for the

Not all Japanese are enthusiastic about the rapid pace and change of modern life. Elderly Japanese, such as the person at the left, often retain traditional customs of dress even while shopping.

Western-dressed Japanese workers, who may wear traditional clothing at home or only on festive occasions.

The Japanese home is a blend of the old and the new. Most urban homes are furnished largely in Western style, with perhaps one room decorated in the traditional Japanese manner. In such chairless rooms, reed mats called tatami cover the floor and tables are low to the ground. Most Japanese prefer to sleep on a futon or bed roll, rather than a Western-style bed. Almost all Japanese homes, both traditional and modern, have a color television set, a washing machine and dryer, a refrigerator, a vacuum cleaner, and other small electric appliances. The majority of homes, however, do not have central heating.

Family Patterns

Since the mid–1950's, a dramatic change has occurred in the structure of the Japanese family. Until that time it was common for two or even three generations of a family to live under one roof. In this **extended family** the eldest son remained at home and brought his wife to live with him. Younger sons set up their own households and daughters went to live with their husbands. Then as Japan became more urban and more industrialized, the extended family in the urban areas became less common. The **nuclear family** is now typical.

234

Like modern Japan itself, the contemporary Japanese home mixes the old and the new. A nuclear family might relax in front of a TV set while sitting on cushions on a tatami-covered floor. Parents often prefer to wear kimonos while at home.

For the Japanese today, the nuclear family has both advantages and disadvantages over the extended family. In the nuclear family a couple has greater privacy and independence. But the sense of security provided by the extended family is missing. The decline of the extended family has also created a vacuum in the care of the elderly. In the past, the extended family developed as the eldest son or the unmarried daughters began to take on the responsibility of caring for the elderly in the household. With the rise of the nuclear family, the elderly have been left to care for themselves.

The problem of caring for the elderly is complicated by the aging of Japan's population. Life expectancy in Japan today is 80 years for women and 75 for men. At the same time that people are living longer, the rate of natural increase has slowed, giving Japan a less than 1 percent annual increase in its population. In 1989, 16 percent of the population was 60 years of age or older. In 1970 only 10 percent of the population was in that age bracket. By the year 2000, the percentage of people 60 or older is expected to reach 20 or higher. For many of Japan's elderly, old-age pensions and social security payments are inadequate. This is one important reason why Japan is a nation of savers. In the years to come, increasing pressure will be put on the Japanese government to provide more help for the elderly. In the meantime, both the young and the old are changing their living patterns.

Increasingly Japanese women are finding challenging careers in politics. Takako Doi, left, leader of the Japan Socialist Party, waves as she takes to the streets of Nagoya to campaign for Socialist candidates before a Parliamentary election.

The Status of Women

The economic and social status of women is slowly beginning to show improvement. Since the 1970's more and more Japanese women have found jobs outside the home. While women occupy few important positions in government and industry, great strides in removing unequal treatment have been made by women in the television industry, journalism, and the world of fashion. United States and Western European companies in Japan have hired women managers, providing role models for women to follow. Most Japanese women who have jobs outside the home are employed by small companies and family businesses or work in agriculture and the service sector.

About half of middle-class women stop working when they get married or when their first child is born. Many of these women reenter the labor force when all their children are of school age. In lower-class families, it is common for women to work outside the home even after they have a child. Of rising concern in Japan, as in the United States, is the supervision of children who come home from school to an empty house.

Although women have a subordinate status outside the home, within the home their role has been dominant. Husbands have usually spent long hours at work and have taken few vacations. Consequently many men have had little daily involvement with their families. They have left it to their wives to raise the children, make most decisions regarding the household, and control family finances. It has been common, for example, for a husband to hand his paycheck over to his wife, in turn receiving a weekly allowance. But many younger men are beginning to display a new attitude toward work and the family. These younger workers are resisting the traditional pattern of working long hours and socializing with co-workers after hours. Instead they are leaving work at an hour that allows them to eat supper with the family and to become more involved in family decision making. They are also using their well-earned affluence to take family vacations, sometimes in the United States and Europe.

Education in Japan

Japan's educational system has gained world renown for its excellence, rigor, intensity, and competitiveness. When Japanese students have taken the same tests as students of other nations, they consistently have outperformed them in mathematics, science, and geography. Virtually everyone in Japan is literate. Japan provides free public education through six years of elementary school and three years of junior high school. The students attend school five and one-half days each week for 240 days each year. In contrast, students in the United States attend school five days a week for 180 days.

Most students go on to three years of senior high school. About 90 percent of Japanese students obtain a high school diploma. Public as well as private schools charge tuition although in the case of public schools, it is low. About 40 percent of college-age students pay tuition to attend the many public and private two- or four-year colleges and universities in Japan.

To get into a particular college, a student must take the competitive examination offered by that school. Students often attend special cram schools that hold sessions after regular school and on weekends to prepare for the grueling examinations that are given every February and March. Students put up with the rigorous study that leads to the test-taking because it is vital to get into a top-rated institution. Without a diploma from a prestigious university or college, it is impossible to get a job that offers the pay, benefits, and lifetime security that are offered to graduates of top schools.

After the rigors of cramming for the tests, college is usually easy, and almost everyone passes. Students who fail to get into a particular college or university will sometimes wait a year and take the entrance examination a second time. Some students, whom the Japanese call "ronin" after the masterless samurai of the past, even take the examination three or four years in a row.

Criticism of the School System

In recent years, many Japanese have begun to criticize their nation's school system. These critics contend that the Japanese educational system places too much pressure on youngsters to study and to do well on examinations. They say that the school system at all levels puts too much emphasis on memorization and fails to develop creative thinking. They complain that the pre-college levels of education encourage conformity and deny students the opportunity to explore their own individuality. The Japanese educational system also takes its toll on the entire family. Fathers take second jobs and work long hours to pay for the cram schools. Mothers, whom the Japanese call "education mamas," often devote their main energies to ensuring that their children, especially their sons, are well prepared for the entrance examinations.

Japanese Workers

In both the private and public sectors, about 30 percent of the Japanese work force, including managers, highly skilled technicians, and professionals, have lifetime employment. These employees will rarely be laid off. If their jobs are phased out, they are retrained and reassigned to other jobs. With a vested interest in the company's well-being, lifetime workers strive to maintain product quality and to increase their productivity. They know that if they do well their company will do well. In part for this reason, labor-management relations for companies with a large work force of lifetime employees tend to be harmonious. Most workers with lifetime status are represented by a company union. Long strikes are uncommon. Workers and union representatives usually make reasonable wage demands. For its part, management is open to suggestions from workers.

The remainder of Japan's work force, especially women and unskilled workers, have no guarantees of lifetime employment. Employees at small and middle-sized companies often have little job security. Even at large companies, some of the workers have a temporary status. When business slows down, these temporary workers are the ones who are laid off. Their wages and fringe benefits are also less than those that are granted to lifetime employees.

Discrimination in Japan

Japan's expansion has brought great benefit to many of its people, but some, including the elderly, orphans, the physically and mentally handicapped, and other minorities, have not shared in their nation's prosperity. Unlike some countries, Japan has not set up many programs to provide for minorities and the needy. In the prewar period, people who needed help got it from relatives or from public charities. In recent decades the Japanese government has passed laws to expand public assistance to the needy. The situation has improved, but far more still needs to be done. As for other minorities, they can count on little government support.

In each large Japanese city, day laborers, the unemployed, the homeless, alcoholics, and others with no visible means of support live in dirty, crime-infested areas. Then too there are the **burakumin,** who in outward appearance look just like other Japanese, but who are considered outcasts. Other Japanese would never consider marrying a burakumin. The origin of this class is not clear. Centuries ago in Tokugawa times, they were called "eta" and were involved in occupations thought to be unclean, such as butchering and tanning. Discriminatory regulations were imposed on them.

Estimates put the number of burakumin between 1.5 million and 3 million. But the exact number is unknown because most burakumin try to hide their origins. While legal discrimination against burakumin was abolished in 1871, they still encounter forms of prejudice and discrimination in education, housing, and employment. The burakumin are often poor, uneducated, and live in ghettos. Criminal behavior and juvenile delinquency are more common among the burakumin than among other Japanese.

More than 700,000 Koreans live in Japan. After the burakumin, Japanese–Koreans are the second largest minority group

The End of an Era

In January 1989, Emperor Hirohito died at the age of 87. His death brought to an end the Era of Showa, or "Shining Peace," the name given to his reign when he assumed the Chrysanthemum Throne in 1926. According to legend, Hirohito was the 124th emperor in an imperial line that had begun over 2,600 years ago. Hirohito's 64-year reign spanned the years of Japan's rising militarism, the era of post-World War II reconstruction, and the emergence of Japan as an economic superpower.

For the first 20 years of his reign, in keeping with Japanese tradition, Hirohito was regarded as a living god. But in 1946, Hirohito renounced the concept of imperial divinity. From that time on, Hirohito became Japan's symbol of state, representing a democratic, peace-loving Japan.

Hirohito's death has aroused a long dormant controversy over his role in Japan's prewar and World War II aggressions. Most historians argue that Hirohito personally opposed Japan's policy. But like most emperors before him, he had little power. A few historians, however, insist that Hirohito approved of and actively participated in the planning of his country's assault on China and its surprise attack on Pearl Harbor.

At present little evidence has surfaced to support the minority view. What is known is that in 1945 Hirohito was able to break the cabinet deadlock over whether to surrender or to continue fighting by siding with those who were pushing for a decision to surrender. Many historians argue that Hirohito was not capable of assuming the role of an aggressive military leader. He was vastly more comfortable studying marine biology than dealing with matters of state. Much of the credit for the Japanese acceptance of their role under the American Occupation, however, goes to Hirohito and his desire to abide by the symbolic role the constitution set for him.

According to Japanese tradition, Hirohito is now to be known by the name of his reign, becoming Emperor Showa. The emperor of Japan is now his son Akihito, and in 1989, Japan entered the Era of Heisei—"Achieving Peace."

in Japan. Between 1930 and 1945, thousands of Koreans were forcibly brought to Japan to work. When the war ended, many Koreans stayed in Japan. Their descendants were born in Japan and speak Japanese. Still most Japanese–Koreans are classified by the Japanese government as resident aliens. The government makes it very difficult for them to acquire citizenship, and as non-citizens, they are not entitled to vote in Japanese elections. Like the burakumin, Japanese–Koreans are discriminated against in countless ways both by Japanese citizens and by the Japanese government.

Quality of Life

In other nations, economic development has often brought about a rise in the crime rate, drug abuse, juvenile delinquency, and a sense of alienation. But Japan has largely managed to avoid many of these problems. The crime rate is unusually low. In most areas of most large cities, it is quite safe to walk alone on the streets at night. Drug abuse is negligible. While juvenile delinquency increased rapidly for a time during the 1970's and 1980's, it is still low compared with other nations. As for alienation, or a sense of antagonism toward one's environment, most of the Japanese people appear to be reasonably content with their quality of life and the shape of the society of which they are a part. Most of all, the Japanese appear proud of their nation's record of achievement, proud of their heritage, and proud to be Japanese.

Check Your Understanding

1. What price does the Japanese consumer have to pay for Japan's high standard of living?
2. Why is Japan's affluence not fully demonstrated in the living patterns of most Japanese families?
3. How has the status of women changed in the 1970's and 1980's?
4. Why is Japanese education so rigorous?
5. What effects does the education system have on individuals and the family?
6. *Thinking Critically:* Discuss the advantages and disadvantages to Japan and the Japanese people that result from the move to living in nuclear families.

CHAPTER REVIEW

■ Chapter Summary

Section 1. The Liberal Democratic Party has controlled both houses of Japan's National Diet since 1955. From time to time, opposition parties have tried to form a coalition to oust them from power but have never managed to agree. The main opposition parties are the Japan Socialist Party, which advocates increased spending for social welfare; the Komeito, which advocates a foreign policy more independent of the United States; the Democratic Socialist Party, which takes positions similar to the Liberal Democratic Party; and the Japan Communist Party, which wants Japan to sever all ties with the United States. The LDP retains its popularity because of its flexible approach and its success in fostering Japan's economic prosperity and growth.

Section 2. In the 1970's, in response to the oil shortages engineered by OPEC, Japan began to shift its economic priorities from heavy to high-technology industries. It concentrated in such fields as robotics, electronics, and the manufacture of appliances because these industries used small inputs of raw materials and energy. Japan's economic successes in the global economy brought reprisals from around the world in the form of protectionism from nations wishing to lessen competition for their domestic industries and to regain for themselves a more favorabie balance of trade with Japan. The United States and Western Europe voiced their concerns over Japan's growing trade surpluses and their own increasing trade deficits, restrictions on imports into Japan, and Japan's growing investment base abroad.

The major change in Japan's relations with the nations of East Asia and Southeast Asia has been an increase in Japan's foreign aid. Japan has viewed this foreign aid as a means of increasing its own economic presence in these countries. In spite of its enormous economic prestige, Japan has undertaken very little leadership in foreign affairs and is unlikely to pursue a position of power in world affairs.

Section 3. A direct result of Japan's economic growth and prosperity is the transformation of Japan into a land of affluence. But that very affluence has brought its own set of problems to the Japanese, who have one of the world's highest standards of living. As one of the world's most densely populated countries, the Japanese pay high prices for food, land,

and housing. With government encouragement the natural increase in population has slowed in recent years, producing a significant decrease in Japan's youthful population while its elderly population increases. Beginning in the mid–1950's, the Japanese family structure changed, moving from the extended to the nuclear family household. This change also made the problem of caring for the elderly more difficult, and will probably force the Japanese government to provide more social services for its people.

The Japanese secure lifetime jobs by successfully completing courses in Japan's rigorous educational system and passing competitive examinations to the nation's top colleges and universities. The educational system has been criticized, however, for the toll it exacts on students and their families and for emphasizing memorization and conformity at the expense of creativity and a sense of individual identity. Women have made some strides toward equality and a lessening of discrimination in the workplace. The burakumin and Japanese–Koreans, as well as other minorities, still experience severe forms of discrimination. Most Japanese, however, are content with the quality of their lives and proud of their nation's accomplishments and heritage.

■ Vocabulary Review

Define: coalition, welfare, faction, robotics, protectionism, trade surplus, trade deficit, standard of living, per capita income, metropolitan area, extended family, nuclear family, burakumin

■ Places to Locate

Locate: Tokyo, Nagoya, Osaka, Kitakyushu

■ People to Know

Identify: Tanaka Kakuei, Takeshita Noboru, Nakasone Yasuhiro, Fukuda Takeo, Uno Sousuke

■ Thinking Critically

1. Why might the Liberal Democratic Party itself be considered a coalition?
2. How do Japan's economic priorities influence its foreign relations with the United States, the Soviet Union, South Korea, and Southeast Asia?
3. How has Japanese affluence affected its social patterns?

■ Extending and Applying Your Knowledge

1. In a series entitled the "Asian Challenge," an article in the February 13, 1989, issue of *Newsweek* discusses the obstacles American manufacturers face in getting their products into the Japanese market and the causes. Secure a copy of this issue of the magazine and report on the obstacles discussed in the article, which is entitled "Still Only a Half–Open Door."

2. Examine the *Readers' Guide to Periodical Literature* for recent articles on Japan and the social trends that are developing there. Select one of these trends to research and report on in class.

APPENDIX

BIBLIOGRAPHY

General Works

Akutagawa, Ryunosuke. *Rashomon and Other Stories,* trans. by Kojima Takashi. Liveright, 1952. A collection of short stories by one of modern Japan's most gifted writers.

All-Japan: The Catalogue of Everything Japanese. Intro. by Oliver Statler. Morrow-Quill, 1984. A well-illustrated, panoramic survey of Japanese culture through the ages.

Anderson, Joseph L., and Donald Ritchie. *The Japanese Film: Art and Industry.* Princeton University Press, 1982. A history of Japanese cinema, with a foreword by the famous director, Akira Kurasawa.

Earhart, H. Bryan. *Japanese Religion: Unity and Diversity.* Wadsworth Publishing Company, 1982. A survey of religion in Japan, past and present.

Gibney, Frank. *Japan: The Fragile Superpower, 2nd. rev. ed.* Meridian, 1986. Discussion of contemporary Japanese business, society, culture, and politics.

Hall, John W. *Japan: From Prehistory to Modern Times.* Delacorte Press, 1970. A solid political and cultural history of Japan.

Hane, Mikiso. *Modern Japan: A Historical Survey.* Westview Press, 1986. A solid survey of Japanese history from the Meiji Restoration to the mid-1980's.

Hearn, Lafcadio. *Kwaidan: Stories and Studies of Strange Things.* Charles E. Tuttle, 1970. A collection of Japanese folktales by a master story-teller.

Mishima, Yukio. *The Sound of Waves,* trans. by M. Weatherby. Knopf, 1956. A prize-winning novel of teen-age life in a Japanese fishing village.

Mishima, Yukio. *The Temple of the Golden Pavilion,* trans. by Ivan Morris. Putnam Perigee, 1980. A superb novel furnishing sensitive insights into the nature of Zen Buddhism.

Paine, Robert Treat, and Alexander Soper. *The Art and Architecture of Japan.* Penguin Books, 1985. An introduction to Japanese painting, sculpture, and architecture that contains many illustrations.

Reischauer, Edwin O. *Japan: The Story of a Nation,* 3rd. ed. Knopf, 1981. An outstanding appraisal of Japanese history.

Richie, Donald. *The Inland Sea.* Century, 1986. A beautifully written travelog of Japan's Inland Sea area.

Statler, Oliver. *Japanese Inn.* Random House, 1961. Masterful sketches of life and manners in Japan from Tokugawa times to the postwar period.

Varley, H. Paul. *Japanese Culture: A Short History.* Praeger, 1972. A well-written introduction to Japanese culture.

Japan Before Perry *(Chapters 1–4)*

All-Japan: The Catalogue of Everything Japanese. Intro. by Oliver Statler. Morrow-Quill, 1984. A well-illustrated, panoramic survey of Japanese culture through the ages.

Ernst, Earle. *The Kabuki Theater.* University Press of Hawaii, 1974. A thorough description of kabuki.

Harris, Townsend. *The Complete Journal of Townsend Harris,* 2nd. rev. ed., edited by Mario E. Cosenza. Charles E. Tuttle, 1959. An absorbing record by the first United States Consul General in Japan (1856–1861).

Manyoshu, The. Columbia University Press, 1965. An anthropology of poems compiled during the Nara period.

Morris, Ivan. *The World of the Shining Prince.* Knopf, 1964. Delightful sketches of history, culture, life, and manners in the imperial capital of Kyoto 1,000 years ago.

Murasaki, Shikibu. *The Tale of Genji,* 2 vols., trans. by Edward G. Seidensticker. Knopf, 1976. An excellent translation of Japan's greatest novel.

Nitobe, Inazo. *Bushido: The Soul of Japan.* Charles E. Tuttle Company, 1969. A description of Bushido, the unwritten code of the Samurai, and its impact on modern Japan.

Ruus, Peter. *Feudalism in Japan.* Knopf, 1969. A well-written history of Japan up to the 1850's.

Sansom, George B. *Japan: A Short Cultural History.* Stanford University Press, 1978. An outstanding study of Japan in pre-modern times.

Totman, Conrad. *Japan Before Perry: A Short History.* University of California Press, 1981. A survey of Japan from earliest times to 1853.

Totman, Conrad. *Tokugawa Ieyasu: Shogun.* Heian International, Inc., 1983. A detailed and exciting biography of one of Japan's great leaders.

Yoshikawa, Eiji. *Mushaski,* trans. by Charles S. Terry. Harper & Row, 1971. An historical novel depicting the adventures of one of Japan's great swordsmen.

The Meiji Era, 1853–1945 *(Chapters 5 and 6)*

Craig, William. *The Fall of Japan.* Dial, 1967. A sobering account of the final years of the war against Japan in the Pacific.

Feis, Herbert. *The Road to Pearl Harbor.* Princeton University Press, 1950. One of the best studies of Japanese foreign policy and Japanese-American relations on the eve of World War II.

Feis, Herbert. *Japan Subdued: The Atomic Bomb and the End of World War II,* rev. ed. Princeton Univertiy Press, 1966. A sound and objective study of the decision of the United States to use the atomic bomb.

Fukuzawa, Yukichi. *The Autobiography of Fukuzawa Yukichi,* trans. by Kiyooka Eiichi. Hokuseido, 1960. The memoirs of the "Benjamin Franklin" of early modern Japan.

Lord, Walter. *Day of Infamy.* Holt, Rinehart and Winston, 1957. A carefully reconstructed account of the Japanese attack on Pearl Harbor.

Reischauer, Edwin O. *Japan: The Story of a Nation,* 3rd. ed. Knopf, 1981. An outstanding appraisal of Japanese history.

Statler, Oliver. *Japanese Inn.* Random House, 1961. Masterful sketches of life and manners in Japan from Tokugawa times to the postwar period.

Japan from the Occupation to the Present   *(Chapters 7 and 8)*

Anderson, Joseph L., and Donald Ritchie. *The Japanese Film: Art and Industry.* Princeton University Press, 1982. A history of Japanese cinema, with a foreword by the famous director, Akira Kurasawa.

Christopher, Robert C. *The Japanese Mind: Goliath Explained.* Linden Press, 1983. A readable survey of Japanese society in the 1980's.

Gibney, Frank. *Japan: The Fragile Superpower,* 2nd. rev. ed. Meridian, 1986. Discussion of contemporary Japanese business, society, culture, and politics.

Hall, John W. *Japan: From Prehistory to Modern Times.* Delacorte Press, 1970. A solid political and cultural history of Japan.

Hane, Mikiso. *Modern Japan: A Historical Survey.* Westview Press, 1986. A solid survey of Japanese history from the Meiji Restoration to the mid-1980's.

Trager, James, ed. *Letters from Sachiko.* Sphere (Abacus), 1984. A Japanese woman's views of contemporary Japan.

Vining, Elizabeth G. *Windows for the Crown Prince.* Lippincott, 1952. A warm account of the experiences of an American who tutored Emperor Akihito when he was young.

Vogel, Ezra F. *Japan as Number One: Lessons for America.* Harvard University Press, 1979. A sympathetic portrait of Japanese business and society.

White, Merry. *The Japanese Educational Challenge: A Commitment to Children.* The Free Press, 1987. An explanation of why the Japanese educational system has been so successful.

GLOSSARY

This Glossary contains definitions for the social studies terms used in this volume about Japan. These terms are printed in bold type the first time they appear in the text. The page number following each definition below is the page on which the word is first used. Often words have more than one meaning. The definitions given below are the ones that will be most helpful to you in reading this book.

alliance   association among nations or groups based upon mutual purpose, interest, or advantage (56)

anarchism   theory that advocates the end of all government (151)

archipelago   group of islands (2)

aristocracy   privileged upper class (42)

authoritarianism   system of rule demanding absolute obedience to authority (151)

Bakufu   military government of feudal Japan (57)

balance of trade   condition that exists between imports and exports of a country; the balance is favorable when exports exceed imports, unfavorable when imports exceed exports (135)

barter system   system of trade by which people exchange one good for another good (72)

birth rate   number of births per 1,000 people (195)

buffer zone   region or territory located between unfriendly rivals that acts as a deterrent against military action (87)

bunraku   Japanese puppet plays (106)

burakumin   impoverished person in Japan (239)

calligraphy   expert use of the brush in Japanese writing (47)

capital   resources used to produce goods and services (132)

capitalism   economic system in which businesses are privately owned and in which there is open competition in a free market (200)

castle town   cluster of homes, farms, and shops that developed around the fortified castle of a daimyo (71)

centralized government   government in which authority is concentrated in a single organization or unit (85)

Charter Oath edict establishing guidelines for the transition of government from Tokugawa rule to the Meiji Restoration (122)

cloistered emperor real ruler of Japan during Fujiwara domination (43)

coalition union that is convenient and often temporary between parties with a common interest or goal (216)

cold war non-military political, economic, and diplomatic conflicts between Communist and non-Communist countries in the post-World War II era (202)

commendation act by which farmers in feudal Japan, while continuing to farm their lands for a fee, put them under the control of wealthy aristocrats in return for protection (42)

communism system of government in which the state owns all lands and controls production of goods and services; one political party maintains power with the goal of distributing all goods equally to the people (151)

conscription compulsory enrollment in a military service (38)

conservative person who prefers the existing social and political order (151)

constitution document that sets forth the guiding principles and basic laws of a constitutional government (128)

constitutional government government guided in its basic operation by either a written or an unwritten constitution (128)

consumer goods materials such as food and clothing purchased by people for their own use (131)

coup seizure of power through force (45)

culture all the tools and objects people make and use, their language, religious beliefs, customs, traditions, foods, clothes, and activities (12)

daimyo local lord in feudal Japan who exercised great power through the warriors who owed loyalty to him (71)

democracy form of government based on rule by the people (151)

dynasty line of families that transfers its right to rule by inheritance (34)

emperor monarch who rules an empire (24)

ethnic group set of people sharing a common culture and often a common geographical location (13)

extended family social unit of parents, their children, and one or more aunts, uncles, or grandparents living in the same household (234)

extraterritoriality provision by which Western nations were granted special privileges in Japan (136)

faction dissenting minority within a group (45)

family planning program or method of population control (195)

feudalism social and political system in which upper-class landowners gave lower classes protection and land in exchange for labor or military service (42)

fief land granted to a feudal vassal by a higher lord (87)

genro "elder statesmen" who formed the oligarchy or group that was the real ruling power in the Meiji Restoration (130)

go-kenin vassals bound to the Minamoto lords by ties of loyalty and service so strong that they almost equalled kinship (58)

guild organization formed by medieval merchants of the same trade or artisans of the same craft whose purpose was to protect its members and set policies and standards (72)

haiku poem of only three lines with the syllables in each line following the fixed sequence of 5, 7, 5 (111)

han estates surrounding Edo granted to hereditary vassals and minor vassals loyal to Ieyasu and located within the buffer zone set up by Tokugawa Ieyasu (88)

haniwa clay figurine artifacts found in mound burial crypts of early Japanese ancestors (28)

imperialism policy by which a nation extends its control over other lands to gain an economic or political advantage (136)

indemnity compensation for damages suffered by a nation during war (139)

inflation rising prices caused by a scarcity of goods and an abundance of money and credit (132)

institution relationship or behavioral pattern in the life of a nation or society; also an established organization (12)

kabuki colorful play celebrating tales and legends of feudal Japan in dance and song (107)

kami Japanese term that refers to unseen forces of nature (18)

kamikaze literally "divine wind"; term applied to special squadrons that flew suicidal missions in World War II to protect Japan from invasion. (64)

kana Japanese writing system (16)

liberal supporter of moderate political change and social and economic reform (151)

liberalism   political philosophy that emphasizes progress and reform (128)

light industry   manufacture of food, textiles, and other goods that do not require heavy machines (135)

loyalist   member of a group who advocated the full restoration of the emperor's power in Japan (116)

mandate   territory administered by a League of Nations grant after World War I (145)

market town   town that developed at the junction of frequently traveled roads or around sheltered harbors (72)

mediator   person who serves as a go-between for two other parties in a dispute (141)

megalopolis   densely populated urban area comprising several cities linked by transportation (7)

mercenary   paid professional soldier, usually of foreign background (51)

metropolitan area   area that surrounds a large city as well as the city itself (233)

militarism   policy of glorifying war and promoting the build-up of military power (167)

moderate   person opposed to extreme views (161)

monopoly   control of a service or product and its price by a single source (73)

nationalism   feeling of devotion to and pride in one's country (67)

naval parity   equality in number and tonnage of combat ships with those of other nations (163)

no-war clause   Article Nine of Japan's present constitution, which renounces war as an instrument of government policy (205)

nuclear family   social unit of parents and children living in the same household (234)

oligarch   member of a small ruling group (123)

oral tradition   cultural heritage (stories, folktales, poetry, songs) passed from one generation to the next by word of mouth (16)

paddy   wetland in which rice is grown (7)

per capita income   the average income of all the people in a nation (232)

population density concentration of people in a given area such as a square mile or a square kilometer (195)

prefecture governmental unit of Japan equivalent to a state in the United States (184)

privy council part of the oligarchy that ruled during the Meiji Restoration (130)

protectionism policy that advocates the use of tariffs and other trade barriers to free domestic industries from unwanted foreign competition (222)

protectorate nation, state, or people that depend on a stronger country for defense and foreign affairs (142)

province territory governed as an administrative or political unit of a country or an empire (34)

puppet ruler sovereign, but without real power to rule (41)

radical person who demands revolutionary changes in government (151)

regent acting ruler; often used when a sovereign ruler is underage (31)

robotics manufacturing system that utilizes machines and computers to perform human tasks (222)

ronin masterless samurai (101)

samurai class of warrior nobles in feudal Japan (41)

sankin kotai system of control instituted by Hideyoshi and maintained by subsequent shoguns that required daimyo to build residences in Edo and to visit there at specified times (89)

satori self-enlightenment and understanding; the goal of Buddhist meditation (67)

seclusion laws series of edicts issued by the shogunate to control foreign influences in Japan and to prevent Japanese from leaving the country (92)

self-defense forces army, navy, and air units of Japan's military (206)

shogun military leader who ruled Japan in the name of the emperor from the twelfth to the nineteenth centuries (38)

socialism political and economic system under which the government owns and controls the means of production and operates them for the welfare of all citizens in society (151)

standard of living measurement of a nation's economic well-being (232)

suffrage right to vote (130)

syllabary   alphabet composed of symbols that represent the syllables of a written language (16)

tanka   popular Japanese form of poetry limited to five lines, with the total number of syllables (31) following the fixed pattern of 5, 7, 5, 7, 7 (48)

tenant farmer   peasant who rents farmland (134)

terrorism   use of violence, especially against random victims, to win demands or to influence the politics of a government (163)

titular emperor   figurehead ruler who performed all ceremonial functions during the Fujiwara period (43)

tozama   estates of lords deemed untrustworthy by Tokugawa Shogun and relocated outside the buffer zone surrounding Edo (88)

trade deficit   condition in which the value of a nation's imports exceeds the value of a nation's exports, resulting in an unfavorable balance of trade (208)

trade surplus   condition in which the value of a nation's exports exceed the value of its imports, resulting in a favorable balance of trade (224)

trade union   group of workers in the same trade organized to promote their interests (152)

tradition   set of enduring customs and patterns from the past that influence the present (33)

tsunami   ocean wave caused by an underwater earthquake or volcanic eruption that is capable of traveling thousands of miles and is often destructive (9)

uji   extended family in Yamato society (30)

ultra-nationalist   member of a group that advocated expansion of Japan's sphere of influence through military domination (160)

unconditional surrender   terms under which one nation accepts defeat by another nation or group of nations (181)

vassal   noble in feudal Japan who pledged loyalty and services to a lord in exchange for a grant of land and the peasants who worked the land   (43)

welfare   financial assistance program sponsored by government (216)

zaibatsu   Japan's financial oligarchy during the Meiji Restoration (132)

ACKNOWLEDGMENTS

Text Credits

The Manyoshu: the Nippon Gakujutsu Shinkokai Translation of One Thousand Poems (New York: Columbia University Press, 1965), p. 43. Reprinted by permission of Columbia University Press. Cooper, Michael, ed. They Came to Japan: An Anthology of European Reports of Japan, 1543–1640 (Berkeley: University of California Press, 1965), p. 37. Philippi, Donald L. Norito: A New Translation of the Ancient Japanese Ritual Prayers (Tokyo: Institute for Japanese Culture and Classics, Kokugakuin University Tokyo, 1959), p. 30. Tsunoda, Ryusaku, William T. de Bary, and Donald Keene. Sources of Japanese Tradition (New York: Columbia University Press, 1958), pp. 6–7. Reprinted by permission of Columbia University Press. Keene, Donald, comp. and ed. Anthology of Japanese Literature (New York: Grove Press, 1955, Evergreen Edition), pp. 51–52. Reprinted by permission. Waley, Arthur, trans. The Pillow Book of Sei Shonagan (Woking and London: Unwin Brothers, Ltd., 1957), pp. 25–27. Reischauer, Edwin O., and John K. Fairbank. East Asia, the Great Tradition (Boston: Houghton Mifflin Co., 1960), p. 537. Reprinted by permission of Houghton Mifflin Company. Kirby, John B., Jr. From Castle to Teahouse: Japanese Architecture of the Momoyama Period (Rutland, Vermont: Chas. E. Tuttle, 1962), p. 63. Reprinted by permission of the publisher. Kaempfer, Kaempfer. The History of Japan, trans. by J. G. Schenchzer, 3 vols. (Glasgow: James MacLehose and Sons, 1906, Vol. III), pp. 21–22. Henderson, Harold C. An Introduction to Haiku (New York: Doubleday and Company, Inc., 1968), p. 18. Reprinted by permission of Doubleday and Company, Inc. Shujiro, Watanabe. Japan, 1853–1864 or Genji Yume Monogatari, trans. by Ernest M. Satow (Tokyo, 1905), pp. 7–8. Tiedemann, Arthur. Modern Japan (Princeton, New Jersey: D. Van Nostrand, 1962), quoted on page 132. Truman, Harry S. Memoirs, Vol. I. (Garden City, New York: Doubleday and Company, Inc., 1955), p. 418.

Art Credits

Book designed by George McLean.
Cover concept and design by Hannus Design Associates.
Cover photograph: Jules Zalon/The Image Bank.
Maps: Precision Graphics.
Title Page and Chapter Opener art: Marion Eldridge.
Calligraphy, pages 16 and 17, by Mrs. Fumiko Cranston.

Photographs　**8** (top) Japan National Tourist Organization, (center) Japan Travel Bureau, Tokyo, (bottom) Consulate General of Japan, New York; **14** (top, center) Toge Fujihara, (bottom) Monkmeyer Press Photo Service; **20** (top) Japan Travel Bureau, Tokyo, (bottom) Consulate General of Japan, New York; **26** (left, right) Tokyo National Museum, **29** (left) Tokyo National Museum, (right) Cleveland Museum of Art, Norweb Collection; **31** Imperial Household Collection, Kyoto; **35** Horyuji Temple, Nara; **45** Museum of Fine Arts, Boston, Fenollosa-Weld Collection; **48** Bob and Ira Spring; **50** H. Armstrong Roberts; **51** Spencer Collection, New York Public Library; **56** Tokyo National Museum; **60** (left) Metropolitan Museum of Art, Rogers Fund, 1904, (right) Metropolitan Museum of Art, Gift of Howard Mansfield, 1936; **62** Imperial Household Collection, Kyoto; **68** (top) Werner Bischoff/Magnum, (right) Cleveland Museum of Art, Norweb Collection, (bottom) Japan National Tourist Organization; **72–73** Kobe City Museum of Nanban Art; **79** Consulate General of Japan, New York; **80** (top) Elliot Erwitt/Magnum, (center) F.P.G., International, (bottom) American President Lines, Ltd.; **86** Okura Cultural Foundation; **89** International Society for Educational Information, Tokyo; **94** (left) International Society for Educational Information, Tokyo, (right) Ashmolean Museum, Oxford; **99** (top) Laurie Platt Winfrey, Inc., (bottom left) Japan National Tourist Organization, (bottom right) Tokyo National Museum; **107** Laurie Platt Winfrey, Inc.; **108** (top) Tokugawa Reimeikai Foundation, (bottom left) Japan Na-

INDEX

This index includes references not only to the text of the book but also to charts, graphs, maps, and pictures. These may be identified as follows: *c* refers to a chart; *g* refers to a graph; *m* refers to a map; *p* refers to a picture.

A

MITI *See* Ministry of International Trade and Industry
Mito, *m*4–5
Mitsubishi, 132
Mitsui, 132
Miyazaki, *m*4–5
modernization, in Meiji era, 121–142. *See also* social changes
money *See* economics; economy
Mongolia, *m*138, 161–162
Mongol invasions, 63, 65
mountains, 3, *m*4–5, 6
Mount Fuji, *m*4–5, 6, *p*220
Mount Hiei, 78
Mukden Incident, 162, 167
Murasaki, Lady, 66
Murasaki Shikibu, 49–50
Muroran, *m*4–5
Musashi (ship), 172
Mutsuhito, 121. *See also* Meiji emperor
Mutual Security Pact, 202, 205–206, 216, 266

N
Nagasaki, *m*4–5, 71, *m*91, 92, 176
Nagoya, *m*4–5, 7, 71, *m*91, 233
Nakasone, Prime Minister, 224–225, 230, *p*230
Nanjing, *m*138, 166
Nansei Shoto *See* Ryukyu Islands
Nara, *m*4–5, *p*35, 39, 40; as capital, 36
nationalism, Nichiren's contribution to, 67; following World War II, 198–199. *See also* ultra-nationalists
Nationalist China, 161–166, 207. *See also* Taiwan
natural resources, *c*164, 222
nature, effect of, on Japanese religion, 18–19
Nemuro, *m*4–5
Neo-Confucianism, 97, 100
netsuke, 98
New Guinea, *m*138
Nichiren Buddhism, 32, 66–67, 203
Nihongi (*Chronicles of Japan*), 35–36, 37
Niigata, *m*4–5
Nine-Power Treaty, 158
Nippon, 16
Nixon, Richard M., 207, 208
Nō (drama), *p*68, 75, 107
Nobi Plain, *m*91
Nobunaga, 76, 77–78
North China, 166
North Korea, *m*4–5, 210. *See also* Korea; South Korea
no-war clause, 204–205, 207
nuclear energy, 199
nuclear weapons, 175–176, 210

O
Occupation (Japanese), 181–188
Oita, *m*4–5
Okayama, 71
Okinawa, 3, 137, 172, 175, 184, 208
Okuma Shigenobu, 128
Olympics, 180
OPEC *See* Organization of Petroleum Exporting Countries
Open Door Policy, 169
Organization of Petroleum Exporting Countries (OPEC), 222
Osaka, *m*4–5, 7, 71, *m*91, 104, 233; castle, 79, *p*79, 81
Osaka Plain, *m*30, *m*91

P
Paris Peace Conference, 145–146
Pearl Harbor, 170–171, 172, 181, 240
peasants, in Taika program, 38; and Reform edict, 39; and rise of warrior class, 55; during Tokugawa Shogunate, 96, 97, *p*99, 102, 103; of Meiji era, 133–134; cooperatives, 153
Peking, *m*138
People's Republic of China, 183, 207, 228–229. *See also* China
Perry, Matthew C., 113–115, *p*114, 136
Perry, Oliver, *p*114
Pescadores Islands, 139
Philippines, *m*138, 172, *p*173, 175
Philippine Sea, Second Battle of, 172
Phoenix Hall, *p*20, *p*80
Pillow Book of Sei Shonagon, 48, 50
political parties, *c*6; after World War I, 151–152; and militarism, 167; following Occupation, 200–204; after World War II, 216–220; present-day, *g*218, *p*236
pollution, 194, 200
population, 6, *c*164; postwar patterns, 194–195, 232, 235
Port Arthur, 139, 141
Portsmouth, Treaty of, 141
Portugal, trade with, *p*72, 73–74, *p*73, 93
prehistory, ages of, 27
privy council, 130
protectionism, 222–223
puppet theater *See* bunraku
Pure Land *See* Jodo
Pu Yi, 165
Pyongyang, *m*4–5

R
Record of Ancient Matters See *Kojiki*
Recruit Scandal, 219
Reform Edict, 34, 39